THE PERFECT CRISIS

THE BEGINNING OF
THE REVOLUTIONARY WAR

The publication of this book is made possible
in part by a grant from the Andrew W. Mellon Foundation

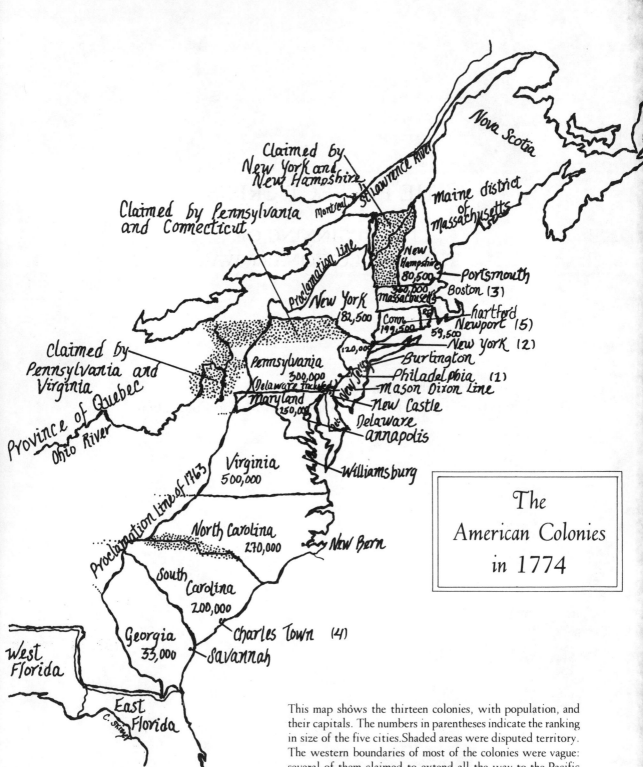

Claimed by
New York and
New Hampshire

Nova Scotia

St Lawrence River

Montreal

Maine district
of
Massachusetts

Claimed by Pennsylvania
and Connecticut

Proclamation Line

New
Hampshire
80,500

Portsmouth

Boston (3)

New York
182,500

Massachusetts

Conn.
199,500

Hartford

Newport (5)

59,500

New York (2)

120,000

Burlington

Claimed by
Pennsylvania and
Virginia

Pennsylvania
300,000
(Delaware included)

New Jersey

Philadelphia (1)

Mason Dixon Line

New Castle

Maryland
250,000

Delaware

Annapolis

Province of Quebec

Ohio River

Williamsburg

Virginia
500,000

Proclamation Line of 1763

North Carolina
270,000

New Bern

South
Carolina
200,000

Georgia
33,000

Charles Town (4)

Savannah

West
Florida

East
Florida

C. Smith

| The |
| American Colonies |
| in 1774 |

This map shows the thirteen colonies, with population, and
their capitals. The numbers in parentheses indicate the ranking
in size of the five cities. Shaded areas were disputed territory.
The western boundaries of most of the colonies were vague:
several of them claimed to extend all the way to the Pacific
Ocean. (Drawn by Carol Skinger.)

THE PERFECT CRISIS

THE BEGINNING OF
THE REVOLUTIONARY WAR

Neil R. Stout

New York • New York University Press • 1976

Library of Congress Catalog Card Number: 76-16343
ISBN: 0-8147-7774-0

Library of Congress Cataloging in Publication Data

Stout, Neil R
  The perfect crisis.

  Bibliography: p.
  Includes index.
  1. United States—History—Revolution,
1775-1783—Causes.   I. Title.
E210.S85   973.3'11   76-16343
ISBN 0-8147-7774-0

Manufactured in the United States of America

To Mainey, Hilary, and Peter
with love

Acknowledgements

I began research for this book in 1969 with the help of a small summer grant from the Graduate College of the University of Vermont; otherwise, it has had no direct subsidies. I typed it myself. Nevertheless, this book owes a great deal to many persons, including the following:

The Sir George Williams University History Department, who paid me enough for part-time teaching so that I was able to spend my sabbatical year from the University of Vermont in Cambridge, Massachusetts; my family, who made financial sacrifices so that I could research and write instead of teaching summer and evening courses; Deborah Clifford, who gave me a reader's ticket to the Boston Atheneum; Ann Gould of the University of Vermont library, who made my task much easier by allowing me to keep Force's *American Archives* far longer than library rules allowed; John Buechler and Catherine Mazza for their help in finding illustrations; the staffs of many libraries, especially Harvard University, Boston Atheneum, and Cambridge Public libraries; the historians who invited me to join their Wednesday sessions at Warren House, Harvard University, especially Pauline Maier and Richard D. Brown; David Reimers of New York University, who called this book to the attention of the New York

University Press; my colleagues in the University of Vermont History Department, especially Nick Muller, Mark Stoler, Harold Schultz, and Bill Daniels; my students, who read and discussed parts of the book and gave me much encouragement, especially Brian Burns, John and Sally Krueger, Andrea Booth Rebek, Carol Clark, and Louise Roomet; and finally, my best editor and strongest supporter, my wife Mainey. Thank you all.

N.R.S.

Contents

Introduction

On the evening of December 16, 1773, a group of Americans superficially disguised as Indians dumped 90,000 pounds of the East India Company's tea into Boston Harbor. On the morning of April 19, 1775, eight other Americans lay dead on Lexington Common, shot down by British troops marching to Concord. This book is about the sixteen months separating these two events, the period during which America's first civil war began.

The question of why there was an American Revolution has been debated by historians for two centuries. This book, however, is not so concerned with the *why* of the American Revolution, a political protest movement that began more than a decade before 1774, as with *how* it turned into the War for American Independence.

At the beginning of 1774 there was no inevitable reason for war to break out within the next sixteen months or even sixteen years. By August the war clearly could have begun at any time. A commander more dilatory than Thomas Gage, if such a man existed, might have delayed the beginning of hostilities for a few months beyond April 19, 1775; but only a change in attitude amounting to a surrender by either side could have postponed it beyond the summer of 1775.

The year 1774 is unique because only in that year did both sides come to realize that their constitutional differences would not be settled by peaceful means. The British government had to be prepared, as it was not during the Stamp Act crisis of 1765, to back its policies with force of arms. The Americans had to be willing, as they were not during the Townshend Act crisis of 1768, for armed resistance to those policies. The Americans proved to be the more realistic. The British government overreacted to the Boston Tea Party, and then underestimated the amount of force it would need to enforce its "Coercive Acts." The American radicals, on the other hand, included some practical revolutionaries who recognized the probability of war long before the British and the American moderates. A large part of this story is how, during 1774, these practical revolutionaries prepared America militarily, politically, and psychologically for the break with England.

Much of the story takes place in Massachusetts, because the colony was the focus of British efforts throughout 1774; but if the struggle had been confined to Massachusetts, the outcome would have been very different. At the beginning of 1774, few people believed that American union was possible; by September it was a reality. Each colony moved in its own way and for its own reasons, but the result was that Britain had to face not just one recalcitrant colony but an outraged people who were already thinking of themselves as Americans, not as British colonists. Perhaps this was the most revolutionary thing of all about the American Revolution.

List of Illustrations

LIST OF ILLUSTRATIONS

At length the perfect crisis of American politics seems arrived and a very few months must decide whether we and our posterity shall be slaves or freemen.

   —Dr. Thomas Young to John Lamb, May 13, 1774

CHAPTER I

A Happy Country

America in 1774

> The ease with which people can maintain a family, induces the young men to marry very young; one may see many young couples married and set up for themselves here, whose ages put together would not make above thirty years. This I think is a very clear proof of a happy country.
> —Patrick McRobert, a Scottish traveler, 1774

The average man or woman of 1774 could have found no better place in the world to live than in the thirteen British colonies in America. Had it not been for the rapidly worsening dispute with England, the picture of the colonies would be one of a well-established, reasonably tranquil society that was able to deal with its problems sensibly and adequately. It was an unlikely place for a revolution.

I. THE PEOPLE

Two and a half million people lived in the thirteen colonies in 1774. Three-fifths of them came from English stock. Most of the rest were of Scottish, Irish, or Welsh ancestry, or had been, like the Dutch, Swedish, and French settlers, so Americanized that they were little different from their English neighbors. The Germans, by their own choice, and the Negroes, who had no choice, were the only large groups that remained unassimilated. Almost all Indians lived beyond the effective boundaries of the colonies and were not counted as part of their population. By language, ancestry, and attitude, the typical colonist was an Englishman, although he was becoming more and more self-consciously an American.

The American population was increasing at a phenomenal rate, doubling every twenty years. The British government officially noted that the colonies' "vast increase in territory and population" made tighter imperial regulations "of immediate necessity," before they became too big for the mother country to control. In May 1774 Benjamin Franklin wrote in a London newspaper that the surest way of "humbling our rebellious Vassals of North America" was for Parliament to require "that all the Males there be c-st-ed," insuring that within fifty years "we shall not have one rebellious Subject in North America," and effectually stopping the emigration that was worrying some British officials.

Part of America's extraordinary growth came from an upsurge of immigration after the end of the Seven Years' War, but most of it was the result of natural increase. Americans married young, quickly remarried when widowed, and had large families. Both owed much to the fact that land was relatively available and cheap, while labor was scarce and expensive; Patrick McRobert's statement was not much of an exaggeration. Early and fecund marriages made, of course, for a very young population; more than half of it was under sixteen, and most of the rest under forty.

Besides being youthful, the population was overwhelmingly rural. Only one out of ten Americans was an urban dweller; and, in spite of the remarkable growth of cities, the population was getting more rural every year. Again the availability of cheap land was responsible. With the end of the long series of French and Indian Wars in 1763, settlement broke out of the tidewater and piedmont. By 1774 one-quarter of the colonists were living in the "back country." Against the craving for new land, British attempts to force orderly settlement of the west, such as the Proclamation of 1763, proved futile and had been largely abandoned by 1774. Daniel Boone is only the most famous of the many Americans who by 1774 had crossed the Appalachian Mountains and made a good start at settling the present states of Tennessee, Kentucky, and West Virginia, while in Pennsylvania and the Carolinas the back country folk comprised nearly half the population. Even in areas settled for a century or more, in 1774 a person was far more likely to live on a farm than in a city or even a village, although the farm was generally much smaller than it had been fifty years earlier.

II. THE REGIONS

The population was almost evenly divided by the line Charles Mason and Jeremiah Dixon had recently surveyed between Pennsylvania and Maryland, then as now the accepted boundary between north and south. In 1774 the south had not yet become self-consciously "southern," but Maryland, Virginia, the Carolinas, and Georgia shared characteristics that set them apart from the middle and New England colonies. For one thing, 28 percent of the southerners were black, compared to only 4 percent in the north. If one excludes the southern back country, nearly four out of every ten southerners were black.

The southern economy, too, was distinctive. A warm climate and rich soil enabled the southern colonies to grow crops which had a ready market in England and northern Europe: tobacco in Maryland and Virginia, rice and indigo in South Carolina and Georgia, so that they were sometimes called the "staple colonies." Unlike the other regions, the south traded directly with the mother country under strict imperial controls. Economic ties helped preserve cultural ties with England, and southern colonists tried harder to be "English" than northerners. On the other hand, many southerners keenly resented the economic subordination direct trade brought. Perhaps 75 percent of tobacco profits went to England in taxes, commissions, and freight and insurance charges. Furthermore, most planters were locked in perpetual debt to British mercantile houses that prospered by filling orders to maintain the planters' lifestyle. In 1774 Thomas Jefferson charged that Virginians then owed more than £2,000,000 sterling and had become "a species of property annexed to certain mercantile houses in London."

The great planters dominated the social, economic, political, and even religious life of the south. Nevertheless, there was a great deal of difference between the Virginia tobacco planter who lived on his land and struggled to make it pay and the South Carolina rice nabob who maintained a town house in Charleston and summered in Newport, Rhode Island. Neither had much in common with the back-country farmer or the black slave. Carl Bridenbaugh has described the southerners as "without question the least homogeneous human group in all America."

The four middle colonies—New York, New Jersey, Pennsylvania, and

Delaware—were often called the "bread colonies," for their main exports were grain and flour. They produced for a world market, yet had little direct trade with England, and felt the effects of the British Navigation Acts less than the other regions. Over 600,000 people lived in the middle colonies in a society that was prosperous, rapidly expanding, religiously tolerant, and politically conservative. Otherwise, it is hard to generalize about the middle colonies. Delaware had much in common with the plantation south, while parts of New York resembled New England. Pennsylvania was the fastest growing of the thirteen colonies, partly because the Penn family had a liberal land-sale policy. New York, on the other hand, was one of the slowest—in 1774 she ranked eighth in population, just behind Connecticut—because eastern New York was divided into large estates where land was rented, not sold, and the west was still dominated by the powerful Iroquois Confederation. Nevertheless, New York City was growing faster than any other American city.

The four New England colonies of Connecticut, Rhode Island, Massachusetts, and New Hampshire were also known as the "eastern colonies," and their people were already called "Yankees." In 1774 New England was the most homogeneous, the slowest growing, and the least prosperous of the regions; but it was also the most democratic, the most politically active, and the most disaffected toward England.

Nearly 700,000 people dwelt in New England, almost all of English ancestry. Even though New England's soil and climate were less suitable for commercial agriculture than the other regions', most Yankees, like most other colonists, lived on the land. New England had few significant agricultural exports, but she produced most of the dried and salted fish and a large part of the timber products exported by the colonies. Much of the produce of the other regions were carried in New England's ships; and the ships themselves, sold in the other colonies or in Britain, were a major New England export. A Yankee might farm part of the year, spend the winter in lumbering or home manufacturing, and then be a sailor on a vessel taking his farm products and handiwork to markets as far away as the West Indies.

New England always had an unfavorable balance of trade with England, which she redressed with profits from the carrying trade and, especially, from commerce with the West Indies. The sugar islands—especially the French ones—needed New England lumber and provisions, and were glad to buy the poorest-quality fish, unmarketable elsewhere, to feed their slaves. New England, in turn, was by far the largest purchaser of West Indian molasses, a waste product of sugar production, which she converted into rum. New England exported nearly 2,000,000 gallons of rum a year. The molasses trade, however, was the most heavily taxed of all colonial commerce—one reason for New England's disaffection. John Adams later reminded Americans that molasses was "an essential ingredient" of their Revolution.

While these three regions embraced all the inhabitants of the thirteen colonies, some of them were really part of a fourth "region" with its own characteristics, the back country. Every colony except Rhode Island and Delaware had a back country. Even Connecticut claimed and settled a part of the back country in the Wyoming Valley of Pennsylvania. Most of the back country, however, lay south of New York. In Pennsylvania and the south, the back country comprised more than half the land area, nearly half the population, and certainly more than half the white population.

III. COMMUNICATIONS

Ninety percent of the Americans were rural dwellers. The majority of them probably never saw a city or even a big town. Only twenty municipalities had populations of more than 3,000; only five of them, with a combined population of only 104,000, could be called cities. Philadelphia, with 40,000 souls, was much the biggest American city and one of the largest in the British empire, New York, with 25,000, was the fastest growing. Boston's 16,000 was nearly the same it had been thirty years before. Charleston (still called Charles Town) was the only city in the south, with 12,000 people, up from 8,000 in 1760. Newport, Rhode Island, with 11,000, was more than 2,500 larger than any of the fifteen or so smaller municipalities in America. Yet for all their insignificant size, the cities dominated American government, commerce, culture, and communications. To a very large extent, the American Revolution was born in the cities.

All the important urban centers were Atlantic ports, and even the smaller municipalities were on navigable waterways. Thus they were the first to receive news from the rest of the world, and they were the source of news for the hinterland. Although the fastest, surest, and safest transportation was still by water, by 1774 regularly scheduled stagecoaches and post riders traveled by post road between major cities. In the back country, the Great Wagon Road, stretching 700 miles from Georgia to Pennsylvania, was the most traveled land route in America. Letters, newspapers, and word of mouth all served to disseminate news throughout the colonies. News from Boston found its way with astonishing speed (though often with considerable damage to accuracy) all the way to the Ohio Valley.

The most important medium of communication was the press. During 1774 and early 1775, American printers, located mostly in the cities and larger towns, ran off thousands of broadsides and pamphlets, dozens of almanacs, two magazines, and thirty-eight newspapers. Every colony except New Jersey and Delaware, already served by New York and Philadelphia printers, had at least one newspaper, and of the rest, all but Georgia and New Hampshire had at least two. Most papers were new; only fifteen of them had been in print before 1764. All but the biweekly *Boston Chronicle* and the triweekly *Pennsylvania Evening Post* were weeklies. Circulation was tiny by modern standards, around 1,500 or 1,600 per issue. The Tory *Rivington's New-York Gazetteer* had the largest subscription list in America with 3,600.

But colonial newspapers' readership far exceeded their subscription lists, and their circulation went far beyond their immediate localities. Their good rag paper stood up to the dozens of hands that might pick them up in taverns and coffeehouses. The *New-York Mercury* boasted in 1762 that it circulated in every town and village of Connecticut, Rhode Island, and New Jersey, every capital from Nova Scotia to Georgia, as well as the West Indies, Great Britain, and Holland. Americans writing to correspondents in England often referred them to American newspapers. Furthermore, printers served as postmasters in the colonial postal service, and newspapers exchanged with other colonial printers were carried free of charge. Thus an important story in the *Georgia Gazette* would eventually find its way into the *New-Hampshire Gazette* and most of the papers in between.

It is almost impossible to overestimate the importance of the press in disseminating ideas in colonial America. Any educated American was likely to be versed in the philosophy of John Locke, whose principles were constantly discussed in newspapers, pamphlets, and books. As Bernard Bailyn has pointed out in his masterly *Ideological Origins of the American Revolution,* pamphlets did much to convince Americans that there was a ministerial plot against English liberty. American unity from the Stamp Act on was promoted by newspaper accounts of what the other colonies were doing: thus Massachusetts was prodded into action by newspaper reports of the Virginia Stamp Act resolves, Boston was heartened by news of resistance to the Tea Act in the other colonies, and the need for a continental congress was fully debated in the press long before it was actually convened.

[6]

IV. THE GOVERNMENTS

At the beginning of 1774, the colonial governments were long established and seemed more conducive to stability than to revolution. The fact that many of them had been overthrown by the end of the year is a good indication of how revolutionary 1774 was.

Most of the colonial governments had been functioning for at least a century, and there was little evidence of discontent with the *structure* of government in 1774. While all the colonies had been founded either by chartered companies or by individual proprietors, by 1774 eight of them had been converted into royal colonies. Connecticut and Rhode Island still clung to the seventeenth-century corporate charters that gave them virtually complete control of their internal affairs, while Maryland was still owned by the Calvert family and Pennsylvania and Delaware by the Penns. But whether royal, corporate, or proprietary, the structure of government was essentially the same in every colony.

The executive power was exercised by a governor who was appointed by the king or the proprietor, except in Connecticut and Rhode Island, where the governors were elected annually. Governors had very broad powers, including an absolute veto of acts of their legislatures and patronage that extended to the appointment of all militia officers, all judges down to the lowliest justice of the peace, and, in most colonies, members of the Council, which was both an advisory body to the governor and the upper house of the legislature.

Fourteen men served as governors of the thirteen colonies during 1774. They were, by and large, men of outstanding ability and experience for their jobs; and in anything like normal circumstances, all of them could have retired with honor and a personal sense of a job well done. As it was, only one—Jonathan Trumbull of Connecticut—chose the winning side in the American Revolution. Everything about the governors should have lent itself to stability. Only two colonies—Massachusetts and New York—underwent a change in governors during 1774, and both of these were supposed to be temporary.

Their average age in 1774 was fifty-two years—fifty, if one omits Cadwallader Colden, who was born in the year of the Glorious Revolution, 1688. At the beginning of 1774 they averaged just over five years in their governorships and over twenty years in some office in the colonies. Half of them were native Americans, and all but three had lived in America for so long that they, too, were considered colonists. No doubt their age and long time in office contributed to their conservatism, but they cannot be called outsiders foisted on the colonies by a cynical British government. Influence had a role in all eighteenth-century political appointments, but the only clear-cut example of nepotism among the governors was William Franklin, who was granted both an Oxford M.A. and the governorship of New Jersey to please his natural father, Benjamin Franklin!

Many of the governors had substantial reputations outside of politics. Thomas Hutchinson's *History of Massachusetts-Bay* was the best piece of historical scholarship written by an American during the colonial period. Cadwallader Colden was a famous scientist. William Bull studied medicine at Leyden and became the first native born American to receive the M.D. degree. Five governors had been British army officers, while three others had served in the colonial militia. Half of them had academic degrees in an era when college training was rare for politicians or anyone else.

Their personalities and rapport with their constituents varied. Some, like the two proprietary governors, Robert Eden of Maryland and John Penn of Pennsylvania and Delaware, were genuinely popular and only regretfully turned out of their posts during the War for Independence. Others, like Josiah Martin of North Carolina and Colden of New York, would have fought with their legislatures under any circumstances. Only Thomas Hutchinson of Massachusetts was roundly hated by his constituents.

The governors' greatest problem was having both American and English responsibilities. As royal governors, they were literally servants of the crown. This did not bother Americans so long as the governors did not try to serve the British Parliament as well; for by 1774 only a few Americans would acknowledge that Parliament had any power at all over the colonies. They still vowed allegiance to King George III, but his support of Parliament's claims had markedly reduced the affection Americans had for him. Thus, even as the king's personal representatives, the governors were caught in the middle of the dispute between Parliament and the colonists.

During 1774, as in the preceding decade, the main burden of opposition to Great Britain was carried by the lower houses of the colonial legislatures. These bodies had increasingly equated themselves with the British House of Commons, and by 1774 many of them were calling themselves "parliaments," rather than houses of representatives. Their greatest powers—and the ones they were disputing with Parliament—were those of taxation and appropriation. They guarded these prerogatives as jealously as had the English parliaments that beheaded Charles I and drove James II from his throne; and they never tired of pointing to those precedents.

By eighteenth-century standards, the lower houses were chosen democratically. Every colony had property qualifications for voting and holding office, but these qualifications had been set in England, where land was scarce and labor plentiful. In practice, few adult white males were legally excluded from the political process, although it was seldom that anything like a majority of them bothered to exercise their vote. The basis for representation in New England was the township, with each town annually voting for representatives. In the other colonies elections were generally county-wide and held somewhat less frequently.

In every colony except Pennsylvania there was a two-house legislature. The upper house, called the Council, was in most colonies appointed by the king or proprietor. Councilors were supposed to be—and usually were—the wealthiest and most conservative gentlemen in the colonies—men who could be counted upon to support the governor and official British policy.

The government of Massachusetts was something of a hybrid. It was a royal colony whose governor was appointed by the king, but it also had a charter dating from 1691 which provided that the Council be elected annually by the House of Representatives. Thus the Council was much more responsive to popular will in Massachusetts than in the other royal colonies. Parliament tried to change that in 1774, making the Massachusetts Council appointive, as in the other royal colonies.

At the colony level, government was thrown into turmoil during 1774. Before the year was out, most colonies were forced to shift to some extralegal government, such as conventions and provincial congresses. Local government, however, continued to function during the crisis. America was never in a state of anarchy, even when the legal colonial governments had ceased to function. New England's order was sustained by its town meetings and boards of selectmen, the other colonies by their county courts and vestries.

At first glance, there seem to be wide differences between the local governments of New England and the other colonies. The New England town meeting is often cited as an example of pure democracy in action; the electorate met whenever necessary to thresh out the town's problems and choose officers to keep things running smoothly. By contrast, in a colony like Virginia, the vestry was a self-perpetuating body and the county court very nearly so. In practice, however, the differences are less apparent. The New England towns tended to elect the same men and the same families to office year after year. Virginia was undoubtedly ruled by county oligarchies, but they stayed in power not by a kind of local "divine right," but because they had proved to be responsive to the needs of their constituents. Local government reflected American society.

[9]

V. AMERICAN SOCIETY

American society in 1774 was filled with paradox and contradiction. Perhaps this has always been true in America, but it was especially evident in 1774.

To begin with, the colonists had hardly begun to think of themselves as "Americans." When a John Adams or a Thomas Jefferson spoke of "my country," he meant Massachusetts or Virginia, even when he was promoting a union of the colonies. It is true that Patrick Henry told the Continental Congress in 1774 that "the distinctions between Virginians, Pennsylvanians, New Yorkers, and New Englanders are no more. I am not a Virginian, but an American." His listeners, however, knew that the point of Henry's oratory was to get more votes for Virginia in Congress.

The concept of a single "America" was more prevalent in England. During the debates over the Coercive Acts, members of Parliament tended to use "America" and "Massachusetts" interchangeably. No colonist would have done such a thing. By the end of 1774, however, the sense of a common cause and a common enemy had begun to break down the parochialism of many colonists. The delegates to the First Continental Congress returned with at least the beginnings of a national identity.

Another paradox lay in the class structure. Jackson Turner Main, who has made the most comprehensive study of the social structure of revolutionary America, has concluded that insofar as "class" requires that men know their own place in the order of society, America certainly "was both classless and democratic by comparison with the America of 1900 or with England in 1776." Nevertheless, Main found that Americans did recognize that there was a social hierarchy within which individuals could move up and down. They often expressed this by referring to the "better sort," the "middling sort," and the "meaner sort" of persons.

The main criterion for social standing in America was wealth. Any man who had an estate of at least £2,000 was in the top 10 percent economically, and probably socially, as well. At the bottom were those who had less than £50 worth of property and generally depended upon someone else for wages or support. This group included around one-fifth of the white population and virtually all of the blacks; perhaps 30 percent of the whole population would be recognized as part of the "meaner" or "lesser" sort of men. The great mass of colonists—at least 70 percent of the white population—lay between these extremes.

Since status was based mostly on wealth in America, the social structure of America differed significantly from that of England or continental Europe. America had no hereditary nobility. Ancestry was not a negligible factor in American social class, but the most important thing a patriarch could leave to his heirs was not his name but his money.

Social mobility was commonest among the lowest-class whites. While about 20 percent of the white population at any time could be classed as the "meaner sort," a large number of them were immigrants, indentured servants, apprentices, young men and women who hired themselves out in order to save a stake, and those with "no fixed address," such as soldiers, sailors, and teamsters. Most of these could and did move up to the middle class. Only 5 to 10 percent of the whites were locked into a permanent proletariat by lack of talent, ambition, temperance, or luck. With black Americans, whether slave or free, no amount of these qualities was likely ever to get them into even the lowest stratum of the middle class. They and a few other groups were victims of a prejudice so alien to the spirit of revolutionary America that a few Americans, at least, were beginning to be bothered by it in 1774.

The Negroes comprised the largest non-English group in the colonies, nearly one-fifth of the population. While there had been blacks in the colonies since 1619, most of them had arrived only in the past sixty years. All of them had come to America as slaves, and almost all of them were still slaves. Although at least 85 percent of the slaves were held south of the Mason and Dixon Line, slavery existed in every one of the colonies. No colony had a black majority in 1774, although some counties in the lowland south were as much as 70 percent black. Nowhere did even free blacks enjoy equality with whites. Most colonies had, or thought they had, a race problem. Civil disturbances were often officially attributed to "sailors, Negroes, and boys," sometimes as a plausible cover-up for the activities of the "respectable" citizenry. Wherever there was a large concentration of blacks, not only in the south but in New York City, whites feared a black uprising. In spite of, and partly because of, racial prejudice, blacks were Americanized Englishmen in almost everything except color and status; all traces of Africanism were ruthlessly stamped out.

While blacks were the main victims of American prejudice, other groups suffered disabilities as well. The Germans—10 percent of the colonial population concentrated mainly in Pennsylvania and the southern back country—clung to their language, their churches, and their own settlements. Benjamin Franklin spoke for many Pennsylvanians when he railed against the influx of "Palatine Boors" who would "shortly be so numerous as to Germanize us instead of our Anglifying them," but Franklin also published a German-language newspaper

[11]

and assiduously courted German votes. Pennsylvania's laws were published in both English and German.

Jews, and indeed anyone who was not a Trinitarian Protestant Christian, experienced both legal and social disabilities, though they were not as great as those suffered by religious dissenters in most of the rest of the European world. Scots came in for a lot of public and private criticism, partly carried over from England, and partly because Scotsmen often served as agents for British mercantile houses in America. The Scots, however, proved quite capable of taking care of themselves in both Britain and America.

One way to achieve status was through education. Illiteracy was a handicap. New England had the broadest educational system, which may have been a factor in the region's greater democracy. A college degree was such a scarce commodity—no more than one out of every thousand Americans ever attended college—that it automatically conferred status. Philip Vickers Fithian, a young Princeton graduate hired to tutor the children of Robert Carter, a wealthy Virginia planter, wrote that Virginia society was based on wealth "excepting always the value they put upon posts of honour, & mental acquirements." Fithian was told that a Princeton graduate "would be rated, without any more questions being asked, either about your family, your Estate, your business, or your intention, at 10,000 £; and you might come, & go, & converse, & keep company, according to this value."

Recognition of this road to success helped create what the Reverend Ezra Stiles called "College Enthusiasm" during the three decades before 1774. In 1745 the only colleges in British North America were Harvard, Yale, and William and Mary. By the end of 1774 they were joined by Dartmouth, Brown, Columbia, Rutgers, Princeton, Pennsylvania, and Delaware. While most students came, of course, from at least well-to-do families, there were always openings for bright youngsters like John Adams, son of a small farmer.

It should be noted, however, that American social mobility was not as easy in 1774 as it had been fifty or a hundred years earlier. The economic opportunities were not as great after the country became more settled, except for those willing to brave the hazards of the back country or the frontier. Farms in the older regions were getting smaller and less fertile at the same time land was getting scarcer and more expensive. Although by European standards, the rich were still not very rich nor the poor very poor, the difference in life styles between rich and poor tended to advertise their social differences. In addition, family was becoming more of a barrier to instant aristocracy. This was particularly true in New York and the south, but family connections were important even in New

England, as witness the long rule of Massachusetts by the Hutchinsons and Olivers, with their "River God" allies in the Connecticut valley.

The perquisites of aristocracy, such as a seat in the Council, deference in political matters, and invitations to the right social functions, were getting harder to be commanded by mere wealth. Some of the young men who had become successful in business or the professions, like John Adams, Patrick Henry, or Christopher Gadsden, felt that the top of the ladder of success was being blocked by the old guard. Part of their radicalism was the result of thwarted ambition.

Whatever the realities of the American class structure, a number of persons on both sides of the Atlantic saw dangerous "leveling" tendencies in America. During the debate over the Coercive Acts, Member of Parliament Sir Richard Sutton told a story to illustrate the extreme lengths to which Americans had carried democracy: "He knew a gentleman who went to a merchant's house at Boston, and he asked the servant if his master was at home. 'My master!' replied the servant, 'I have no master but Jesus Christ: John Such-an-one (naming his master) is at home, if you want him.' " Thomas Hutchinson charged that Sam Adams packed the Boston town meeting with the lower classes, and Daniel Horsmanden, chief justice of New York, complained that Rhode Island's "government, if it deserves such a name, is no better than a downright democracy." Nearly every English traveler in America noted, with satisfaction or alarm, that the wealthy and powerful had to act familiar with their inferiors, especially if they were running for office.

On the other hand, it is evident that "leveling" had a long way to go. Harvard still kept its class lists according to social standing, rather than by alphabet or scholarly achievement. The light turnouts for elections and the continued election of wealthy individuals—in some cases generation after generation—indicates that deference was still strong in America, partly because most American aristocrats had done something to prove their worth to the community, like making a lot of money or serving competently as elected or appointed officials.

America's religious life was just as paradoxical. Many colonies had established churches; Anglican in the south and Congregationalist in New England. Even Rhode Island, founded as an experiment in religious freedom, limited full citizenship to Trinitarian Protestants. America had gone through one of history's biggest revival movements—the Great Awakening—during the 1740s, and its effects were still felt in 1774. Political speeches and even business transactions were liberally sprinkled with biblical quotations. Newspapers and

[13]

magazines constantly printed theological discussions. America probably had more religious sects living side by side than any other area of the western world.

However, church membership was probably the lowest in American history. Even in New England, founded as the "New Wilderness Zion" and where Sunday blue laws were still strictly enforced, only one person in seven was a church member. South of New England the average was less than half that. This was not because the churches made admission to communion difficult; indeed, the clergy were so worried about the loss of membership that there were hardly any restrictions. It is evident that, whatever Americans' private religious beliefs, they were not much taken with organized religion.

But that is not to say they found religion unimportant. New England was in an uproar in the 1770s over persistent rumors that an Anglican bishophric was to be established in the colonies. Nor did the colonies where the Anglican church was established much care for the idea of an American bishop. So long as the bishop stayed in London, control of the parishes was in the hands of the vestrymen. The Anglican church in America was fully as congregational in its polity as the Calvinist churches.

Colonial politics had strong religious overtones, but they were only overtones. The Quaker party of Pennsylvania was run by two non-Quakers, Benjamin Franklin and Joseph Galloway, and was much more concerned with opposing the Penn family than with promoting any of the tenets of the Society of Friends. Connecticut was politically, as well as religiously, divided between the "New Lights" and the "Old Lights" (the latter being the less committed to the "old-time religion"), but by 1774 the religious conflict was so complicated by the fight with England and an internal struggle over the Susquehannah Land Company that it is impossible to tell where religion left off and other conflicts began. New York had long been the scene of political battles between the Livingston (Presbyterian) and DeLancey (Anglican) parties, but in 1774 they both were mainly concerned with the Revolution and how to keep the lower classes from seizing power.

In 1774, then, America was both happy and discontented, stable and fluid, English and American, democratic and elitist. In the face of all the paradoxes and internal conflicts, it is little wonder that many Englishmen and Americans as well were certain that the colonies could never unite in opposition to British policy or anything else. How they accomplished this task is the theme of this book.

CHAPTER II

Molasses, Stamps, and Tea

The Dispute with England to 1774

> What do We Mean by the Revolution? The War? That was
> no part of the Revolution. It was only an Effect and
> Consequence of it. The Revolution was in the Minds of the
> People, and this was effected, from 1760 to 1775, in the
> course of fifteen Years before a drop of blood was drawn at
> Lexington.
>
> —John Adams to Thomas Jefferson, 1815

As John Adams pointed out to his old friend and sometime antagonist, the year 1774 marks the conclusion—not the beginning—of the American Revolution. To understand the importance of 1774 we must, if only briefly, review the dispute between England and America through the Boston Tea Party.

I. MR. GRENVILLE AND THE EMPIRE

Until 1760 Great Britain had not tried very hard to control the internal affairs of her American colonies. Although Britain consistently stuck to the theory that her control over the colonies was absolute, in fact she attempted to exert that control only rarely, as in the short-lived Dominion of New England in the 1680s. She was hardly more consistent in her efforts to control American trade. Parliament began to regulate American trade in 1651, and although it laid taxes on certain American imports and exports as early as 1673, the purpose of these taxes was not to raise revenue but to regulate trade, a power most Americans conceded in theory. In practice, they obeyed only those regulations which did not harm their trade, as is especially attested by the record of the Molasses Act of 1733. This act put a tax of sixpence per gallon on all foreign molasses, which would have doubled its cost and halted trade between England's North American colonies and the French and Spanish West Indies. The act was seldom enforced, and the trade went on even when England was at war with France and Spain.

Under the lax application of the British imperial system, the colonies grew and prospered. Occasionally English politicians influenced by grumbling taxpayers suggested that Parliament should levy direct taxes in the colonies. Most British governments, however, seem to have recognized the wisdom of Sir Robert Walpole, who is said to have replied to such a suggestion with: "I will leave that for some of my successors, who may have more courage than I have."

In April 1763, George Grenville became prime minister of a government that desperately needed a new source of revenue. Great Britain had a huge national debt, a vastly enlarged empire, and a plethora of new responsibilities. Grenville and most other politicians agreed that a considerable military establishment must be maintained in North America. Large numbers of former French and Spanish subjects were now ruled by King George III in Canada and Florida. Potentially hostile Indians must be kept from attacking frontier settlements; but so also must the Americans be kept from encroaching on Indian lands. Not least was the problem of finding employment for large numbers of army and navy officers. The military estimates for the British government's 1763 budget were therefore the largest in the nation's peacetime history; a large part of those forces were to be stationed in America.

No one was sure just how much all this would cost (Grenville's guess of £350,000 per year for the army in America proved to be reasonably accurate); but it was certainly more than Britain could willingly pay. Drawing on the experience of military enforcement of the Molasses Act during the last years of the war, Grenville was convinced that America could shoulder part of the burden. The army and navy in America could help enforce tax collections that would pay for their existence, and at the same time bring the colonies under closer imperial control. It should not be surprising that Grenville's first venture into colonial affairs was to continue, strengthen, and formalize army and navy

[16]

enforcement of the trade and revenue laws and to reform the customs service. During the summer of 1763 absentee customs officials were ordered to their posts in America, naval officers of the North American squadron were commissioned as deputy customs officers, and, most importantly, the Molasses Act of 1733 was ordered to be rigorously enforced. It was never designed to produce revenue, but to exclude foreign sugar products from British imperial trade. Grenville enforced it, however, to impress both the colonists and colonial officials that Parliament could command obedience to its laws. The law was soon revised to make it a real revenue producer when Grenville secured passage of the Revenue Act of 1764, better known as the Sugar Act.

Purely as a revenue measure, the Sugar Act was a success, the only successful tax Parliament ever imposed on the American colonies. The molasses tax, especially after it was lowered to a penny a gallon in 1766 and imposed on British as well as foreign molasses, yielded enough revenue to allow the customs service, for the first time, to pay its own expenses, with enough left over to help support other parts of the British colonial program.

Had the British government been content with the molasses tax and the other duties imposed by the Sugar Act, the history of British North America might be different. Merchants grumbled but paid, and the economic catastrophe they predicted did not materialize. Some Americans tried to make a constitutional issue of the molasses tax from time to time after 1764, but with little success; possibly the molasses trade was too important to New England's economy to make it susceptible to the kind of resistance later used for the Townshend duties. Furthermore it could be rationalized as an act to regulate trade even though, especially after 1766, the Sugar Act was a palpable revenue measure. It is evident that the continued payment of the molasses tax was a continual embarrassment to the American radicals.

The molasses tax, however, did not produce all the revenue needed to maintain military forces in America. Announcing his intentions when he introduced the Sugar Act in 1764, George Grenville expected to make up the difference with a stamp tax on American newspapers, diplomas, licenses, deeds, wills, ship clearances, and legal documents. The Stamp Act was passed in March 1765, to go into effect in November. Unlike the Sugar Act, which had been opposed largely on grounds of economic hardship, the Stamp Act opened up the whole constitutional issue of the colonies' relationship to the British Parliament.

The Virginia House of Burgesses was the first legislature to object to the Stamp Act. Toward the end of May 1765, after the House had finished most of its regular business, young Patrick Henry rose to suggest that George III reflect on the fate of Julius Caesar and Charles I, and then presented seven resolutions against the act. Even the generally conservative burgesses heartily approved four of them: their thrust was that Virginians enjoyed all the rights of Englishmen, the most important of which was to be taxed only "by themselves, or by persons chosen by themselves to represent them." The other three, which the burgesses turned down, declared that Parliament was attempting "to Destroy AMERICAN FREEDOM," that Virginians were not bound to obey any act of Parliament "designed to impose any Taxation upon them," and anyone who argued otherwise "shall be Deemed, AN ENEMY TO THIS HIS MAJESTY'S COLONY." The colonial newspapers, however, printed all seven of Henry's resolutions as if all had been passed by the House of Burgesses.

Following what they thought was Virginia's lead, other colonial legislatures added their objections to the Stamp Act. Massachusetts called for an intercolonial congress to meet in New York City in October to "implore relief" from the Stamp Act. The twenty-seven delegates to the Stamp Act Congress were anything but radical; nevertheless, they clearly stated the constitutional case against Parliament's taxing Americans: "it is inseparably essential to the Freedom of a People, and the undoubted Right of *Englishmen,* that no Taxes be imposed on them, but with their own Consent, given personally, or by their Representatives." Furthermore, "the People of these Colonies are not, and from their local Circumstances cannot be Represented in the House of Commons in *Great Britain."* This stand, which was soon universally expressed in the more epigramatic "no taxation without representation," remained the basis of the constitutional dispute between England and America for the rest of the revolutionary period.

Opposition to the Stamp Act was not confined to statements of constitutional principles, however. On August 14, 1765, a Boston mob tore down the business office of the Massachusetts stamp distributor-designate, Andrew Oliver. Twelve days later the mob, much uglier now, settled some old scores with William Story, an officer of the vice-admiralty court; Benjamin Hallowell, comptroller of customs; and Thomas Hutchinson, who was both chief justice and lieutenant governor.

Taking their cue from Boston, other cities fomented popular uprisings. By November 1, the day the Stamp Act was supposed to take effect, all the stamp distributors in the colonies had been forced to resign or were otherwise prevented from exercising their commissions. Merchants had quit importing British goods. At first all operations requiring stamps were suspended, but before the end of the year most had gone back to business as usual, in defiance of the Stamp Act. Except briefly in Georgia, not a penny was collected under the Stamp Act in the thirteen colonies.

Meanwhile, George III had replaced George Grenville with the marquis of Rockingham. Moved by complaints of British merchants who were hurt by American nonimportation rather than by colonial resolves and riots, the Rockingham government agreed to repeal the Stamp Act less than five months after it became law. Parliament conceded nothing on the constitutional issue, however; it simultaneously passed a "Declaratory Act" claiming for itself the power to make laws "to bind the colonies and People of America . . . in all cases whatsoever."

It would be impossible to overestimate the effect of the Stamp Act crisis on the American Revolution. It forced Americans, as the Sugar Act had not, to examine their constitutional relationship to Great Britain; and, ignoring the Declaratory Act, most of them thought their constitutional stand had been vindicated. Thomas Hutchinson later wrote that "the repeal of the Stamp Act, notwithstanding the Declaratory Act which accompanied it, was considered throughout the colonies not as a mere act of favor . . . but as a concession made to the claim of exemption from taxes while not represented." By 1766, said Hutchinson, the colonists developed new ideas about the degree of their subordination to Parliament. " 'No representation, no taxation, ' became a very common expression. 'No representation, no legislation, ' designing men knew would obtain by degrees, and become as common." Hutchinson was right. On July 1, 1769, the Massachusetts legislature unanimously resolved "that no man can be taxed, or bound in conscience to obey any law, to which he has not given his consent in person, or by his representative."

The Stamp Act brought a revolution in American politics. Nothing else so united Americans during the whole revolutionary era as did their opposition to the Stamp Act, and perhaps nothing else in American history produced such a widespread mass uprising.

After the Stamp Act crisis, the "common" people were less inclined to defer to their "betters" than they had been before. They still elected aristocrats to office, but now they held them accountable to the public will. English fears that America was becoming democratic were exaggerated, but not entirely un-founded. On the other hand, this "leveling" tendency—and especially the emergence of mob action as an instrument of politics—frightened some of those who had ardently opposed the Stamp Act. Thereafter they were inclined to balance the theoretical tyranny of a Parliament several thousand miles away against the more imminent danger of local mobs. A good many of those who

[19]

became Tories in 1774-75 did so because of their memories of the Stamp Act riots.

II. COERCION AND CONCILIATION

After the repeal of the Stamp Act, Great Britain had a new government—the Pitt-Grafton ministry—and an old problem, the need for money to finance its American operations. The government was one of the oddest amalgams in the history of any major nation. It was formed by the erstwhile "Great Commoner," William Pitt, but Pitt was now the earl of Chatham. His voice could no longer be heard in the House of Commons, but it was seldom heard in Lords either, for Chatham was physically and mentally ill. The nominal prime minister, the young duke of Grafton, had few strong principles about anything and exercised little leadership. America had a true friend in the secretary of state for the southern department (the office responsible for colonial affairs), the earl of Shelburne, but Shelburne was also in Lords, and he was thoroughly distrusted by much of Parliament. The most prominent commoner in the government was the chancellor of the exchequer, Charles Townshend, whose views on America were much the same as those of the leader of the opposition, George Grenville. Townshend, a brilliant but erratic man, got the name "Champagne Charlie" for a speech satirizing his fellow ministers made under the influence of the bubbly wine. As a result, for more than two years Parliament made American policy with little leadership from the government.

Early in 1767 Townshend told Parliament that he had a plan to make Americans pay taxes willingly. While he thought the distinction was "perfect nonsense," he claimed that both Chatham and the Americans had objected only to "internal" taxation by Parliament, such as the Stamp Act; "external" ones, such as the Sugar Act's taxes on imports, were acceptable. (In fact, Benjamin Franklin was the only American to make such a distinction, and that was only to help secure repeal of the Stamp Act. As John Dickinson soon pointed out in his famous "Letters from a Farmer in Pennsylvania," a tax for revenue was "internal" and unconstitutional however it was collected.)

Even George Grenville was not fooled. He told Townshend that Americans would "laugh at you for your distinctions about regulations of trade," but he forced Townshend to carry out his program by helping defeat a government motion to extend an English land tax, costing the treasury £500,000 in revenue.

[20]

The three "Townshend Acts" which became law in July 1767 levied taxes on paper, paint, lead, glass, and tea imported into the colonies; created a new American Board of Customs Commissioners to make collections more efficient; and suspended the New York legislature until it should agree to supply the British army as required under the Quartering Act of 1765. On the surface, at least, the acts would have done little to alleviate Britain's colonial problems. Tea was the only important item taxed, and Townshend himself estimated that the taxes would yield an annual return of only £40,000.

New York was not the only colony that had failed to abide by the Quartering Act, but the real purpose of the acts was to establish precedents by which the constitutional issue would be resolved in favor of Parliament, and that is what the Americans feared. If New York could be forced to supply the soldiers, so could every other colony; even Shelburne agreed to this. If Americans acquiesced in paying import duties that were palpable revenue taxes, then the principle of the Declaratory Act was established. Perhaps more important, the money collected from the Townshend duties was specifically to go toward "defraying the charge of administration of justice, and the support of civil government, in such provinces where it shall be found necessary." In other words, British colonial officials would be freed of the control colonial assemblies had always exercised through their power of appropriation.

Townshend's plan (if that is what he really had in mind—he died in September 1767) might have worked. Americans were divided and anxious to avoid repeating the excesses of the Stamp Act crisis. Despite radical opposition, New York voted to supply the troops. The most noteworthy American protests, the "Massachusetts Circular Letter" and Dickinson's "Pennsylvania Farmer" letters, were firm in tone but did not breathe defiance like Patrick Henry's Stamp Act Resolves. But the British government, still smarting from the Stamp Act defeat, seemed determined to force a crisis. The conciliatory Shelburne was eased out of his supervision of colonial affairs by the creation of a new secretariat for the colonies. Soon both Chatham and Shelburne resigned.

The new colonial secretary, the earl of Hillsborough, believed in talking tough. He called the "Pennsylvania Farmer" letters "extremely wild." The "Massachusetts Circular letter" (which had passed only with difficulty in Massachusetts and was getting little notice from the other colonial assemblies) was "of a most dangerous and factious tendency, calculated to inflame the minds of [the King's] good subjects in the colonies." Hillsborough instructed Governor Francis Bernard to dissolve the Massachusetts legislature if it failed to rescind the Circular Letter and ordered all the other colonial governors to dissolve their legislatures if they should show "a disposition to receive or give any countenance to this seditious paper."

The results of Hillsborough's orders were the exact opposite of what he had intended. Massachusetts refused to rescind by a vote of 92-17; more importantly, the radicals were once again strengthened and the conservatives discredited. The other American legislatures might have ignored the Massachusetts Circular Letter if Hillsborough had not challenged their prerogatives. Now they had to take notice of it, thus creating colonial unity where little had previously existed.

The most serious confrontation between Parliament and America came in Boston. Although Philadelphia and New York had more trade, Boston was the largest importer of the items taxed by the Townshend Acts, and was chosen to be headquarters for the new American customs board. Thus Boston could be isolated, just as New York had been on the issue of supplying the troops. As Charles Paxton, one of the customs commissioners, put it: "If the laws of trade are enforced in Massachusetts government, the other provinces will readily submit."

The commissioners certainly expected trouble. They repeatedly demanded that troops and naval vessels be sent to Boston to protect them, even though the Bostonians subjected them to nothing worse than social ostracism. On June 10, 1768, however, the commisioners got the riot they had expected and may even have wanted. Backed by the fifty-gun warship *Romney*, the commissioners seized John Hancock's sloop *Liberty* for the technical violation of loading without a customs permit. For their temerity, the commissioners' houses were sacked, and they had to flee, first to the *Romney* and then to Castle William, a fort on an island far out in Boston harbor. There they remained until October, refusing to return to their duty until troops should be stationed in Boston for their protection. Soldiers were finally sent to occupy Boston on Hillsborough's orders. Perhaps the *Liberty* riot justified them; but Hillsborough had issued the orders on June 8, two days before the riot, thus lending credence to the view that the government had expected and desired a confrontation with Boston all along.

Four regiments of redcoats landed in Boston in October 1768, and the town remained under military occupation until March 1770. The soldiers' stay was not a happy one. The redcoats were constantly harassed, and the most remarkable thing about the "Boston Massacre" of March 5, 1770, in which severely provoked troops fired into a mob, is that it was so long in coming.

[22]

Thereafter the remaining troops were quartered in Castle William, out of harm's way for either side.

In February 1769 Parliament overwhelmingly passed a series of resolutions and an address to the king asserting that Massachusetts's actions were "illegal, unconstitutional, and derogatory of the rights of the Crown and Parliament of Great Britain," that the Massachusetts Circular Letter was a call to rebellion, and that certain Massachusetts leaders should be brought to England to stand trial for treason under a statute from the reign of Henry VIII.

Once again the American response was just the opposite of what England had hoped. Far from being intimidated and fragmented by Parliament's resolutions, the colonies drew more closely together to defend their rights. Followed by others, the legislatures of Virginia and South Carolina adopted vigorous protests against Parliament's February resolves. Against the wishes of many colonial merchants who feared enforcement by committees of radicals, a reasonably effective nonimportation and nonconsumption movement was instituted. Thus Parliament unwittingly helped to keep the American radicals in the ascendant during 1769 and early 1770.

The Townshend Acts—the cause of all the trouble—were a failure. All the items except tea could be produced in America, so the Townshend taxes served mostly to protect nascent American industry. As for tea, both Americans and Englishmen had long patronized smugglers better than than they had legal importers. The Townshend Acts produced only £13,202 (about one-third what Townshend had predicted) in 1768. Under nonimportation, receipts under the act fell to £5,561 in 1769 and £2,727 in 1770.

After the February outburst, however, Britain shifted to a much more conciliatory attitude toward America. In May 1769 Lord Hillsborough sent the colonial governors another circular letter, repeating Parliament's assertion of absolute power over America, but going on to state that the government would not ask Parliament for new American taxes. Furthermore, the ministry intended to seek repeal of all the Townshend taxes except that on tea. The ministry kept its promise. The repeal went through during the 1770 session, and Parliament never again passed a bill that taxed America.

Part of the reason for Britain's dramatic shift in actions—if not in official policy—toward America must lie in Lord North's emergence as the leader of the government. Frederick North, a commoner who bore the courtesy title "Lord North" because he was heir to the earldom of Guilford, had been chancellor of the exchequer since Charles Townshend's death in September 1767. He quickly

[23]

became the "strong man" (if an individual so dependent upon the king's favor can be so called) in the weak Grafton government. He became prime minister of a government composed of "King's Friends" in January 1770 and remained in office for the next twelve years. North's image in America has been one of an evil plotter, partly because the English Whigs and the great Whig historians of the nineteenth century so despised him. Actually, North's inclinations were always toward avoiding trouble with America or anyone else; but as George III was the most immediate source of trouble, North never had a free hand. North was the leader of the conciliatory policy in 1769, and he continued it after he became prime minister.

And, for a time, conciliation worked, in spite of the fact that none of the basic differences between England and her American colonies were reconciled. Neither side abandoned its stand on the constitutional relationship between Parliament and America. The Sugar Act continued in force. The archbishop of Canterbury and the Society for the Propagation of the Gospel in Foreign Parts still designed to establish an Anglican bishop in Calvinist America. Redcoats were still stationed in America, but few of them remained in Indian country. The tea tax was still law. Nevertheless, 1770 through 1772 was a period of calm in which the American Revolution appeared to have collapsed.

One reason for the hiatus is that Americans were simply tired of the turmoil that had existed for more than five years and were glad to accept North's gestures as an excuse to rest. Merchants had never been happy with the nonimportation and nonconsumption agreements, and they were even unhappier with the emergence of "popular parties," as the political organizations opposing British policy came to be known, and the "new men" who led them. The merchants and other conservatives seized upon the repeal of the most unimportant parts of the Townshend Acts as justification for abandoning nonimportation. By September 1770 commerce with England was fully resumed. Furthermore, the Boston Massacre, after momentarily increasing anti-British feeling, soon turned to reaction against the radicals and their tactics, especially when the massacre trials showed that the soldiers acted under extreme provocation. Finally, the postwar depression was at last over by 1770, ending economic discontent as an incentive for revolutionary activity.

[24]

III. SAM ADAMS AND THE REBIRTH OF THE REVOLUTION

The revolutionary movement was not dead, of course, but it was significantly changed as a result of the collapse of 1770. Such men as Samuel Adams in Boston, Alexander McDougall in New York, Charles Thomson in Philadelphia, and Richard Henry Lee in Virginia never ceased their revolutionary activities; but they had learned that they could not count on the moderates and "summer soldiers." They rebuilt their organizations around trusted activists, and they paid a great deal more attention to building intercolonial cooperation. The American Revolution emerged from the quiet times of 1770 through 1772 a much stronger and better organized movement than before.

More than any other individual, Sam Adams was responsible for the course the revolution took after 1770. Like all successful revolutionaries, Adams was an utter Machiavellian. This fact has caused considerable embarrassment to some American historians, who would prefer their revolutionaries to rely on sweet reason rather than demagoguery, manipulation, and terrorism.

Most of the leaders of the American Revolution were successful merchants and professional men. Adams, by contrast, failed in everything he tried except revolutionary politics. He was born in 1722, the son of a well-to-do owner of a malting house who was active in the Caucus Club, a little group of operators who had long directed Boston politics. The elder Adams was financially ruined in the Land Bank scheme in the 1740s, largely through the work of Thomas Hutchinson and his father, whose belief in hard money was supported by the British government.

Sam was not the man to recoup the family fortune. He was educated at Harvard (B.A. 1740, M.A. 1743), and after giving up on both theology and law, he worked for a time in the countinghouse of the elder Thomas Cushing. At the end of a few months it was evident to both Sam and the Cushings that he was not cut out to be an accountant. He went into business for himself and failed. Then he inherited his father's malting house and lost that, too. With that he became a public servant.

Sam Adams had always had a lively interest in politics. At Harvard he immersed himself in the theories of John Locke and became an avid joiner of political clubs. At some time, possibly out of deference to the memory of his father, he was admitted to the Caucus Club, the inner circle of Boston politics, where his ability as a propagandist soon made him a valued member.

[25]

Samuel Adams

Adams started in public office at the bottom. In 1753 he was elected town scavenger. Three years later he became tax collector, surely the one job in Boston for which he was most poorly fitted. Sam was one of those rare individuals to whom money means nothing, and only a practical wife kept his personal affairs going. To make matters worse, the postwar depression made tax collection difficult, and Sam was not the type who pressed delinquents overhard. Naturally he was quite popular, but by 1765 he was £8,000 in arrears. Had he not by that time been a leader of the radical Popular Party, Sam might well have ended in debtor's prison, rather than in the thick of the fight for independence. Instead, in 1765 he was elected as one of the four Boston members of the Massachusetts House of Representatives. In 1766, in the aftermath of the Stamp Act crisis, the house elected him its secretary, a post he continued to hold until 1780.

In the meantime, the Caucus Club became the Sons of Liberty; and, with Adams as their leader, added mob violence to their backroom activities. Boston had always had its mobs who fought for fun as often as anything else—especially on Guy Fawkes or, as it was known in Boston, Pope's Day. Adams united and controlled the mob, so that from 1765 on, the mob was Sam Adams's militia. There is no doubt that he was responsible for the Stamp Act riots in Boston and the wanton destruction of the home of his old enemy, Thomas Hutchinson.

Samuel Adams's contribution to the revolutionary movement did not lie solely in his pen and his ability to use the mob. He was constantly on the lookout for men who could add something to the movement, such as wealth, intellect, or respectability. Among his protégés were John Adams and Josiah Quincy, Jr., two rising young lawyers who gave much of their considerable legal and literary talents to the cause. Two of the outstanding pamphleteers were young physicians, Joseph Warren and Benjamin Church. The prize catch was a young merchant who had inherited a large fortune from his uncle, but whose craving for fame and popularity far exceeded his love of money. Sam Adams gave John Hancock what he craved by engineering his election to the Massachusetts House in 1766. By electing him, Sam told John Adams at the time, Boston had done "a very wise thing:" they had "made that young man's fortune their own." Nor did Adams neglect the lower classes in his search for talent; William Molineux, a shopkeeper, Paul Revere, an artisan, and Ebenezer Mackintosh, the chief bully of the South End mob, are only the most famous examples of the class that formed the bulk of Adams's following.

Trusted followers outside of Boston included Elbridge Gerry, a Marblehead merchant, and James Warren, a *Mayflower* descendant who was sheriff of

Plymouth County. Allied with Adams, although certainly not controlled by him, were such prominent politicians as James Otis, James Bowdoin, and Thomas Cushing of Boston, Robert Treat Paine of Taunton, and Major Joseph Hawley of Northampton. They often disagreed with Adams's tactics, but they just as often went along with him for their own reasons. They wanted nothing to do with Adams and his radicals during the quiescent period of 1770 through 1772.

During those inauspicious times, Sam Adams carried on almost alone. Between August 1770 and December 1772 he contributed over forty articles to such radical newspapers as the *Boston Gazette* and *Massachusetts Spy,* thus keeping the issues of the revolution before the people. More important, he built a revolutionary party that was much more than the strictly Bostonian institution it had been through 1770. In 1771 Adams first mentioned local associations to promote American liberty in a letter to Arthur Lee in London. All that remained was for an issue to present itself that would get others to buy the idea.

Adams's first opportunity to implement his plan came in his own province of Massachusetts. In 1772 it was revealed that the salaries of Governor Thomas Hutchinson and the judges of the superior court were to be paid from customs receipts, not by legislative appropriations. The Boston town meeting demanded that the governor tell them if it was true, to which Hutchinson replied that it was none of the town meeting's business.

Sam Adams was no doubt pleased with this response and used it as a pretext for moving that the town appoint a committee to communicate with the other towns on the province. The committee quickly produced a "Statement of Rights," a "List of Infringements and Violations of those Rights," and a "Letter of Correspondence with the Other Towns." Despite their radical tone, these documents were well received. Two of the first responses came from Plymouth and Marblehead, where James Warren and Elbridge Gerry got their towns behind Boston, thus giving greater weight to the colony-wide appeal. By January 1773 a hundred towns had formed Committees of Correspondence.

The Committees of Correspondence were probably the greatest gift of Sam Adams to the revolutionary movement. The committees were perfectly legal, for they were regularly chosen by the town meetings. Their avowed purpose was simply to communicate the sentiments of each town, but it gave the Boston radicals for the first time a chance to disseminate their views throughout the colony. Thus Sam Adams built a propaganda machine and ultimately a true revolutionary party. Most of all, the Committees of Correspondence brought unity to the revolutionary movement. With the information gathered from the local committees, the Boston committee could act as a central command post, issuing orders for local action and coordinating the efforts of the whole.

In the meantime, an opportunity arose for adopting the idea of intercolonial Committees of Correspondence, which Samuel Adams had suggested to Arthur Lee in 1771. The Royal Navy schooner *Gaspee* and her commander had made themselves unpopular in Rhode Island by their overzealous enforcement of the trade and revenue laws. On June 9, 1772, the *Gaspee* ran aground in Narragansett Bay, possibly lured into shoal waters by a canny Rhode Island captain, and during the night a group of the leading citizens of Providence burned her. The reaction of the British government was mild enough, considering that the destruction of a Royal Navy vessel by a foreign country would have been deemed an act of war. It appointed a royal commission to investigate the incident and to turn its findings over to the local authorities for action. Radical propagansists, however, ascribed to the *Gaspee* Commission powers to interrogate and arrest citizens for any reason, using the army and navy if need be, and to turn them over to the admiral of the North American squadron to be transported to England to be tried for treason. The *Providence Gazette* called the commission "a Court of Inquisition, more horrid than that of Spain," and most Americans seemed to agree.

Patrick Henry, Thomas Jefferson, and Richard Henry Lee seized the opportunity to get the Virginia House of Burgesses, in March 1773, to set up a "standing committee of correspondence and enquiry" to acquire information about acts of Parliament and the ministry that might endanger America, and to correspond with committees set up by other colonial legislatures about the *Gaspee* Commission or anything else. The Boston Committee of Correspondence saw to it that all the towns of Massachusetts knew about the Virginia plan, adding that Virginia had offered "to bring our sister colonies into the strictest union," to "RESENT IN ONE BODY any steps that may be taken by administration to deprive ANY ONE OF US of the least particle of our rights and liberties." In May the Massachusetts legislature adopted the Virginia resolutions, and most of the other colonial legislatures soon followed. As the Reverend Ezra Stiles, a radical Rhode Island clergyman, predicted, the ultimate result was the formation of a continental congress. Although the *Gaspee* Commission failed to find any culprits, and thus to provide an issue, it had produced the machinery for intercolonial organization by the middle of 1773. Within a few months America had an issue.

[29]

IV. THE BOSTON TEA PARTY

When it introduced the Tea Act in the spring of 1773, the British ministry was not trying to reopen the constitutional dispute with America. It was, in fact, following a policy of ignoring any American activities that might once again antagonize Parliament. The purpose of the act was simply to bail the East India Company out of deep financial trouble. High taxes and the company's monoply of tea imports in the British empire had made the price of the commodity so high that most tea lovers brewed smuggled leaves. It has been conservatively estimated that Americans imported at least three-quarters of their tea illegally, and that still made them relatively more law abiding than tea drinkers in the British Isles. One result was that as of 1773 the East India Company was on the verge of bankruptcy, and had 18,000,000 pounds of tea deteriorating in its warehouses.

Under the Townshend Revenue Act, tea exported to America was granted a rebate of all the duties collected in England, but a duty of threepence per pound was imposed on the tea when it reached America. American sales did go up; however, American dislike of the Townshend duty and the continued high cost of East India Company tea kept them lower than either the company or the government had hoped. The company therefore petitioned the government for permission to sell tea directly through its agents in America, rather than by auction in London, thus removing middlemen's costs. It also requested that the threepenny duty be removed or at least collected in England, not America; but this was denied because the ministry was afraid that Parliament would consider it a surrender to American demands and vote against the whole bill.

The resulting Tea Act passed on May 10, 1773, gave Americans the opportunity to buy tea, legally imported and paying the Townshend duty, that was cheaper than either that smuggled or available to Englishmen. At another time in history they might have welcomed such an advantage, but the events of the past decade made Americans suspicious of the motives behind any such "concessions" from Parliament. The Tea Act was viewed almost universally in the colonies as an attempt to seduce Americans into paying an unconstitutional tax. By the fall of 1773 the revolutionary movement was again in full swing and more united than it had been since the Stamp Act.

Many factors went into this extraordinary response to the Tea Act, but the most important was the fear on the part of the revolutionary leaders that it could be enforced. Already they were most embarrassed (and their opponents never tired of reminding them of the fact) by the continued payment of "unconstitutional" taxes on molasses, sugar, and wine under the Sugar Act. Furthermore, the collapse of nonimportation in 1770 still rankled, and more especially the fact that (again as their opponents liked to remind them) a considerable amount of tea was imported legally, and not just by "friends of government," either. John Hancock's ships brought in 45,000 pounds of duties tea during 1771 and 1772, and Boston was the leading tea importer on the continent. The inescapable fact was that tea was a very popular drink in America in 1773, despite a heavy newspaper campaign warning of dire consequences from consuming the brew and extolling the virtues of infusions of sassafras bark, moss, and other substances. There was a real and legitimate fear that most Americans would be able to swallow their constitutional principles if they could wash them down with inexpensive Hysong and Bohea. And, once the tea tax was paid, who knew what other taxes would follow?

But if the Tea Act presented a threat, it also presented an opportunity. United American resistance had defeated the Stamp Act, and the Tea Act resembled the Stamp Act in many ways. The constitutional issue was easy to understand: it was the familiar "no taxation without representation." Again, as in the Stamp Act, the government had failed to anticipate resistance and thus to provide for adequate enforcement measures. Finally, like the stamp distributors, the tea consignees were American residents who were vulnerable to public opinion and mob action. Superficially, at least, the resistance to the Tea Act followed the same lines as resistance to the Stamp Act had eight years earlier.

In important ways, however, the Tea Act crisis differed from the Stamp Act crisis. Resistance to the Stamp Act was far more spontaneous and universal. The difference in the role of the merchants is especially striking. Where they had led the way in opposing the Stamp Act, they were reluctant and coerced followers at best in the Tea Act crisis, even though they had something to fear from the creation of an East India Company monopoly in the colonies. What they feared even more, however, was the breakdown of order and commerce that had attended the Stamp Act and Townshend Act crises. At the same time, the radical leaders had learned during the earlier crises that they could not count on the merchants; the abandonment of nonimportation in 1770 had been led by the merchants. Even more important, the Tea Act provided the radicals with an opportunity to recapture the initiative they had lost to the moderates in 1770.

By the spring of 1774, resolutions against the Tea Act had been passed by popular meetings throughout America; but the focus of resistance came, not surprisingly, in the four great seaports: Philadelphia, Charleston, New York, and Boston. What was unusual was that Philadelphia, the quietest of the big towns, should have taken the lead. On October 16, 1773, a mass meeting of 700 inhabitants resolved that the Tea Act "has a direct tendency to render assemblies useless and to introduce arbitrary government and slavery," and that anyone who aided in landing or selling dutied tea "is an enemy to his country." The meeting also appointed a committee to request the tea consignees to resign their appointments. Most of them did, with little prodding. The firm of James & Drinker held out until December 2, then acknowledged that public opinion dictated that the tea not be received, although they recommended that it be landed and stored. While James & Drinker had been subjected to no violence, neither had they received any assurance from Governor John Penn that he would give them aid if the situation turned violent.

Meanwhile, the former consignees passed the word to the popular leaders that the ship *Polly,* with a load of tea for Philadelphia, had left England in September. On November 27 two handbills signed "THE COMMITTEE FOR TAR-RING AND FEATHERING" were circulated in the City of Brotherly Love. The first, addressed to the Delaware pilots, promised to attend to anyone who piloted the *Polly* into the harbor. The second, addressed to the *Polly*'s master, Captain Ayres, charged that the tea under his care "has been sent out by the India Company, under the auspices of the ministry as a trial of American virtue and resolution." After assuring the captain that Pennsylvanians would not be found wanting, the committee asked:

> What think you Captain, of a halter around your neck—ten gallons of liquid tar decanted on your pate—with the feathers of a dozen wild geese laid over that to enliven your appearance?
> Only think seriously of this—and fly to the place from whence you came—fly without hesitation—without the formality of a protest—and above all, Captain Ayres, let us advise you to fly without the wild geese feathers.

Captain Ayres, however, showed little obstinacy when he and the *Polly* arrived in Pennsylvania waters on Christmas Day, the day after Philadelphians heard the news of the Boston Tea Party. Although he made it up the Delaware River without a pilot, simply by following a larger ship, Ayres readily heeded a command that he anchor in midstream, without coming to dockside or entering at the customhouse. On December 27 Ayres heard a meeting of 8,000 people resolve that the tea should not be entered or landed. The next day *Polly* headed back to London without unloading the tea or anything else in her cargo. Neither Governor Penn nor the customs officers made any move to stop her. Thus Philadelphia, after making the initial move toward defying the Tea Act and hurling threats that would have delighted a Sam Adams, handled the actual confrontation with a characteristic lack of violence.

Charleston was another city that narrowly escaped having a tea party at the East India Company's expense. South Carolina had missed the uproar over the passage of the Tea Act, and it was not until the middle of November 1773 that Peter Timothy's *South Carolina Gazette* began reprinting northern denunciations of the act and suggesting that steps ought to be taken to stop the landing of duties tea. On December 2, however, before anything was done, the tea ship *London,* Captain Curling, arrived in Charleston. The next day a hurriedly convened mass meeting dominated by mechanics beat down merchant opposition, succeeded in getting the tea consignees to resign and demanded that the tea be returned to England. Captain Curling, however, had already entered his cargo at the customhouse, and by law all duties had to be paid within twenty days or the cargo would be seized. The merchants sought to escape the domination of the mechanics by forming a "Chamber of Commerce" on December 9; but the planters, who had led the opposition to Parliament in previous disputes, rallied to the side of the mechanics. Finally, all three groups held a joint meeting on December 17, but they agreed on nothing except the fact that the tea should not be landed or sold.

Governor William Bull then took the initiative. On December 22, exactly twenty-one days after the *London*'s cargo was entered at the customhouse, Bull ordered the customs collector to seize the tea for nonpayment of duties. The seizure was carried out with no opposition. The tea was stored in a warehouse where it remained until the outbreak of hostilities in 1775; then it was auctioned to help buy arms. It was only through the vigilance of the mechanics and planters that the tea never paid the duty. Had anyone agreed to pay the duty, or had Governor Bull acceded to the East India Company's request in February 1774 that the tea be sold at auction, the patriots would have taken a bad defeat.

Sam Adams was outraged that the Carolinians had allowed the tea to be landed. He wrote to the Charleston Committee of Correspondence that through their lack of unity "the grand cause was neglected. . . . Must then the liberties of the present and future ages be sacrificed to some unhappy feuds in Carolina?" Adams knew that in England and some parts of America Boston's Tea Party would be unfavorably contrasted to Charleston's moderation.

In New York the radicals had fallen on particularly hard times. The triumvirate of Isaac Sears, Alexander McDougall, and John Lamb had taken a beating from the conservative DeLancey faction in 1770 and had been virtually silent ever since. They were desperate for an issue that would propel them back into an effective role in New York politics; when the *New-York Mercury* printed the Tea Act on September 6, 1773, it must have seemed like a gift from the gods. New York newspapers, especially John Holt's *Journal,* were quickly filled with denunciations of the act, answered in kind by James Rivington's Tory *Gazetteer.* An extraordinary number of broadsides circulated, arguing all sides of the issue. Most important, the triumvirate staged a series of public meetings during October and November, culminating on November 29 in the reorganization of the Sons of Liberty. On that day "a great number of the principal gentlemen of the city, merchants, lawyers, and other inhabitants of all ranks," adopted the "Association of the Sons of Liberty of New York." In five resolutions the association denounced anyone who aided in importing the duded tea, whether the duty was collected in America or England, and promised "That whoever shall transgress any of these resolutions, we shall not deal with, or employ, or have any connection with him." The association was circulated throughout the city "to give an opportunity to those who have not yet signed to unite with their fellow-citizens, to testify their abhorrence to the diabolical project of enslaving America."

In the face of public demands, the tea consignees resigned their commissions on December 1, 1773, claiming that until then they had thought the tea was to come in duty free. They petitioned Governor William Tryon and his Council to take charge of the tea when it should arrive. The governor and Council decided to bring the tea into New York Harbor under the escort of the warship *Swan,* land it, and store it in the military barracks, much as New York's stamps had been handled in 1765. At first this solution was acceptable to the populace, but a week later came news that Boston had demanded that the tea be taken back to England without landing. William Smith, a conservative Whig who was on the Council, recorded in his diary that the "Liberty Boys now changed their tone," and demanded that New York send its tea back, as well.

Tryon wavered. He was anxious to avoid a confrontation with the New Yorkers because, as William Smith put it, "he is determined to be popular here, to save himself from the Imputation of a Want of Prudence in Carolina," where he had used force to put down the Regulators. Tryon told his Council that he would not use force to land the tea. Thereupon Sears and McDougall called another mass meeting for December 17. A thousand people attended the meeting, at which they heard letters from Philadelphia and Boston stressing their determination to return the tea. The mayor was allowed to present a message from the governor asking that the tea be stored in the fort until word should come from England about what to do with it, but Tryon's proposal was shouted down. The last remaining sentiment for storing the tea disappeared on December 21, when Paul Revere rode into town with news of the Boston Tea Party.

As it turned out, New York's tea ship was forced far off course by storms, and did not arrive off Sandy Hook until April 18, 1774. Although Tryon had gone back to England to consult with Lord Dartmouth about some boundary disputes, everything had been prepared since December, and Tryon told one of his last Council meetings that there would be no trouble. Captain Lockyear left his ship, the *Nancy*, outside New York harbor. She was provisioned, her angry crew prevented from abandoning her, and, on April 25, she headed back to England. One of her passengers was Captain James Chambers, whose ship *London* had arrived on April 22. The *London* was allowed to dock because her captain was something of a local hero; in October a mass meeting had voted its gratitude to him because a report from London said he had refused to carry East India Company tea to America. Other captains charged, however, that Chambers was not above bringing in duxied tea on his own. Chambers denied it, but when a committee searched the *London* and found eighteen chests of Hyson, New York finally had its tea party. Chambers did not stick around to complain. Abandoning his ship, crew, and cargo, the captain grabbed the first ship out of New York: fittingly, the tea ship *Nancy*.

New York's tea party, however, was only one of several that took place in 1774; and, like the rest, it has been lost in the more important events of that year. The only tea party that took place during 1773 was in Boston, the one city where destruction of the tea could guarantee a massive reaction on the part of England. It can truly be said that the last crisis of the American Revolution began in Boston harbor on December 16, 1773; but it was the result of so many coincidences that one wonders if fate had taken a hand.

Lagging behind Philadelphia and New York, Boston was late in taking up the Tea Act as an issue. In fact, had it not been for the example of those cities, Boston might well have been caught as short as Charleston in her preparations to resist landing the tea. The Boston Committee of Correspondence ignored the Tea Act through September 1773, and it was not until October 11 that denunciations of the act began to be printed in the radical *Boston Gazette*.

Until October the Massachusetts radicals were occupied in a struggle with their old enemy, Governor Thomas Hutchinson. In his address at the opening of the legislature in January 1773, Hutchinson bitterly denounced Massachusetts's Committees of Correspondence and charged that the recent declarations of Boston and other towns against Parliament's ability to legislate for the colonies were nothing less than claims of independence—claims which, Hutchinson said, had no historical backing, for until recent times Massachusetts had always recognized the supremacy of Parliament. The legislature's reply, in large part the handiwork of Sam Adams, used the governor's own *History of Massachusetts-Bay* to refute Hutchinson's arguments. After piously expressing dismay that Hutchinson should have brought up the matter of independence, Adams stated that "absolute uncontrolled power" was more to be feared than total independence, although independence was something that the Massachusetts legislature would never think of, unless agreed to by a congress of all the colonies.

A series of exchanges between Hutchinson and the legislature followed until the governor, on March 6, sent the legislators home—but not before the House of Representatives had sent a petition to the king and a letter to Lord Dartmouth that substantially repeated the list of grievances drawn up by the Boston Committee of Correspondence the previous November. (Still trying to avoid a parliamentary debate over America, Dartmouth kept the letter quiet until the session was over.)

Hutchinson may have thought that the logic of his speeches to the legislature would appeal to the voters in the May election. If so, he got a rude shock almost as soon as the new House convened. On May 28 the House approved the Virginia resolves for intercolonial Committees of Correspondence. Worse yet, on June 2 Sam Adams placed before the House a number of private letters written by Hutchinson and Lieutenant Governor Andrew Oliver to Thomas Whately, a British official who had died in 1772. Benjamin Franklin, the London agent for Massachusetts, had somehow procured these letters and sent them to Speaker Thomas Cushing with the injunction that they must be kept secret.

But Sam Adams had no intention of keeping them secret. Not only did he read them to the House of Representatives, he contrived to get a carefully edited version of them printed in the newspapers. Especially damning was Hutchinson's statement that "there must be an abridgement of what are called English liberties. . . . I doubt whether it is possible to project a system of government in which a colony 3,000 miles distant from the parent state shall enjoy all the liberty of the parent state."

The house voted 101-5 that the letters showed a design "to overthrow the Constitution of this Government, and to introduce arbitrary Power into the

[36]

province." A few weeks later, on June 23, the House sent a petition to the king to remove Hutchinson and Oliver from the government of Massachusetts "forever." Writing to Lord Dartmouth on June 26, Hutchinson did not deny the letters but defended them as true; nevertheless, he asked for leave to come to England to defend himself against the House's charges. Three days later he prorogued the legislature. It was not to meet again until after the Boston Tea Party.

Sam Adams was sure he had Hutchinson and his allies on the run. He moved to follow up his advantage by reopening the issue of officials' salaries—including those of Hutchinson, Oliver, and the superior court judges—from Townshend Act revenues. Adams had used this issue to get the Committees of Correspondence started the previous November. Now he was able to get the House—the day before Hutchinson prorogued it—to order the judges to refuse to accept a salary from anyone but the legislature. In choosing to concentrate on this issue, Adams and the Massachusetts radicals nearly missed the opportunity presented them by the Tea Act. As late as October 21, 1773, the Boston Committee of Correspondence was sending out circular letters to other colonies harping on the threat independent salaries posed for American liberties, and mentioning the Tea Act only as an afterthought.

Once the news of widespread opposition to the Tea Act began coming in from Philadelphia and New York, however, the Bostonians quickly made up for lost time. The *Boston Gazette* opened the attack on October 11, and a week later published the names of the tea consignees. They included two of Governor Hutchinson's sons and members of the Clarke family, who had incurred the enmity of the Boston patriots by breaking the nonimportation agreement in 1770. Throughout the rest of October and November, the newspapers conducted a war of words, with denunciations of the Tea Act, the consignees, and the British ministry filling the pages of the *Boston Gazette* and *Massachusetts Spy,* answered in kind by the conservative *Boston Evening Post* and *Boston News-Letter.*

Neither side paid much attention to accuracy, but the pro-tea forces published one charge that was both true and damaging. On November 11 the *Boston News-Letter* published customhouse accounts revealing that Boston had imported over 3,000 chests of tea since the Townshend duty had gone into effect in 1768. The charge was not answered because it was unanswerable, and it was picked up by newspapers in the other colonies. Letters soon began arriving from the other colonies charging that the Boston patriots were all talk and no action. Thus the Bostonians had to prove their sincerity, or all their hopes of intercolonial

[37]

cooperation against Parliament would be dead. This time Boston would have to live up to its own advice.

New York, Philadelphia, and Charleston had a much easier time meeting their commitments, for in those cities public resolutions and newspaper and pamphlet denunciations had been enough to make all the tea consignees resign before the tea arrived. Boston's consignees were a great deal more stubborn, partly because they knew they had the backing of Governor Hutchinson, plus a regiment of redcoats in Castle William and a considerable number of warships in the harbor.

Shortly after midnight on November 2, the consignees were handed "summonses" signed only "O.C." demanding that they appear at the Liberty Tree at noon on the following day to resign their commissions. A few hours later, the North End caucus and the Boston Committee of Correspondence met jointly to draw up a resolution to be presented to the consignees, including a threat to make them "feel the weight of their just resentment" if they failed to show up at the Liberty Tree. At the appointed hour, however, the gathering of 500 did not include a single consignee; they were gathered several blocks away in Clarke's store. Escorted by most of the crowd at the Liberty Tree, a delegation was sent to demand the consignees' presence. When they refused to have anything to do with such an illegal gathering, the crowd stormed Clarke's store. The consignees fled to the counting room on the second floor (the eighteenth-century equivalent of a bank vault) and, after an hour and a half, were able to go home unmolested. Round one went to the consignees.

Since the consignees had scorned the "illegal" meeting at the Liberty Tree, Boston next confronted them with a perfectly legal town meeting. On November 5, usually given over to Pope's Day festivities in the town, the Bostonians instead gathered at Faneuil Hall where, with John Hancock as moderator, they adopted the Philadelphia resolutions of October 16 and appointed a committee to demand the consignees' resignation. The consignees, however, could not be found, although the committee, headed by Hancock and Sam Adams, went all the way to Milton and back looking for them. Frustrated once again by the consignees, the town meeting broke up the next day.

On November 17 Hancock's ship *Hayley* arrived from London with news that four tea ships were already headed for Boston. A town meeting was immediately called for the next day; but before it met, a mob gathered outside the Clarke residence, where the family was holding a dinner in honor of Jonathan Clarke, who had just returned on the *Hayley.* The mob confined itself to verbal abuse until Jonathan imprudently fired a pistol from the upstairs window; then it broke every window in the house. But the mob did not force its way into the house; it

melted away after an hour without even securing a promise that the Clarkes
would attend next day's town meeting. The meeting again demanded the
consignees' resignation, and again they refused. The town meeting dissolved and
did not meet again until March 5, 1774.

Although the consignees had ignored both official and unofficial demands that
they resign, as well as threats of everything from social ostracism to death, they
knew that they could not hold out indefinitely without aid. Therefore, on
November 19, they petitioned the governor and Council to take custody of the
tea when it arrived and hold it until it became safe to sell it. It might have
worked in another royal colony, but the Massachusetts councilors were elected
by the House of Representatives. They did not act until November 29, when
they accepted a report by a committee of James Bowdoin, Samuel Dexter, and
John Winthrop that denounced parliamentary taxation, independent salaries for
colonial officials, and the Tea Act. If the consignees wanted personal protection,
let them apply to the justices of the peace, not the Council. Finally, the Council
could not approve the landing of the tea, let alone taking charge of it for the
consignees. The first tea ship had arrived the day before; already 5,000 people
from Boston and surrounding communities were meeting to decide on how to
prevent its landing. The consignees' nerve began to fail in the face of the
Council's report. Before the day was over, the consignees and customs
commissioners had fled to Castle William, and even Governor Hutchinson
retired to his estate in Milton.

Meanwhile, the radicals abandoned the town meeting as the forum for their
demands and shifted to the Committees of Correspondence and mass public
meetings. On November 22 the committees of Boston, Cambridge, Brookline,
Dorchester, and Roxbury met jointly to agree to prevent the landing of the tea
and to ask aid of the other towns.

On Sunday, November 28, the tea ship *Dartmouth* arrived in Boston harbor.
Although the sabbath was still strictly observed in Boston, the town selectmen
met anyway, hoping that the consignees would offer them proposals to present
to a regular town meeting the next day. But the consignees did not come
forward, and the Committee of Correspondence had plans of its own. By
Monday morning it had blanketed the town with handbills calling for a mass
meeting of the people of all the surrounding towns to meet in Faneuil Hall at
9:00 A.M. The meeting quickly resolved that the tea should be sent back to
England, but still people poured in, until a huge crowd had gathered outside in
Dock Square. The meeting, calling itself the "Body of the People," adjourned to
the larger Old South Meeting House a few blocks away, where 5,000 people

[39]

again resolved to send the tea back without paying the duty. At 3:00 P.M. the "Body" met again, this time to send a guard of twenty-five men to Griffin's Wharf to make sure that the *Dartmouth* was not unloaded.

The next day the "Body" met again, to receive proposals from the consignees; but by that time they had fled to Castle William, leaving a letter with John Scollay, chairman of the board of selectmen, claiming that they were powerless to send the tea back but would agree to have it stored until they received instructions from the East India Company. This, of course, was unacceptable; and the temper of the meeting was not improved by the arrival of Sheriff Stephen Greenleaf with an order from Governor Hutchinson for the illegal meeting to disperse forthwith. The "Body" voted unanimously to ignore Hutchinson's order.

At this point the young artist John Singleton Copley, who was married to a Clarke daughter, asked the gathering if it would guarantee safe passage and a fair hearing to the consignees if he could persuade them to appear in person. The "Body" agreed, and gave Copley two hours to produce the consignees. It was dark when Copley returned, alone. The consignees said that their position was completely explained in the letter to Scollay, and they had no reason to appear at the meeting. Copley said, however, that the consignees would make no attempt to unload the tea, nor would they interfere if the people themselves sent it back. The "Body" voted the reply unsatisfactory, but, after ordering an account of their proceedings sent to New York, Philadelphia, London, and the other New England ports, they adjourned. Considering the tinderbox atmosphere in which they were held, the meetings of November 29 and November 30 had been surprisingly orderly.

Nevertheless, nothing had been solved. Unlike those in the other ports, the Boston tea consignees had not resigned. Once it had entered Boston harbor, the tea ship *Dartmouth* had to enter its cargo at the customhouse; and, once entered, had to pay all duties within twenty days or be seized. Furthermore, it could not leave the port until the governor had issued a clearance. Hutchinson not only refused to do this, he ordered the Royal Navy warships in Boston harbor to stop the ship if it tried to leave. Hutchinson obviously thought he held the upper hand. Once the waiting period expired, he could legally move to seize the tea for nonpayment of duties and have it brought ashore. Since he had a number of Royal Navy ships, with their sailors and marines, plus a regiment of redcoats near at hand, it was certainly in his power to do this. And, as both Hutchinson and the patriots well knew, once the tea was landed, no one in the other colonies would ever trust Boston again.

[40]

The twenty-day period of grace would be up on December 17. As that day approached, two other tea ships, the *Eleanor* and the *Beaver,* joined the *Dartmouth* at Griffin's Wharf. The three vessels held over 90,000 pounds of tea worth some £9,000 and subject to £1,125 in duties. Meanwhile, news came from New York and Philadelphia that all their tea consignees had resigned, but neither port had seen a tea ship. Thus Boston had no precedent from the other ports, but it did get a number of sharp reminders that Bostonians had been willing to buy duted tea in the past.

On Monday, December 13, 1773, the Committees of Correspondence of Boston and its nearest neighbors met again to call another mass gathering of the "Body of the People" from as many towns as possible. The "Body" met on Tuesday, December 14, and chose as its moderator Samuel Savage from Weston, fifteen miles away. The "Body" remained in almost continuous session for the next three days. First it tried—and failed—to get Customs Collector Richard Harrison to issue a clearance for the tea ships. On Thursday, December 16, the last day of grace, 5,000 people, many of them from outside Boston, gathered at Old South Meeting House at 10:00 A.M. The *Dartmouth*'s owner, Francis Rotch, once again explained that he could not send his vessel out of Boston harbor without official permission. Rotch was sent to Milton to make a final plea to Governor Hutchinson for a clearance. When he returned at 5:45 P.M. it was to report that Hutchinson had refused. Thereupon Sam Adams rose and said: "This meeting can do nothing more to save the country."

Adams's statement may have been a prearranged signal, or it may merely have summed up the feelings of the multitude. At any rate, it was answered by war whoops. Within a few minutes, blanketed and painted "Indians" were filing toward Griffins's Wharf. A large crowd watched silently as they boarded the three tea ships and, in three hours' hard work, tore open 342 chests of the East India Company's tea and threw it overboard. Boston had answered the challenge of Parliament, Governor Hutchinson, and, most importantly, the rest of America.

CHAPTER III

The Coercive Acts

The question now was, not about the liberty of North
America, but whether we were to be free, or slaves to our
colonies.
—Earl of Buckinghamshire in Lords, February 1, 1774

They will be Lyons, whilst we are Lambs, but if we take the
resolute part they will undoubtedly prove very meek.
—General Thomas Gage to King George III,
February 4, 1774

There is indeed a great business in agitation, and has been
for some time; but, without the thorough-bass of opposition,
it makes no echo out of Parliament. Its Parliamentary name
is Regulations for Boston. Its essence, the question of
sovereignty over America.
—Horace Walpole to Sir Horace Mann, May 1, 1774

Bearing the first account of the Boston Tea Party, John Hancock's ship
Hayley arrived in England on January 20, 1774. Her remarkably quick passage

brought the incident to England's attention at a time when tempers were already inflamed against Boston. Out of this atmosphere came the "Coercive Acts" that insured a break between America and England.

I. THE ORDEAL OF BENJAMIN FRANKLIN

The focus of ill feeling toward Massachusetts at the beginning of 1774 was Benjamin Franklin, a sixty-eight-year-old Pennsylvanian who had resided in London since 1764. In 1770 the Massachusetts House of Representatives chose Franklin, already the London agent (lobbyist) for Pennsylvania, Georgia, and New Jersey, as its agent. Thus Franklin was the instrument through which Massachusetts's complaints against Governor Thomas Hutchinson and British colonial policy were transmitted to the British government.

In 1774 Franklin was by far America's best-known son and perhaps the most illustrious citizen of the British empire. By the time he was forty, Franklin had made a fortune as a printer, enabling him to turn to other pursuits. His experiments with electricity had gained him fellowships in the American Philosophical Society, the French Royal Academy, and the English Royal Society, as well as an honorary doctorate from St. Andrews University. He had enhanced his reputation for literary wit, begun years before in *Poor Richard's Almanack,* with essays published in European journals. And with all this, Benjamin Franklin found time to become a master of political intrigue at every level from local fire companies to the most exalted strata of the British government.

Franklin's vast reputation, satirical wit, and able advocacy of the American cause were bound to make enemies of powerful English politicians. Lord Hillsborough, the hard-line colonial secretary, resigned in 1772 when the Privy Council voted against him on an American land company scheme. Hillsborough blamed Franklin, who was heavily involved in the company, and most politicians either agreed or were careful not to disabuse Hillsborough of his opinion. The new colonial secretary, the earl of Dartmouth, was thought to be a friend of America. Perhaps he was, but his strongest desire was for America to keep quiet. Franklin's presentation of petitions and statements of right—especially one denying that Parliament had any power at all over Massachusetts—endeared neither the colony nor Dr. Franklin to his lordship. Dartmouth tried to talk Franklin out of following his instructions to present such petitions to the king; after that failed, he delayed passing them on.

Franklin further irritated Dartmouth and the ministry by publishing, during

[43]

Dr. Franklin

THE
WESTMINSTER MAGAZINE,
For JULY, 1774.

For the WESTMINSTER MAGAZINE.

Il a ravi le feu des Cieux.
Il fait fleurir les Arts en des Climats Sauvages.
L'Amérique le place à la tête des Sages.
La Grece l'aurait mis au nombre de ses Dieux.

BENJ. FRANKLIN, Esq. L.L.D. and F.R.S.

THE

BRAVE DEFENDER of his COUNTRY (AMERICA)

AGAINST THE

OPPRESSION OF TAXATION WITHOUT REPRESENTATION;

AUTHOR OF THE

GREATEST DISCOVERY IN NATURAL PHILOSOPHY

SINCE THOSE OF SIR ISAAC NEWTON.

VIZ.

That LIGHTNING is the same with the ELECTRIC FIRE.

[With an Elegant ENGRAVING of that GENTLEMAN.]

THE Character of this truly great Man is well known to the Public.
The Encomiums he deserves would offend his Modesty. We therefore chuse
to decline expatiating farther on the subject.

the fall of 1773, two pieces of biting satire. *Rules by Which a Great Empire May Be Reduced to a Small One* went through British colonial policy since 1763 point by point: suppose the colonies are inclined to revolt and treat them accordingly, so that your suspicions will become reality; send the worst men to govern them; scorn their offers of voluntary grants in favor of novel taxes, and proclaim your power of taxation is unlimited; deprive them of their constitutional rights; send the army and navy to enforce your policies, and give them more power than your civil officials.

An Edict by the King of Prussia was an obvious hoax, though it temporarily fooled some of the denser English aristocrats. It purported to be an edict of Frederick the Great to the effect that, since England had never been emancipated, she must be made to yield increased revenues to the august house of Hohenzollern. Duties were to be laid on English commerce. English manufactures and wool production were forbidden. Finally, thieves, murderers, perverts, and other criminals were to be transported from Prussia to England. In both satires Franklin outlined, with but little exaggeration, the actual policy of the British government toward America. Both pieces were widely reprinted. It is little wonder that Dartmouth and his fellow ministers were rapidly getting a bellyful of Dr. Franklin.

In the meantime, Franklin had somehow acquired a number of private letters from Governor Thomas Hutchinson and his deputy, Andrew Oliver, to Thomas Whately, a Grenvillite who had died in 1772. Franklin, who never revealed how he came by the letters, sent them to Thomas Cushing, speaker of the Massachusetts House of Representatives. The upshot was that on August 21, 1773, Franklin presented Dartmouth with still another petition, this one requesting Hutchinson's and Oliver's removal from office.

Once again Dartmouth delayed passing the petition on until Parliament was not in session. A hearing before the Privy Council was scheduled for January 1774. By that time Dartmouth had received a letter from Hutchinson claiming that he was the victim of a plot hatched in London, and that indeed the radical faction in Massachusetts never took a step without directions from Franklin. Hutchinson's accusation was not true, but another incident helped give it credibility in England.

William Whately, a banker, was outraged at rumors that he had put his late brother's letters into Franklin's hands. Whately believed the culprit was John Temple, a former member of the American customs board who had generally upheld the American side. Whately's charges and Temple's denials and countercharges were carried in the newspapers. Both men thought their honor was sullied. On December 11, while Franklin was out of town, Whately and Temple fought a duel. Unlike most eighteenth-century English duels, which were pretty decorous affairs, Temple and Whately went at each other with swords and pistols until Whately was too wounded to continue. Still neither man thought honor was satisfied. They agreed to fight to the death as soon as Whately was mended. When he heard of it, Franklin moved to prevent further bloodshed. On Christmas day his letter appeared in the London *Public Advertiser* absolving Temple and taking on himself full responsibility for the purloined letters.

The hearing on the petition for Hutchinson's and Oliver's removal finally took place on January 29, 1774, exactly a week after news of the Boston Tea Party first appeared in the London papers. Franklin, of course, represented the petitioners. Hutchinson and Oliver had their own agent, Israel Maduit, who retained as counsel Alexander Wedderburn, the solicitor general of England. The hearing quickly turned from a defense of Hutchinson and Oliver into a trial of Franklin and Massachusetts.

Alexander Wedderburn was the government's master of invective. He had left the Scottish bar rather than apologize for insulting a judge of sessions. He had no strong political convictions; he had entered English politics as a follower of Lord Bute, then became a defender of John Wilkes, and it was said that North bought him off with the solicitor generalship in order to escape his barbs in the House of Commons. It was no coincidence that he was picked to examine Franklin before the Privy Council, because Franklin's by no means blameless conduct over the letters provided the North ministry with a beautiful opportunity to discredit the serious charges against Hutchinson and British policy brought by the Massachusetts House. Lord Shelburne guessed what the ministry was about; "it is the opening of a new plan of American government," he told Lord Chatham a few days after he attended the hearing.

Wedderburn disposed of the letters by arguing that, far from upholding the petitioners' claim that Hutchinson and Oliver were enemies of English liberties, they were an accurate appraisal of the state of affairs in Massachusetts. Wedderburn hauled out every action of Massachusetts since the Stamp Act to show that the colony had long been virtually in a state of rebellion. The final proof, said Wedderburn, was the petition itself. The legislature's denunciation of such outstanding public servants and upholders of law and order as Hutchinson and Oliver was proof positive that Americans were not, in fact, ready to enjoy all the liberties of Englishmen.

Then, before his audience had time to examine this bit of reasoning closely,

Wedderburn shifted his attack to Franklin. This is what the Privy Council—including almost all of the North cabinet—had come to hear. To their delighted applause, Wedderburn engaged in "the most severe Phillipic [sic] on the celebrated American Philosopher, in which he loaded him with all the licensed scurrility of the Bar, and decked his harangues with the choicest flowers of Billingsgate." General Thomas Gage wrote to Hutchinson: "I suppose no man's conduct and character was before so mangled and torn, as Dr. Franklin's was at this time."

The Privy Council's decision, not surprisingly, was that the charges contained in the petition were not only without merit, but they were calculated for the "seditious purpose of keeping up a Spirit of clamour and discontent" in Massachusetts. Franklin was stripped of his office as deputy postmaster general for America. In addition, his influence in England was destroyed just at the time when it was most needed. Thus the Coercive Acts were debated at a time when neither Franklin nor America's best friends were in any position to offer effective opposition.

II. THE MINISTRY AND THE BOSTON PROBLEM

On the evening of January 29, after listening to Franklin's humiliation by Wedderburn, the cabinet—the inner circle of the British government—met to decide what to do about the Boston Tea Party. Of the seven men who gathered on that evening, only the prime minister, Lord North, was a member of the House of Commons. North and Dartmouth, the colonial secretary, were the most inclined to be lenient with America, but neither was a very forceful personality. The earls of Sandwich, Suffolk, and Gower, the strongest personalities in the cabinet, had been advocating a hard line toward America ever since the Stamp Act. Lords Rochford and Apsley could be counted upon to vote with the majority on anything. The cabinet made no substantive proposals on January 29, but it agreed that "in consequence of the present disorders in America, effectual steps to be taken to secure the Dependence of the Colonies on the Mother Country." The cabinet ministers knew that they would be supported in a tough American policy by King George III, and the king had made himself the strongest political leader in Britain. North was the king's man, and all the cabinet ministers depended upon the king's goodwill for their offices. Even had they been inclined to take a more charitable view of Boston's activities, the king would probably have forced them to take drastic measures.

On February 4 the king had a meeting with General Thomas Gage, commander in chief of the British army in North America ever since 1764. Perhaps George III heard only what he wanted to hear; perhaps Gage said what he thought the king wanted to hear. At any rate, Gage made a very favorable impression on His Majesty. As the king related the interview to Lord North, Gage offered to return to America "at a day's notice if the conduct of the Colonies should induce the directing coercive measures." The king thought Gage's "language was very consonant to his Character of an honest determined man; he says they will be Lyons, whilst we are Lambs but if we take the resolute part they will undoubtedly prove very meek; he thinks the four Regiments intended to Relieve as many Regiments in America if sent to Boston are sufficient to prevent any disturbance."

It seems incredible that Gage, who was no fool, really thought that Boston could be controlled with only four regiments—about 1,400 men. Indeed, Gage later told the historian George Chalmers that "he desired at length that a much larger force than four weak regiments might be sent out, and the Town of Boston declared in rebellion, without which his hands would be tied up"; but an officer who was present later told General Frederick Haldimand that Gage had in fact assured the king that he had enough troops to bring Boston to reason. At any rate, king and cabinet operated under the assumption that coercion would require little military force. If Gage was responsible for this miscalculation, he got his just reward by being sent back to America as both commander in chief of the army and governor in chief of Massachusetts Bay Colony.

The evening of the day of Gage's audience with the king, the cabinet met at Lord Rochford's residence to decide how to implement the policy agreed to on January 29. The ministers decided that both the town of Boston and the individuals responsible must be punished for the Boston Tea Party. First, both the seat of government and the customhouse must be moved out of Boston by executive order. Second, the cabinet sent a report of the events surrounding the Tea Party to the government's legal officers, Attorney General Edward Thurlow and Solicitor General Alexander Wedderburn, with the following queries: "Do the acts and proceedings . . . amount to the crime of High Treason?" and "If they do, who are the persons chargeable with such crime, and what will be the proper and legal method of proceeding against them?"

Lord North expected an immediate answer to these questions, but it was not until the following Friday, February 11, that Thurlow and Wedderburn were ready to answer. They were of the opinion that the Boston Tea Party was indeed an act of "High Treason; namely to the levying of war against His Majesty."

[49]

Furthermore, those who were involved in the committee that confronted the Clarkes and other consignees to demand their resignation, the leaders of the "Body of the People," the committee that put a guard over the tea ships, the Committee of Correspondence, and possibly even the Boston selectmen, the town clerk, and members of the Massachusetts House of Representatives were all guilty of high treason. Among the names specifically listed by Thurlow and Wedderburn were Sam Adams, John Hancock, Joseph Warren, William Molineux, Thomas Young, and Benjamin Church. All could be prosecuted in Massachusetts courts or, if arrested by a royal commission or on a warrant signed by a secretary of state, they could be brought to England for trial. However, Thurlow and Wedderburn did not think there were presently in England any witnesses upon whose testimony a court would convict; the only one available was James Scott, captain of Hancock's ship *Hayley,* whose testimony "as it stands, is scarce sufficient to affect any person with the crime of High Treason."

Dartmouth moved quickly to round up more witnesses. On Saturday, February 19, twelve people who had lately arrived from Boston were examined under oath before the Privy Council. Once again Thurlow and Wedderburn were asked if there were enough evidence for arrest warrants. On Monday, February 28, the attorney and solicitor general "gave their opinion that the charge of High Treason cannot be maintained against any individuals on the ground of the depositions taken at the Council Board on the 19th inst."

The cabinet ministers already had their pens ready to sign the arrest warrant when Thurlow and Wedderburn dropped their bombshell. It was not entirely a matter of concern for the English constitution. Thurlow reportedly walked out of the meeting with these words:

> Don't you see that they want to throw the whole responsibility of the business upon the solicitor general and me? And who would be such damned fools as to risk themselves for such —— fellows as these? Now if it was George Grenville, who was so damned obstinate that he would go to hell with you before he would desert you, there would be some sense in it.

Thus, despite the wishes of North, Darmouth, and the king, there would be no treason trial of Americans in England; and experience had shown that it was futile to hope American courts would punish anyone for the outrage.

While the cabinet was wasting a month on chimerical plans for a treason trial, it also groped for ways to punish the whole town of Boston. On February 11

[50]

Thurlow and Wedderburn told Dartmouth that the treasury had sufficient authority to order the removal of the Boston customhouse to some other port. This would have been a serious blow to Boston, since ships could neither load nor unload without first being cleared by customs. The same day, on Dartmouth's instructions, the treasury board drafted instructions to the American customs commissioners to remove themselves and all other customs officers from Boston. Two days later, the cabinet decided to instruct Admiral Montagu, commander of the Royal Navy's North American squadron, to close Boston harbor to all ships that did not have customs clearances specifically allowing them to enter that port.

By February 19, however, the cabinet began to have second thoughts. At that meeting the ministers took up the larger problem of Massachusetts's denial of Parliament's authority, and decided to bring in a bill to alter the colony's charter. They also decided to close the port of Boston by act of Parliament, not by executive decree. Partly this change of tactics was dictated by doubts as to the strict legality of closing the whole port by executive order, rather than just the customhouse. In part it may have been that the ministers wanted to be sure that Parliament would share the responsibility if anything went wrong. Certainly a very important consideration was the fact that the whole issue had revolved around Parliament's authority to legislate for the colonies. Closing the port of Boston by act of Parliament would help to establish the principle of parliamentary supremacy.

III. THE BOSTON PORT ACT

On March 7 the king sent a message to both houses of Parliament about "the violent and outrageous proceedings at the Town and Port of Boston," expecting that they would pass laws not only "to put an immediate stop to the present disorders, but will also take into their consideration, what farther regulations and permanent provisions may be necessary to be established for better securing the . . . just dependence of the Colonies upon the Crown and Parliament of Great Britain." North, in Commons, and Dartmouth, in Lords, then laid before their houses 109 documents relating to the tea disturbances in the colonies. North noted that while some of the papers related to the other colonies, "there was no outrage committed but at Boston," and they were included only to indicate that Boston was trying to spread the poison of its resistance to its neighbors.

On March 14 North at last promised to bring in a bill that would punish Boston and indemnify the East India Company. The Boston Port Bill, introduced four days later, went far beyond the earlier plan to remove Boston's customhouse by executive order. The port, defined as everything lying between Nahant Point and Alderton Point, was to be closed indefinitely to all shipping. After June 1, 1774, the only vessels that would be allowed to enter the port, aside from military transports and royal navy ships, were those carrying food and firewood. Even these, however, had to call first at Marblehead and there be unloaded and reloaded. They could continue to Boston only if they had on board a customs officer and armed guards, and they had to leave Boston empty. After June 14 no cargo was allowed to be taken out of Boston by water.

The port was to remain closed until certain vaguely worded conditions had been met. The East India Company had to be reimbursed by the town of Boston for the damages (unspecified in the bill) suffered "by the destruction of their goods sent to the said town of Boston." The governor of Massachusetts had to certify that "reasonable satisfaction hath been made to the officers of his Majesty's Revenue and others, who suffered by the riots and insurrections" during November and December 1773 and January 1774. These would presumably include the Clarkes and John Malcom, a customs officer who had been tarred and feathered in January. Until all these things were done, the king was forbidden by the law to open any part of the port of Boston. After they were done, he was not to reopen the port until it was proved to the satisfaction of the Privy Council "that peace and obedience to the laws shall be . . . restored in the said town of Boston." Even then the king did not have to open the whole port, but only such "open places, quays, and wharfs" as he saw fit.

In retrospect, the Boston Port Bill seems to have been a massive overreaction. At the time, however, given the feelings in England, it probably seemed mild enough. In January the *Middlesex Journal* thundered that the government's proper course would be to "hang, draw, and quarter fifty of them"; by March it had raised its demands to "about one hundred of these puritanical rebels in Boston." One member of Parliament, Charles Van, gave his opinion "that the town of Boston ought to be knocked about their ears, and destroyed. Delenda est Carthago . . . I am of opinion you will never meet with that proper obedience to the laws of this country, until you have destroyed that nest of locusts." About the mildest—albeit commonest—opinion expressed in and out of Parliament was that it had been a mistake to repeal the Stamp Act. Even Benjamin Franklin was dismayed and privately conceded that Boston should make reparations.

There was never any doubt that the Boston Port Bill would pass. The opposition was already weak and fragmented, and support of Boston was not a promising rallying point. The two Englishmen most revered by Americans

[52]

joined in the denunciation. William Pitt, earl of Chatham, called the tea destruction "certainly criminal." Colonel Isaac Barre, whose impassioned speech against the Stamp Act had provided the American radicals with the name "Sons of Liberty," was so upset with Boston that he got his genders mixed: "I think Boston ought to be punished; she is your eldest son."

The only serious attempt to change the Port Bill came from Mr. Rose Fuller, a former West Indian planter who had a seat in Commons. Fuller moved an amendment that would have allowed the bill to take effect only if Boston refused to pay. Lord North disagreed. He claimed that "Boston had begun many years ago to endeavor to throw off all obedience to this country," and this was the first time that Parliament had ever tried to punish the town for it. North recalled that the repeal of the Stamp Act contained a clause requiring reimbursement for sufferers from the Stamp Act riots, but that Boston had never paid. The matter went beyond Boston, said North. "Let this Bill produce a conviction in all America, that we are in earnest, and that we will proceed with firmness and vigour; that conviction will be lost, if they see us hesitating and doubting." Charles James Fox tried to amend the bill so that the port would be restored as soon as the East India Company was paid. Neither Fuller's nor Fox's amendments got much support. On Friday, March 25, the bill came up for its final reading. In spite of the impassioned opposition of Edmund Burke and John Sawbridge, the Port Bill passed without a division of the house. By Wednesday, March 30, it had passed Lords, and the next day the king signed the Boston Port Act into law.

A few Englishmen—mostly Londoners who disliked the North government and merchants who would suffer from any suspension of Boston's trade—thought Parliament had gone too far. The *London Chronicle* pointed out that Parliament's punishment of Edinburgh in 1737, cited by the ministry as a precedent for the Port Act, was much less severe. Boston destroyed some East India Company tea; Edinburgh murdered a crown officer. Edinburgh was represented by counsel and witnesses; Parliament refused even to consider petitions from William Bollan, agent for the Massachusetts Council, on the specious grounds that he had no official standing because he was not approved by the governor and house, as well. After four months' debate, Edinburgh was fined £2,000; it took only seventeen days to decide upon a measure that would cost Boston at least £500,000.

Other papers wondered why Scottish ministers were so anxious to punish Boston, when their own countrymen had flocked to the banner of Charles Edward Stuart in 1745. In general, however, English public opinion supported the Port Act. Most seemed to agree with the king's statement to Lord North that the feebleness of the opposition to the Port Act proved the rectitude of the measure.

IV. THE MASSACHUSETTS GOVERNMENT ACT

Had the ministry been content with punishing Boston, the history of the year 1774 might have been very different; even in Massachusetts there was a sizable body of opinion that the town had behaved badly. But as the king's message of March 7 had pointed out, mere punishment did not go to the heart of the matter: there must be reforms to keep anything of the sort from happening again. Both Hutchinson and his predecessor, Sir Francis Bernard, had long argued that the real problem was the structure of Massachusetts government. Hutchinson blamed the lack of support from his elected Council for his failure to take steps to protect the tea. Thus on the Monday after Commons passed the Port Bill, March 28, Lord North informed the House that he would bring in a bill to alter the government of Massachusetts.

The problem, North stated baldly, was that there was too much democracy in Massachusetts. "I propose, in this Bill," said North, "to take the executive power from the hands of the democratic part of Government." The government was in the hands of the people, and the people were rioters; therefore "little obedience to the preservation of the peace is to be expected from them." The governor was almost powerless to put down or prevent civil disturbances because he could not act unless at least seven members of his Council concurred; but since the Council's "dependence is on the democratic part of the constitution," it was impossible to get its consent to any peace-keeping measures. Furthermore, the Council's consent was required for appointing justices of the peace, county judges, sheriffs, and other magistrates. North wanted the governor to have the sole power to appoint and remove them. Much of the agitation had emanated from town meetings; North wanted town meetings to be held only with the governor's consent. Finally, "their juries are improperly chosen"; that is, the town meetings annually elected persons to serve jury duty, rather than being picked by a magistrate.

After North made his presentation he answered a number of questions. No, he assured Sir Fletcher Norton, he did not intend to abolish the Massachusetts House of Representatives or strip the Council of its legislative function. Lord George Germain, a cashiered army officer who would eventually succeed Dartmouth as colonial secretary, said North had not gone far enough. The

[54]

Council ought to be appointed by the king, as it was in the other royal colonies, and the town meetings should be completely abolished. "I would not have men of a mercantile cast every day collecting themselves together, and debating about political matters," said Germain. "I would have them follow their occupations as merchants, and not consider themselves as Ministers of that country." Germain wanted the towns to be governed by self-perpetuating corporations, as in England; "I should then expect to see some subordination, some authority and order." North replied that he agreed with everything Germain had said.

Not much attention was paid to the speakers who took the side of Massachusetts, among them Thomas Pownall, former governor of the colony and England's greatest authority on colonial government. Pownall tried to explain how Massachusetts's government worked, and claimed there were no more respectable citizens of the empire than the Bay colonists. Horace Walpole caught Parliament's attitude in his diary: "Governor Pownall owned the mob governed in the Massachusetts, but that they were sober, religious, and fond of government."

In spite of North's very complete outline of his proposed bill, the text of the "Bill for the Better Regulating the Government of the Province of Massachusetts Bay" was not presented to Commons until Friday, April 15. It was the longest and most technical of the bills dealing with Massachusetts, and ultimately it was the one that caused the most resistance in America. Briefly, the Massachusetts Government Bill would amend the Massachusetts Charter, granted in 1691 by William and Mary, as follows:

(1) The Council, to consist of between twelve and thirty-six members, would be appointed by the king, to serve during his pleasure. This would bring Massachusetts into line with the practice in the other royal colonies.

(2) Even though the Council was no longer elected, it was stripped of its power to veto the governor's appointment and removal of justices of the peace, judges, sheriffs, and attorneys general. This would make the Massachusetts Council significantly weaker than those in the other royal colonies.

(3) Justices of the Superior Court of Judicature, the colony's highest court, were to serve during the king's pleasure, rather than during their good behavior. The matter of judges' tenure had been a friction point between England and the colonies for years.

(4) Town meetings could be held only once a year to choose town

officers and elect members of the House of Representatives. Other meetings could be held only with the governor's written permission, and they were required to discuss only the matters on an agenda approved by the governor.

(5) More than half the act was devoted to changing the Massachusetts jury system to make it like that of England. Essentially, it required that jurors be chosen from a list of residents by the county sheriffs, rather than selected from a panel of persons elected by the town meetings.

The opposition was stronger and better organized than it had been during the debate on the Port Bill, but it was never strong enough seriously to endanger the Government Bill's passage. William Dowdeswell thought it was a mistake to tamper with the Massachusetts charter. "The Americans have laboured with unwearied industry, and flourished for near fourscore years under that democratic charter," and had increased their wealth "to the mutual benefit of both countries." The charter, said Dowdeswell, "is more adapted to the spirit of a free people, than any charter that can possibly be framed by any Minister now."

Governor Pownall followed Dowdeswell with an explanation of how Massachusetts government really worked. He pointed out that the Council was not, as some members seemed to think, elected by popular vote, but by a vote of the whole legislature. Selectmen were much like aldermen in England. Finally, all business "of a municipal nature" was done in town meeting; and since many towns were as much as three hundred miles from the capital, the requirement of the governor's permission for town meetings was completely impractical. George Johnstone, who had been a colonial governor, Isaac Barre, who had served in the British army in America, and Constantine J. Phipps, recently captain of a Royal Navy warship on the North American station, all gave informed opinions against features of the Massachusetts Government Bill. There is no indication that Parliament paid any attention to them.

On Tuesday, April 19, there was a break in the discussion of the Government Bill when Rose Fuller moved to repeal the Townshend duty on tea. Fuller pointed out that the tea tax was the cause of the whole problem, and if it were not repealed "the Boston Port Bill, and the other regulations, would be totally ineffectual." Fuller's motion, of course, never had a chance of passing; it lost 49-182. It did, however, provide an opportunity for Edmund Burke to give one of his most famous speeches. The members of Parliament seldom agreed with Burke, particularly about America, but they were always glad to be treated to

Edmund Burke Esq[r].

his eloquence. Burke went through the whole history of the dispute over taxation; and when, after several hours, he asked if he had spoken too long, there were cries of "Go on! Go on!" He argued that the only time Britain had pursued the correct policy was when his own party, the Rockingham Whigs, had repealed the Stamp Act and passed the Declaratory Act in 1766. Burke's speech was a tour de force, but his position was untenable: essentially he was arguing that Parliament could legislate for the colonies "in all cases whatsoever"—as long as it was careful to do nothing the Americans objected to.

With Fuller's motion out of the way, debate resumed on the Government Bill. On May 28 the house refused to receive another petition from William Bollan, agent for the Massachusetts Council. On the following Monday, May 2, it similarly rejected a petition from a number of Americans residing in England. The same day, after a ten-hour debate, the Commons passed the Massachusetts Government Bill 239-64.

The House of Lords also refused to hear Bollan and the Americans. Some lords signed a protest against the bill, and the bishop of St. Asaph composed an eloquent speech containing such lines as "let not the love of liberty be the only crime you think worthy of punishment." Alas, the bishop never delivered his speech in Lords, but reprints of it made the Americans feel better. On May 11 the bill passed Lords. Nine days later the king signed the Massachusetts Government Act into law.

V. THE JUSTICE AND QUARTERING ACTS

The same day that North presented the Massachusetts Government Bill, April 15, he moved, in a voice that "trembled and faultered at every word," for permission "to bring in a Bill for the impartial administration of justice" in Massachusetts. In introducing his motion, North informed the House that Hutchinson was being recalled, and that he would be succeeded by General Thomas Gage, who would take with him four regiments of troops to restore order in Boston. Gage would also continue as commander of the army in America. The Justice Bill, as well as the Quartering Bill introduced two weeks later, were direct results of Gage's appointment.

Gage had made so favorable an impression on the king in his February 4 interview that he was tapped for the job of presiding over the punishment of Boston. Some military types might have welcomed such a commission, but Thomas Gage was instinctively cautious. He was always careful to see that his actions were taken on somebody else's responsibility, an attitude expressed in

the modern army, inelegantly but accurately, as "Cover your ass." In 1774 Gage
had spent nearly twenty years in America, half of them as commander in chief,
and he knew how to keep covered. A governor could request military assistance
only if his Council agreed. Gage had pointedly ignored hints from the governor
of New York in 1765 and the governor of Massachusetts in 1768 that he should
send troops to keep order in their colonies without their getting their councils'
permission. Governor Gage was unlikely to ask General Gage to take any action
that had not been specifically authorized.

On March 30 Gage and his predecessor as army commander, Sir Jeffrey
Amherst, had a meeting with the cabinet. Both agreed that it was hard for British soldiers to get justice from Massachusetts magistrates and juries. There was
some reason for this charge, for Boston justices of the peace had constantly
harassed the redcoats with petty charges during the army's unhappy stay in
Boston from 1768 to 1770. So far as capital crime was concerned, however,
neither of the generals had any precedent to back their contention that fair trial
was impossible. Nevertheless, both said that soldiers accused of capital crime for
doing their duty to suppress a riot would be in very great danger of being
hanged by a Massachusetts court. As governor, Gage could use his power of
pardon, but he much prefered to have the matter taken out of his hands. North
did this with his "Bill for the Impartial Administration of Justice" (called the
"murder bill" in America), which provided thàt the governor of Massachusetts
could shift any trial for a capital crime from Massachusetts to another colony or
to England.

Gage may also have told the cabinet—if it needed any reminding—that the
army had long labored under great difficulties in finding quarters for its troops,
particularly in Boston in 1768; and one of the reasons that the army had not
helped to protect the tea was that the troops were quartered in the provincial
barracks on an island far out in Boston harbor. Like the Justice Bill introduced
and passed after Gage left for America, the Quartering Bill gave the general
considerably more leeway in the way he used his troops.

North's April 15 request for leave to bring in the Justice Bill touched off
another debate. Colonel Barre, now sorry that he had supported the Port Bill,
said that North was proposing nothing more than a license for the army to kill
Americans. Barre challenged North to produce one instance of a British soldier
or official's having been condemned to death by a vengeful American jury. On
the contrary, said Barre, Captain Preston and his soldiers had been acquitted by
a Boston jury in the Massacre trial.

Colonel Barre was joined in his opposition by Captain Phipps, who said he welcomed Gage's appointment because it meant the removal of "one of the worst, one of the most exceptionable servants the Crown ever had, I mean Governor Hutchinson." North gladly seized the opportunity to turn the debate away from his own proposal and Barre's embarrassing reminder about the Boston Massacre trial; he warmly defended Hutchinson. This brought another oratorical blast from Mr. Van, who had earlier proposed a Carthaginian solution to the Boston problem: "If they oppose the measures of Government that are now sent out," declared Van, "I would do as was done of old, in the time of the ancient Britons, I would burn and set fire to all their woods, and leave their country open, to prevent that protection they now have." Van's plan to defoliate Massachusetts was just as realistic as the government's hopes that Massachusetts would swallow the Coercive Acts without fighting.

When North finally brought in the Justice Bill, on Thursday, April 21, only forty-one members were present. Probably most were still recovering from Burke's marathon speech on Fuller's motion to repeal the tea tax. John Sawbridge accused North of a cowardly attempt to enslave America by sneaking the bill in before a thin house. Sawbridge charged that North would also enslave England as well, if he got the opportunity. North made a perfunctory denial that he wanted to enslave America, then silenced the opposition with a magnificent non sequitur: he announced that Boston had had a second Tea Party early in March.

After that, there was really not much the opposition could do. There was little debate when the bill came up for its second reading on April 25, and not much more when it was finally passed, 127-24, on May 6. The opposition was somewhat stronger in the House of Lords. The marquis of Rockingham, a former prime minister who had not uttered a word in parliamentary debates since he left office nearly eight years before, spoke against the bill for three-quarters of an hour. Eight lords signed a dissent to the bill. All this made little difference. On Wednesday, May 18, the Impartial Administration of Justice Bill passed Lords 43-12. The king made it law on the same day as the Massachusetts Government act.

The last of the four laws dealing with Massachusetts, the Quartering Act, aroused almost no debate in Commons. It was brought in on May 2 and passed its final reading exactly one week later. The Lords moved rather more slowly—it took them all of two and a half weeks to pass the bill. Lord Chatham, another former prime minister, came to Lords supported by a crutch and swathed in bandages. Chatham pleaded for the lords to be lenient with America, and he reaffirmed his contention that no English subject could be taxed without his consent. Shortly after Chatham finished speaking, the Quartering Bill passed, 57-16. The king signed it on June 2.

The Quartering Act was the shortest of the Coercive Acts and, in England, the least controversial. It was presented as a needed amendment to the Quartering Act of 1765, an act whose violation had already led Parliament to suspend the New York legislature in Charles Townshend's days. Dartmouth wrote to Gage the day after the act was signed, noting that it was intended to prevent "what happened at Boston in 1770, respecting the quartering the two Regiments sent thither from Halifax, and the Artifices used by forced Construction of the Act of Parliament to elude the Execution of it." Dartmouth's memory was faulty on one point: the incident occurred in 1768, not 1770, but Massachusetts certainly had tried to use the 1765 act to keep the troops in Castle William, rather than in Boston, where they were needed.

The most important part of the Quartering Act of 1774 was this:

it shall and may be lawful for the Governor of a Province to order and direct such and so many uninhabited houses, out-houses, barns, or other buildings, as he shall think necessary to be taken (making a reasonable allowance for the same) and make fit for the reception of such Officers and Soldiers, and to put and quarter such Officers and Soldiers therein, for such time as he shall think proper.

Note that the act did not specifically state that soldiers were to be quartered with families, unless that was what "other buildings" meant. However, Americans (and many historians who have since written about the act) assumed that it gave the army the power to impress lodgings in private households, and they made the act a major issue.

VI. THE QUEBEC ACT

A fifth act dealing with America was passed during Parliament's fateful 1774 session. As all historians have rightly pointed out, it is not properly one of the Coercive Acts. On the contrary, the Quebec Act was the product of a careful study of the problems of French Canada and the trans-Appalachian west after 1760.

Nevertheless, the act was certainly believed in America—especially New England—to be yet another attempt to punish America. It was also considered so in London, where it aroused more opposition than any of the acts dealing with

Massachusetts. Furthermore, there is good reason to believe that the ministry, knowing the act would be unpopular, was happy to have it be considered an act to punish America in order to help get it passed. George III made a speech when he signed the Quebec Act on June 22, noting that the act would help to head off "the dangerous spirit of opposition to my Government, and to the execution of the laws, prevailing in the Province of Massachusetts Bay." Obviously the king thought it was a Coercive Act.

When Canada fell to British forces in 1760, the inhabitants of the newly conquered territory were guaranteed freedom of worship, but few other civil rights. Canada was first ruled by a military governor, and after 1764 by a governor and Council appointed by the king. Almost from the beginning, the English inhabitants of Quebec, many of them from New England, demanded a representative assembly. Since British law forbade Roman Catholics to vote or hold office, any assembly would have to be chosen from and by a few hundred English Protestants. Guy Carleton, who became governor of Canada in 1766, resisted the demands for an assembly, making him something of a hero to French Canadians to this day.

In 1774, when he was called back to England to testify on the Quebec Bill, Carleton said that his province contained only about 360 Protestants, compared to about 150,000 French Catholics. Carleton may have exaggerated, but even the bill's opponents admitted that Catholics outnumbered Protestants by twenty-five to one. Following Carleton's advice, Parliament provided in the Quebec Act that the province should continue to be ruled by a governor and Council, now expanded to include French Catholic aristocrats, which should have all powers of legislation except that of taxation. (The British Parliament kept that power for itself. The Quebec Revenue Act of 1774, passed separately, provided for the government of Canada to be supported from duties on spirits, rum and molasses.)

The Quebec Act reaffirmed the right of Roman Catholics to worship as they chose, and the Catholic clergy were allowed to collect tithes from their communicants. This provision, one of the most enlightened pieces of legislation passed in the eighteenth century, caused an immediate outcry on both sides of the Atlantic. As a scare word, "Popery" filled the same place as "Communism" has in much of the twentieth century.

The French civil law, which had been abolished in 1763, was restored. English criminal law, much more lenient than French and welcomed by the Canadians, was continued.

Most important for America, the boundary of Quebec was extended to include all the trans-Appalachian west that lay north of the Ohio River. This was a sensible attempt to do what the Proclamation of 1763 had failed to do: provide for orderly settlement of the west, protect the rights of Indians, preserve fur resources, and bring some order to the fierce competition of land companies. To its opponents, this part of the act was an attempt to extend popery into free lands, to punish the colonies by taking away their western lands, and to re-create the French and Indian threat that had helped bind the thirteen colonies to England before 1763.

The last of the five acts designed to deal with America became law on June 22, five months to the day after the news of the Boston Tea Party was first published in England. Except for the Quebec Act, the legislation was popular with the electorate. Parliament was sent home and new elections called to take advantage of the popularity of the policy of punishing America. But what was good British politics turned out to be a poor way to preserve an empire.

Lord Dartmouth, America's supposed "friend" in the cabinet, was certain that Parliament had acted wisely. One of Dartmouth's American correspondents, Joseph Reed of Philadelphia, warned him that he could not agree to Parliament's right to tax America. Every colony from Massachusetts to Virginia, said Reed, had resolved to relieve Boston from the distresses of the Port Act. Dartmouth's reply, written on July 11, was both a candid expression of the ministry's attitude toward America and an unwitting prediction that turned out to be all too accurate:

> What then, is the present case? The supreme legislature of the whole British Empire has laid a duty (no matter for the present whether it has or has not a right to do so, it is sufficient that we conceive it has. . . . The question then is, whether these laws are to be submitted to: if the people of America say no, they say in effect that they will no longer be a part of the British Empire; they change the whole ground of the controversy; they no longer contend that Parliament has not a right to exact a particular provision, they say that it has no right to consider them at all as within its jurisdiction.

What Dartmouth thought was *reductio ad absurdum* was, of course, what Americans did say. Almost exactly two years later they presented that view to the world in their Declaration of Independence; and a substantial part of the Declaration addressed itself to the grievances of the Coercive Acts:

[63]

He [the King] had combined with others [Parliament] to subject us to a jurisdiction foreign to our constitution, and unacknowledged by our laws; giving his Assent to their Acts of pretended Legislation: For Quartering large bodies of armed troops among us: For protecting them, by a mock Trial, from punishment for any Murders which they should commit on the inhabitants of these States: For cutting off our trade with all parts of the world: . . . For abolishing the free system of English Laws in a neighboring Province, establishing therein an Arbitrary government, and enlarging its Boundaries so as to render it at once an example and fit instrument for introducing the same absolute rule into these Colonies: For taking away our Charters, abolishing our most valuable Laws, and altering fundamentally the Forms of our Governments. . . .

To the extent that Americans rebelled against the Coercive Acts, the War for American Independence was made in England.

CHAPTER IV

Coercion Resisted

I hear from Many that the [Boston Port] Act has staggered the most Presumptuous. . . . The violent Party seems to break and People fall off from them. . . .

—Thomas Gage, May 1774

If the Opposers of Government may be called only a Faction in the Province, they are at least a very numerous and powerful Faction. . . .

—Thomas Gage, July 1774

Civil Government is near it's [sic] end. . . . Tho' the People are not held in high Estimation by the Troops, yet they are numerous, worked up to a Fury, and not a Boston Rabble but the Freeholders and Farmers of the Country.

—Thomas Gage, September 1774

I. AFTERMATH OF THE BOSTON TEA PARTY

More than four months passed between the Boston Tea Party and the arrival in Boston of news about the Port Act, but the interval was neither tranquil nor marked by passive waiting to see what England would do.

The immediate reaction to the Tea Party was a feeling of exultation. John Adams wrote in his diary: "This is the most magnificent Movement of all. There is a Dignity, a Majesty, a Sublimity, in this last Effort of the Patriots, that I greatly admire." Sam Adams, usually less likely to be carried away than his cousin, wrote to Arthur Lee in London that "You cannot imagine the height of joy that sparkles in the eyes and animates the countenances as well as the hearts of all we meet on this occasion." John Andrews, a Boston merchant who thought destroying the tea was going a bit too far, told his brother-in-law in Philadelphia: "However precarious our situation may be, yet such is the present calm composure of the people that a stranger would hardly think that ten thousand pounds sterling of the East India Company's tea was destroy'd the . . . evening before last."

Some Bostonians, of course, agreed with William Paine's sentiments about "those Devils that call themselves Sons of Liberty—But from such Liberty! good God! deliver us—" or with Daniel Leonard's opinion that the Tea Party was a bigger stain on the reputation of Massachusetts than the Salem witch trials, but they mostly kept their feelings to themselves for the time being.

Beneath the exultation, however, there was some apprehension. John Adams wondered: "What Measures will the Ministry take . . . will they punish Us? How? By quartering Troops upon Us?—by annulling our Charter?—by laying on more duties? By restraining our Trade? By Sacrifice of Individuals, or how." John Andrews feared that if the other colonies allowed their tea to be landed and stored, "poor Boston will feel the whole weight of ministerial vengeance."

The day after the Tea Party, the Boston Committee of Correspondence met in a sober mood. It sent out only four notices of the incident, two of them to the Massachusetts towns of Plymouth and Sandwich. The other two, carried by the committee's trusty messenger, Paul Revere, were directed to Alexander McDougall and Isaac Sears in New York and Thomas Mifflin and George Clymer in Philadelphia. These letters tersely announced what had happened on December 16, then turned to the pressing need for New York City and Philadelphia to form their own Committees of Correspondence. A week later, the Boston committeemen adopted a mutual pledge of support for themselves and anyone else "who may be likely to suffer for any noble Effort they have made to serve their Country."

It soon became apparent, however, that Thomas Hutchinson's government was impotent to do anything about the Tea Party. The Committee of Correspondence settled down to answering the dozens of letters of support that were flowing in. It took time to attempt to heal a dispute among the Marblehead patriots over a smallpox inoculation hospital, supported by members of the Marblehead committee, that fearful townspeople had burned down. Most important, the Boston committee adopted an idea that was to help promote intercolonial unity.

William Goddard, printer of the *Pennsylvania Chronicle*, had closed his printing office in order to try to sell his pet project, a "constitutional post office," to America. He arrived in Boston in March 1774, having already presented his idea to committees in New York and Newport. The Boston Committee of Correspondence immediately grasped the possibilities in Goddard's plan. Ideologically, the postal service established by act of Parliament was just as much "taxation without representation" as the tea tax. On a more practical note, a postal system controlled by the patriots would be far more secure than one whose employees were appointed by the ministry; and if the colonies could agree to form their own post office, they could unite on other matters as well. The Boston committee saw to it that Goddard's plan was published in the *Massachusetts Spy,* and it sent a subscription for establishing a post office to other towns. By the end of 1774, the independent post office was well under way.

In the meantime, the Massachusetts patriots gave ample notice that the Boston Tea Party was only the beginning. By the end of March 1774 they had destroyed more tea and committed several acts of outright terrorism. News of some of them got to England in time to fan the indignation against Boston and speed the passage of the Coercive Acts.

The tarring and feathering of Captain John Malcom was not directly connected with the Boston Tea Party. Malcom, a fifty-year old customs officer who seemed always to be fighting with his family and associates, had just returned to Boston after making himself thoroughly unpopular in several other ports. The circumstances of Malcom's tarring and feathering on January 25, 1774, vary according to whether you read Malcom's own account or that of Isaiah Thomas's *Massachusetts Spy.* Neither was known for letting facts stand in the way of a good story. Furthermore, as Malcom's story made the rounds of

A New Method of Macarony Making, as Practised in Boston ("Macarony" was slang for fashionable dress)

Boston, England, and even France, it attracted considerable embellishments. We do know that Malcom possibly threatened or struck a child who had run into him with a sled; and certainly he got into an argument with a tradesman, George Hewes, and hit him over the head with his cane. Hewes swore out a complaint to a local justice of the peace; but the Bostonians, who must have been waiting for an excuse, got to Malcom before the arresting officer.

Everything in Boston—including Boston harbor—was frozen solid on January 25, 1774. Two days before, the thermometer registered -4°, and one diarist found the ink freezing in his pen as he tried to make his daily entry. On the afternoon of January 25, the temperature rose to 18° under a dull sky, but it was dropping rapidly during the evening when a mob dragged Malcom out of his house to receive "the modern mode of punishment," the Boston euphemism for tar and feathers.

The *Massachusetts Spy,* which had no reason to make the details more gruesome than they actually were, reported that Malcom was thrown into a cart, stripped naked, and given "a modern jacket" of tar and feathers. Then his tormenters "hied him away to the liberty-tree," where they tried to make him resign his customs commission. When he refused, they dragged him to the town gallows and put a noose around his neck. When he still refused to resign, "they basted him for some time with a rope's end, and threatened to cut his ears off," on which he finally agreed to resign. Ann Hulton, sister of one of the customs commissioners, reported that "They say his flesh comes off his back in stakes." Another story said that Hewes tried to give Malcom a blanket, but the mob would not let him. Still another story, which Boston papers later picked up from the London press, said Malcom was given the "water cure"—forced to drink gallons of water until he vomited.

The *Massachusetts Spy* drew an interesting moral from Malcom's lynching: "See reader, the effects of a government in which the people have no confidence! Let those who pretend to dread anarchy and confusion at length be persuaded to join in the only measure to be depended on for their prevention, viz. to put the administration into the hands of men reverenced and beloved by the people." Not everyone agreed. John Rowe wrote in his diary that "this was looked upon by me & every Sober man as an act of outrageous violence."

John Hancock, who could always be counted upon to reflect the mood of his home town, was picked to give the annual Massacre Day address on March 5, 1774. Everyone agreed that it was quite a speech—so good, in fact, that more than one diarist expressed incredulity at the reports that Hancock himself had written it. With even less obeisance to fact than most Massacre orators,

John Hancock

Hancock charged that the Bostón Massacre had been deliberately planned by the British ministry and the Boston Tories. "Ye dark designing knaves," roared Hancock, "ye murderers, parricides! How dare you tread upon the earth, which has drank in the blood of slaughtered innocents, shed by your wicked hands?"

Having warmed up the crowd in the Old South Meeting House with these words, Hancock then turned to more immediate issues. He denounced standing armies, the ministerial plot to pay the salaries of the governor and the judges, and the Tea Act. Had the last succeeded, said Hancock, it would have put Boston's trade in the hands of foreigners, laid taxes on "everything which we consumed," and probably would have led to the sale to a London company of the "exclusive right of trading to America." The people had foiled that plot, but "Restless malice, and disappointed ambition, will still suggest new measures to our inveterate enemies. Therefore let us also be ready to take the field whenever danger calls." Specifically, Hancock called for a continental congress which would secure American liberties and "free ourselves from those unmannerly pillagers who impudently tell us, that they are licensed by an act of the British parliament to thrust their dirty hands into the pockets of every American."

The day after Hancock's speech was a most inopportune time for another tea ship, the brig *Fortune,* to arrive in Boston harbor. Her captain, Benjamin Gorham, had been warned by the vessel's owners not to accept any East India Company tea; and technically he had not, as this tea was purchased at auction in London. The horrified owners immediately tried to send their ship back to London, but the customs collector, Richard Harrison, refused to allow the *Fortune* to depart until her cargo was entered and all duties paid. On Monday, March 7, John Adams confided to his diary: "Twenty Eight Chests of Tea arrived Yesterday, which are to make an Infusion in Water, at 7 o Clock this Evening." At that time, as Adams foretold, sixty "Indians" sent the *Fortune*'s tea to join that of the *Dartmouth,* the *Eleanor,* and the *Beaver.* News of the second Boston Tea Party got to England in time to help pass the Administration of Justice Act.

Not all tea parties needed sea water as an ingredient, nor did the tea even have to have paid the Townshend duty. Since it was impossible to tell the difference between dutied and "honestly smuggled" tea, the ban fell on all alike. Several peddlers had their stocks of tea burned. And Weston, Massachusetts, had a tea party that was in its way more violent than Boston's. On March 17, the *Massachusetts Spy* noted that Captain Isaac Jones, keeper of the Golden Ball Tavern in Weston, had been bragging that he was selling plenty of tea in spite of all the town meeting resolutions against it. "Now if this be true," wrote

[71]

RUSTICUS, "what can be the advantage of our town-meetings and resolves? If it is not true, does not the insolence of this arrogant boaster deserve the severest chastisement?" On March 28, while Jones was away, thirty "Indians" showed up at the Golden Ball. They drank all of Jones's liquor and broke all his windows, glassware, and crockery. When the landlord returned, his guests explained to him the error of his ways. At first Jones tried to claim that his tea had actually been smuggled from Albany (as well it might have been), but he soon discovered that he would get further if he admitted that it was legal and begged everybody's pardon for committing such a heinous offense. It worked. The "Indians" did not run Jones out of town, nor force him to close the Golden Ball. Isaac Jones even continued to offer tea to customers he knew were Tories, but he quit bragging about it.

The air of self-congratulation about the Boston Tea Party persisted well through April, when news at last began to come from England and the rest of America that indicated not everyone supported Boston. On April 25 the first news of the Boston Port Act arrived, followed a few days later by a preliminary copy of the act itself. The Bostonians were rudely shocked. John Andrews wrote his brother-in-law: "Imagine to yourself the horror painted in the faces of a string of slaves condemn'd by the Inquisition to perpetual drudgery at the oar! Such is the dejection imprinted on every countenance we meet in this once happy, but now totally ruin'd town."

Sam Adams, who had never succumbed to Boston's euphoria, was not surprised and was probably secretly gratified at the news of the Port Act. On April 4 he had written a remarkable letter to Arthur Lee in which he predicted not only that Parliament would continue to press its claim of complete sovereignty over the colonies, but that "the evil which they profess to aim at preventing by their rigorous measures, will the sooner be brought to pass, viz.— *the entire separation and independence of the Colonies.*" Adams then went on to paint a glorious and prophetic picture of a great American empire. In the meantime, Adams and his allies had been doing what they could to establish effective independence, whatever they called it, in their final battle with their ancient foe, Thomas Hutchinson.

II. EXIT THOMAS HUTCHINSON

Thomas Hutchinson, the royal governor of Massachusetts Bay, had long been the most formidable enemy of the Boston radicals. Born in 1711 into one of the oldest families in the Bay colony, Hutchinson was as impeccably aristocratic as anyone in America. He had a distinguished record at Harvard, prospered as a merchant, and became the greatest historian produced by colonial America. But above all, Thomas Hutchinson was a politician. In 1737 he was elected to both the Boston Board of Selectmen and the Massachusetts House of Representatives. Nine years later he became Speaker of the House. In this position he worked tirelessly to put Massachusetts on a hard-money basis, ruining Sam Adams's father, among others, in the process. This lost him the support of the Boston electorate, but his reputation in the rest of the colony was so great that after he left the House he was elected to the Council every year from 1749 to 1766. Before being designated royal governor in 1771, Hutchinson had served as lieutenant governor since 1758. In 1760, although he was not a lawyer, Hutchinson was appointed chief justice of the Massachusetts superior court, causing James Otis, whose father was in line for the job, to desert the government party and threaten to set the province in flames. While holding all these posts, Hutchinson was also justice of the peace and of the quorum, probate judge, and commander of Castle William. Hutchinson was able to engross all these offices for himself, and get his relatives and associates, like the Olivers, into the other top jobs, because he was the ablest supporter of British policy in Massachusetts. Royal governors may have had control of patronage, but they asked Thomas Hutchinson whom to appoint. Until Sam Adams rebuilt the Popular party in the 1770s Hutchinson had the closest thing to a political organization in Massachusetts. He was used to having things his own way.

Of late, however, things had not been going well for Thomas Hutchinson. The 1773 legislature had demanded his dismissal because of the famous purloined letters. Hutchinson asked leave to go to England to defend himself, and he repeatedly prorogued the legislature in hopes that things would cool off. The Boston Tea Party, however, destroyed any chance of that. Hutchinson's adamant refusal to allow the tea ships to return to England would have been a canny political move, if he had not underestimated the lengths to which the radicals would go to keep the tea from being landed. When the Boston Tea Party took place, he was not even in town, but at his country estate in Milton.

The next day Hutchinson hurried back to Boston to consult his Council, but he could not gather a quorum. He spent the night in Castle William and called a meeting for December 18 in Milton. Once again, most of the councilors stayed away. Not until December 21 did enough councilors show up to hold a formal meeting, but all they would agree to do was to direct Attorney General Jonathan Sewall to investigate the matter and submit his findings to a grand jury. Even then, the Council rejected Hutchinson's opinion that dumping the tea was high

Thomas Hutchinson

treason; he had to settle for "New England burglary"—breaking open a shop or ship.

On January 26, 1774, Hutchinson at last ended the legislature's seven-month recess. His opening remarks were considerably more restrained than they had been in January 1773. The treasury, he reported, was in the best state ever, the province was completely free of debt, and current expenses could be met with only a small tax on liquor. The problems the governor presented to the legislature were hardly earthshaking; for example, some Indians were demanding that an island (Chappaquiddick) be turned over to them. Hutchinson did note that the king had expressed his disapprobation of the Committees of Correspondence, but he did not denounce them with the same fervor he had shown a year earlier. Hutchinson had been granted leave to come to England, and he wanted to keep things quiet until then.

The House of Representatives, however, did not cooperate with Hutchinson's wishes. It repeated its demand of a year ago that the superior court justices refuse to accept a salary out of Townshend Act receipts and continue to be paid by grants from the Massachusetts legislature, as called for in the 1691 charter. On the same day that the legislative session opened, Judge Edmund Trowbridge caved in to the pressure and signed the pledge. On February 1 the House approved of Trowbridge's gesture and demanded that the four remaining justices do the same by February 8. Three of them complied. One, Nathaniel Ropes of Salem, was dying; a mob extracted his pledge literally from his deathbed. Chief Justice Peter Oliver, however, was defiant. On February 3 he returned a blistering letter that claimed, with some justification, that during his seventeen years on the bench he had been miserably paid, that his services had left him some £3,000 out of pocket, and that he would most gratefully accept the king's salary.

On February 11 the House of Representatives voted 96-9 that the governor and Council should remove Oliver from the bench. Hutchinson replied on February 15 that the Council had no power to do so. If the House desired it, he would pass on their complaints about the chief justice to the king. Hutchinson, of course, knew full well that the king would reject the House's demand.

The next move was suggested by John Adams who, though only thirty-eight years old, already had an enviable reputation as a legal scholar. The House should draw up articles of impeachment against Oliver for high crimes and misdemeanors. True, nothing in the Massachusetts charter gave the House the power to impeach a king's appointee, but since the Massachusetts House of Representatives was the equal of the British House of Commons, it followed that

[75]

it could act on British precedent. The Council, in this case, could try the impeachment as the equivalent of the House of Lords. It is doubtful that anyone, especially John Adams, thought they actually could get away with it, but the House was in a cheeky mood. On February 24 it adopted articles of impeachment against Chief Justice Peter Oliver and appointed a committee of nine to bring the impeachment before the governor and Council. Hutchinson declared that the action was unconstitutional, and he prevented the Council from trying Oliver; but it was the hollowest of victories.

When the superior court next met, no juror would allow himself to be sworn. All claimed that it was improper for the chief justice to sit on the bench while impeachment charges were still pending against him. The court never heard another case under British rule. And if the superior court, which had original jurisdiction in capital cases, could not sit, those walking near the fine line of treason could breathe a little easier.

By early February Hutchinson was almost desperate to embark for England before anything else happened. However, as he explained in a letter to Lord Dartmouth, he could not risk leaving because Lieutenant Governor Andrew Oliver was ill. According to the Massachusetts charter, if neither the governor nor lieutenant governor was present, the Council could exercise all the governor's powers and had in fact done so several times in the past. Hutchinson had every reason to avoid turning the reins of government over to the men who ran the Council in 1774.

Andrew Oliver's illness grew worse. His brother, the chief justice, was afraid to go to his bedside. On March 3 Andrew Oliver died, but even in death he could not escape his old enemies. Sam Adams's Liberty Boys turned Oliver's burial into a public celebration. They even gave three cheers as his coffin was lowered into the grave. Few of Oliver's friends or relatives dared to attend the burial; neither Governor Hutchinson nor his Council was there.

By this time Governor Hutchinson was almost an outlaw in his own capital city. He remained at his country home in Milton for a while, then took up residence in the fort on Castle Island. There is no record of his ever returning to the mainland. When his successor, General Thomas Gage, arrived on May 13, he landed first at Castle William and spent several days in discussions with Hutchinson; but Hutchinson did not accompany Gage to Boston for the ceremonial change of governors.

On June 1, 1774, the day the Boston Port Act went into effect, Thomas Hutchinson left America forever. He expected his absence to be only temporary; that after Gage had seen to the punishment of Boston, he would

[76]

return to the governorship in triumph. His last two weeks in his native land had been heartened by resolutions of support and praise from groups of merchants, lawyers, and Anglican clergymen. But the signers of these resolutions had accomplished nothing except to provide a handy list of Tories who would be dealt with before the year was out. For most people—even the moderates— Hutchinson had become "the damn'd arch traitor."

III. ENTER THOMAS GAGE

H.M.S. *Lively* entered Boston Harbor on Friday, May 13, 1774, bearing an official transcript of the Boston Port Act and the man who was to preside over the end of British government in Massachusetts Bay. Lieutenant General Thomas Gage, commander in chief of the British army in North America since 1764, had been given the dual task of serving as royal governor of the recalcitrant colony and as commander of the troops occupying its capital city. Even as the *Lively* was dropping anchor near Castle Island, a Boston town meeting was in session to condemn the Port Act. Gage found that Governor Hutchinson, Chief Justice Oliver, the customs commissioners, and the tea consignees "were either at the Castle, or dispersed in the Country, not daring to reside at Boston."

Things must not have looked hopeful to Gage as his flag-bedecked barge was rowed toward Long Wharf on Tuesday, May 17. A northeast wind, which is responsible for Boston's reputation for nasty weather, was blowing; the temperature hovered around 50°, and a light drizzle was coming down. As Gage's barge approached the wharf, however, things began to look up. The shore batteries and ships in the harbor fired a salute. The right people were all there: a delegation from each house of the legislature, many of the leading citizens of Boston, and a good humored crowd of people lined the way to the State House. Colonel John Hancock's Corps of Cadets escorted Gage to the State House past several companies of Massachusetts militia, all properly uniformed, and accompanied by a military band.

After Gage was sworn in, he spoke soothing words to the assembled throng and was answered with cheers. Then he went to Faneuil Hall to be treated to a "good Dinner" and "elegant entertainment." Gage responded with a toast to Boston's prosperity, which was well received even if everyone knew that Gage brought with him an act specifically designed to destroy that prosperity. The only thing that marred the occasion was the chorus of hisses that greeted Gage's toast to Hutchinson. Few Bostonians gave any impression that they agreed with

[77]

Thomas Gage

Sam Adams's sour comment: "We suspect studied insult in the appointment of the person who is Commander-in-chief of the troops in America to be our Governour."

Seventeen months later, Gage headed back to England and retirement, as despised as Thomas Hutchinson in Massachusetts and blamed by England for all the civil and military failures she had suffered in America. Perhaps it was the law of averages catching up with him, for no man had escaped being a scapegoat more often than Thomas Gage.

Gage was born in 1719, the second son of the first Viscount Gage, and spent all of his adult life as an officer in the British army. This was not an unusual career for a younger son of the nobility, but it was possible for Gage only because his father, tiring of the severe disabilities suffered by Roman Catholics in England, became a convert to the Church of England. (Both parents resumed their Catholicism before they died, a fact noted by American propagandists.) Helped by good political connections, and following the traditional method of purchasing rank, Gage rose to lieutenant colonel by 1754. The next year his regiment came to America, where he remained for the next twenty years except for a few months in 1773-74.

Gage's first few years in America were not very promising. He commanded the vanguard of General Edward Braddock's ill-fated expedition against Fort Duquesne. Although Gage's troops were ambushed first, the blame was placed on the conveniently dead Braddock. A few years later, Gage, now a brigadier general, was second in command of General James Abercromby's equally disastrous assault on Fort Ticonderoga. Later he was reprimanded by General Jeffrey Amherst for failing to carry out an ordered attack, but his reputation was not permanently damaged by any of these incidents. In 1760, after Canada was at last captured from the French, Gage was made military governor of Montreal, while abler fighters moved on to other battlegrounds. Again his luck held. In 1763 Pontiac's Rebellion broke out, partly due to inept handling by Amherst, the commanding general in North America. Amherst was recalled, and Gage, as the senior army officer in the region, fell into the command. He remained in charge of the British army in North America for the next twelve years.

Gage was doubly fortunate in his promotion, for it enabled him to move to New York City. Both Gage and his wife, the beautiful daughter of the wealthy Kemble family of New Jersey, disliked Montreal. Indeed, Gage had been trying to get leave to come to England to seek a more congenial post. New York suited the Gages well. Gage in turn got along well with the New Yorkers, in spite of several clashes and near-clashes between his troops and the Sons of Liberty and the suspension of the New York Assembly for its failure to supply Gage's soldiers. Even in Boston, which had been occupied by redcoats from 1768 to 1770 and had experienced the Boston Massacre, it was the ministry and governors Francis Bernard and Thomas Hutchinson, not the army commander, who got most of the blame. One may safely conclude that Thomas Gage was amiable, diplomatic, a good administrator, and very lucky; but even these qualities were not enough in 1774.

On the day Gage returned to America, John Rowe wrote in his diary: "God Grant his Instructions be not severe as I think him to be a Very Good man." Rowe's prayer was not answered. Lord Dartmouth's instructions were more severe than Rowe could have imagined. The port of Boston was not only to be shut up, it was to remain so until, among other things, Massachusetts courts themselves punished the perpetrators of the Boston Tea Party and the town had made "a full and absolute submission." Gage was to try "mild and gentle persuasion," but if trouble threatened, General Gage was not to allow the constitutional restrictions on Governor Gage to keep him from using the army to keep order. In addition to the Port Act, Boston was to be further punished by removing the seat of government. On June 1 Gage was to move his residence and the meeting place of the legislature to Salem, and all government officers who were not required by law to operate in Boston were to follow Gage to the new capital.

Dartmouth also had instructions to cover Gage's first problem, the opening of the Massachusetts legislature. The annual elections for the House of Representatives had been held on May 10, just a week before Gage became governor, and the legislature was scheduled to meet in Boston on May 25. On that day, according to the charter, the new House and the old Council would meet jointly to choose twenty-eight men to form the new Council. Dartmouth hoped, not very confidently, that the 1774 Council would be an improvement over that elected in 1773. "There are," wrote Dartmouth, "some amongst those who constitute the present Council there, upon whose Attachment to the Constitution no Reliance can be had in any case where the Sovereignty of the King in His Parliament is in question." Dartmouth had in mind the councilors who had voted the previous November (Dartmouth said September) to accept a committee report which declared that the Tea Act and the Townshend Revenue Act were unconstitutional, and that the government had no responsibility to protect the tea consignees. He ordered Gage to veto the reelection of any councilor who had voted for the report.

The fifteen councilors Gage accepted proved no more malleable than their predecessors. On June 9 they sent Gage an answer to his speech opening the legislature in which the Council expressed hope that Gage's administration "may be a happy contrast to that of your two immediate Predecessors," from whose "machinations (both in concert and apart) are derived the Origin & Progress of the disunion between Britain and the Colonies and the present distressed state of this Province." Gage refused to receive the Council's address because it "contains indecent reflections on my Predecessors . . . I consider this Address as an Insult upon His Majesty and the Lords of his Privy Council, and an Affront to myself."

Gage expected the House of Representatives to be a trouble spot, although in his first report to Dartmouth he said that the news of the Port Act had staggered its "most Presumptious" members. Gage did not intend to give the House any important business until he had moved it to Salem after June 1. The House tried to rush through its business before June 1, to avoid being shifted; but on May 28 Gage, "receiving Intelligence of their Designs, . . . Adjourned them on a sudden to the 7th of June, and then to meet at Salem." Gage thought he had mastered the House, which as yet had only passed a resolution for a day of fasting and prayer, which the governor had vetoed because it "was only to give an opportunity for Sedition to flow from the Pulpits." Later Gage had to report that the fast day was observed anyway, "as generally and punctually as if it had been appointed by authority." Thomas Gage's honeymoon with Massachusetts had not lasted very long.

IV. ENFORCING THE PORT ACT

General Gage's most immediate task, which he shared with the admiral commanding the Royal Navy squadron, was putting the Boston Port Act into effect. Historians have not paid much attention to the actual working of this act, choosing instead to stress its importance in helping to create an American union. Of all the Coercive Acts, however, the Port Act was the only one not nullified by the Americans almost at once. It remained in effect from June 1, 1774, until British forces left Boston forever in March 1776.

Gage arrived in America with detailed instructions from Lord Dartmouth and the treasury board for putting the act into effect. On June 1 the port of Boston was officially closed as a port of entry. On that day the customs commissioners shifted their headquarters to Salem, and all the working customs officers moved

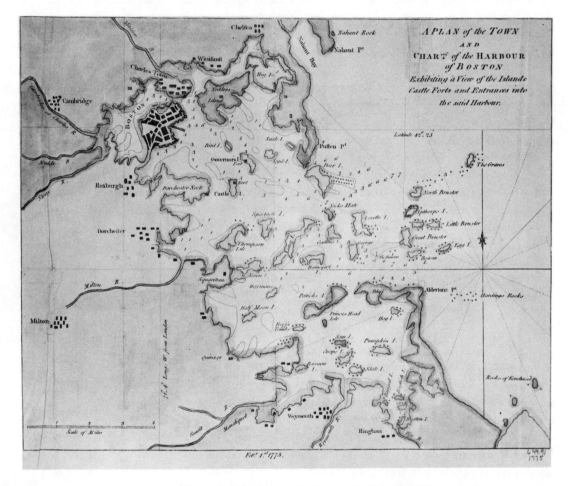

A Plan of the Town and Chart of the Harbour of Boston

their operations to either Plymouth, on Cape Cod, or Marblehead, on Cape Ann. This action alone would have been a severe punishment for the town, for it would have meant that all vessels using the port would have to go far out of their way to enter and clear; but the rest of the Port Act was even harsher. No vessel was allowed to enter Boston harbor unless it contained only food or fuel that had been loaded and cleared at Marblehead and carried a customs officer and armed guards. After June 14 no ship could take anything out of Boston. No vessel of any size was allowed even to move within the confines of Boston harbor, except under terms of the Port Act. Everything else that went in or out had to be carried by land. In every sense, Boston was subjected to a blockade.

Blockading the town of Boston alone would have been easy enough, for it was almost an island connected to the mainland by a neck less than a hundred yards wide. The Port Act, however, closed all of Boston harbor, which it defined as everything from Nahant Point to Alderton Point, the whole coast from Lynn to Hull. Within this large semicircle lay dozens of islands, the mouths of three major estuaries (the Mystic, Charles, and Milton rivers), several good-sized towns, and many creeks, coves, and wharves. Charlestown was hurt as much as Boston, for it, too, was located at the end of a narrow peninsula and depended upon water transportation. The Boston town meeting voted 7 percent of its relief funds to Charlestown's aid.

Even hay and potatoes grown on the islands in Boston harbor could not be taken off by water—and there was no other way. A farmer or storekeeper in Roxbury or Cambridge or Brookline who had always relied on the facilities of Boston itself, or some landing place within the harbor, for carrying his goods, now had to hire expensive cartage to some port outside the limits of the ban. Perhaps the idea behind closing the whole harbor was to make it especially hard for Boston to be served even by land; perhaps the inclusion of other towns was intended to make them bring pressure on Boston to pay for the tea.

Salem and Marblehead, the ports closest to Boston, were seventeen miles away by the usual overland route. The Port Act, however, closed even that route; for it was interpreted to forbid carrying any merchandise on the ferry between Charlestown and Boston. This meant that all freight between Boston and Cape Ann had to be hauled by way of Cambridge and Boston Neck, making the total distance almost thirty miles at the rate of eight dollars a load. John Andrews said that this cost Boston's rum distillers alone at least £6,000 a week. Furthermore, the road was never built to carry such heavy traffic; even in summer it was soon so rutted, said Andrews, that the horses quickly became worn out and skinny from the exertion of pulling the loads. "It is no uncommon

[83]

thing," wrote Andrews, "to hear the carriers and waggoners, when they pass a difficult place in the road, to whip their horses and damn Lord North alternately." The wagons themselves came to be known as "Lord North's coasters." Not even all the food and fuel was allowed to be carried by water. Anything donated to the town of Boston was deemed to be outside the Port Act's exemptions, and thus had to be freighted across Boston Neck.

Boston must trade or die. "The town of Boston, for aught I can see, must suffer martyrdom," wrote John Adams to his wife as soon as he read the Port Act. "It must expire. And our principle [sic] consolation is, that it dies in a noble cause." In this instance, Adams was not exaggerating. By June 12 John Andrews was writing: "Our wharfs are intirely deserted; not a topsail vessel to be seen either there or in the harbour, save the ships of war and transport."

It has been estimated that Boston's population fell by at least one-third by the end of 1774, even though many Tory refugees had fled to the town by then. Those who remained in Boston faced a winter of privation. Even though food and fuel could still be shipped in, workmen who had no jobs and tradesmen who had no customers would have nothing with which to purchase them.

The most serious problem was firewood. Already it was terribly expensive—most of Boston's supply had to be shipped all the way from the Penobscot region of Maine. The Port Act's requirement that firewood be reloaded at Marblehead significantly increased its cost. John Andrews complained that his winter's stock cost twenty dollars more than usual, and twenty dollars was at least one-quarter of the annual wage of a New England workingman. Carl Bridenbaugh has written:

> No feature of the Boston Port Act caused more distress or so contributed to the implacable hatred of the Bostonians toward the mother country than the requirement that all wood boats bound for their port unload and load again at Marblehead, for it at once increased the already high price and decreased the supply of fuel. . . . The pen of Samuel Adams was never needed to labor this grievance—it was too obvious and too real.

The Boston Port Act bore especially hard on Boston's poor. This apparently was not simply a by-product of the act, but one of the features specifically intended by its authors. On August 8 Vice Admiral Samuel Graves, who shared with Gage the responsibility for enforcing the act, wrote to the admiralty:

> I am sorry to acquaint you that these People have already discovered that

the Act does not prohibit Vessels departing this Harbour in Ballast; they are therefore still in possession of a very considerable Trade of building and repairing Shipping, which employs a great number of Handicrafts and other people (I am told that near three thousand) and evidently prevents that general distress among the lower class seemingly intended by the Act as One means the sooner to bring their Rulers to a proper sense of their Duty.

Boston's lower classes, however, never wavered, even when Gage offered extremely high wages to anyone who would hire out to work on barracks and fortifications. The general finally had to seek workmen in New York and Halifax.

John Andrews claimed that "middling people" like himself suffered most from the Port Act, "for the poor (who always liv'd from hand to mouth, i.e. depended on one day's labour to supply the wants of another) will be supported by the beneficence of the colonies; and the rich, who liv'd upon their incomes either as land-holders or usurers, will still have the same benefit from their wealth." Andrews blamed the radicals as much as the British for closing the port, although he was by no means a Tory. There were many people like Andrews who had something to lose and who would have been glad to see the tea paid for. Whether that would have brought the reopening of the port, however, is another matter.

Dartmouth's instructions to Gage made it plain that simply paying the East India Company for its lost property was not a very important consideration. Indeed, several offers to pay for the tea from persons outside of Boston—and even from London—were rejected. What was at stake was "the Sovereignty of The King in His Parliament," which must be acknowledged by Boston's "full and absolute submission." The ministry would not be satisfied until "the ordinary Courts of Justice within the Colony" had found "the Ring-leaders in those Violences" guilty of high treason.

Dartmouth enclosed the affidavits taken before the Privy Council on February 19 and the conclusions of Attorney General Thurlow and Solicitor General Wedderburn that high treason had in fact been committed—but that there was no evidence upon which an English court would convict anyone of the crime. "His Majesty's Subjects in the Province of Massachuset's Bay," Dartmouth informed Gage, "in general cannot give a better Test of their love of Justice, and respect for the Constitution, than in their zealous Endeavours to render effectual a due prosecution of such Offenders." Thus Massachusetts must

[85]

demonstrate its love for the British constitution by doing what Britain's highest legal officers refused to do. Nor would a trial alone be enough. Gage was advised that unless he was certain of getting a conviction, "it would be better to desist from prosecution, seeing that an ineffectual Attempt would only be Triumph to the Faction, and disgraceful to Government." In the meantime, the port would stay closed.

However much it gratified those in England who wanted to be tough with Boston, the Boston Port Act was, by its very harshness, self-defeating. One wonders what would have happened if the ministry had followed its original plan simply to remove the government and customhouse from Boston. Many Americans, certainly a majority of the "better sort," could not go along with the tea destruction. The Port Act, however, distracted everyone's thoughts from Boston's crime to Boston's suffering and aroused the humanitarian instincts of all classes. The cynical demand that Boston seek atonement (with no assurance of its being granted) by abandoning an ideological stand supported by most Americans did even more to make the rest of America come to Boston's aid. On top of this, news of the other Coercive Acts, which affected people who had nothing to do with the Boston Tea Party or any other overt opposition to England, lent credence to the radicals' often-repeated charges that the ministry was bent upon enslaving America. The radicals had much to thank the ministry and Parliament for.

Meanwhile, both the Boston town government and the rest of America addressed themselves to the task of supplying a town of 15,000 unemployed people. On May 13, only three days after the full text of the Port Act arrived in Boston, the town meeting appointed a committee to make plans for relief. Out of this came the Committee of Donations, which, for all practical purposes, was the Boston Committee of Correspondence in another guise. The committee prepared an inventory of "all classes of people . . . suffering by the Port Bill." It spent ten days interviewing the unemployed, then began setting up work relief projects funded by contributions and from the Boston town treasury. The donations committee first hired workmen to repair Boston's streets and dig wells to assist in fire fighting. Then it embarked on grander projects. A brickyard was started on Boston Neck which, by September, was employing more than eighty men. The committee hoped to sell the bricks at cost, to encourage building construction in the town; but it refused General Gage's offer to pay a premium price for bricks with which to build barracks. It encouraged shipbuilding and repair, much to Admiral Graves's dismay. It provided materials for spinners,

The Bostonians in Distress

weavers, shoemakers, ropemakers, and blacksmiths, and tried to find markets for their products.

Boston's plight under the Port Act was treated in much the same way as a natural disaster, such as the great Boston fire of 1760. Boston's people were in need, and the rest of America and even some Englishmen responded magnificently. The donations committee received gifts of food, clothing, and money and saw that they were distributed to the needy. This was very frustrating to the Tories who had been waiting for Boston to get its comeuppance. Samuel Seabury, one of the most vehement Tory pamphleteers, demanded to know "In God's name, are not the people of Boston able to relieve their own poor? Must they go begging . . . from Nova-Scotia to Georgia, to support a few poor people whom their perverseness and ill conduct have thrown into distress?" Others charged that the Boston "malcontents," far from starving, were "sleek and round as robins."

The importance of the donations to Boston went far beyond simple relief of suffering, significant as that was. It gave everyone a chance to participate in the American Revolution in his own small way by contributing a sheep, a cord of wood, a few shillings to those in the forward trenches of the struggle against Britain. Psychologically, the contributions were at least as significant to both givers and recipients as they were as relief measures. When Israel Putnam, America's hero of the French and Indian War, drove his flock of sheep from Connecticut to Boston, he was saying, "You are not alone." And the donations committee, with Sam Adams doing a large share of the work, saw to it that every contribution got a letter of thanks. These letters all stressed that Boston was suffering in the common cause of liberty, and as much as anything else, they helped to unite America.

Not all efforts were simply passive resistance. As might be expected of a people who had for generations nullified whatever imperial regulations they found distasteful, they made General Gage, Admiral Graves, and other British officials work to enforce the Port Act. We have already seen how the Bostonians quickly discovered the loophole in the Port Act that seemingly allowed them to continue shipbuilding and repair. Ships constantly put into Boston Harbor in "distress," claiming that the ancient rule of the sea took precedence over the Port Act. One instance was the schooner *Industry,* supposedly bound from the Bay of Honduras to New York, that suffered storm damage somewhere off Florida. Admiral Graves can be pardoned for wondering why the *Industry* passed up such ports as Charleston, South Carolina, in order to put in to Boston for repairs.

[88]

Within a few weeks after he took command of the Royal Navy's North American squadron on July 1, 1774, Admiral Graves was complaining to the admiralty that he did not have enough ships for all his responsibilities. He had nineteen vessels to cover the whole American coast from Florida to Nova Scotia. Seven were stationed in Boston harbor, but that was too few to stop all the little boats that sneaked around the port using the islands as cover. Furthermore, the Royal Navy was supposed to stop smuggling everywhere else, a job that became especially important when Americans began importing large supplies of arms and ammunition. Whenever Graves sent some of his ships to look for smugglers or gun runners, he had to weaken enforcement of the Port Act. Although the admiralty sent Graves five more warships and authorized him to buy two Marblehead schooners, the admiral had to report in March 1775 that all his efforts to intercept arms shipments reported by British consuls in Europe had been unsuccessful. The last straw was when the Marblehead Committee of Inspection confiscated a box of candles Graves had ordered from England, and refused to give them up until the admiral contributed 1½ percent of their value to the poor of Boston. Graves retaliated by ordering Captain Bishop of H.M.S. *Lively* to press seamen from ships entering Marblehead.

In the end, enforcement of the Port Act had to be eased because the British army was as much under siege in Boston as the townspeople were. There was no formal agreement, but Gage let it be known that he would not be sticky about the Port Act if enough food and firewood came into Boston to supply his 4,000 troops. Suddenly donations were allowed to come in by water. Thus Boston's residents, refugees, and the army made it through the winter of 1774-75.

V. THE PERFECT CRISIS

While the relief measures for Boston were important, they alone could have done no more than delay the town's ultimate capitulation. If Boston was not to bow to the Port Act, she must have the aid of the rest of America in seeking a political solution to the crisis. John Andrews, writing to his brother-in-law in Philadelphia a few days after the text of the Port Act arrived, expressed the hopes and fears of many Bostonians:

Yes, Bill, nothing will save us but an entire stoppage of trade, both to England, and the West Indies, throughout the continent: and that must be determin'd as speedily as absolutely. The least hesitancy on your part to the Southerd, and the matter is over; we must acknowledge and ask foregiveness for all past offenses, whether we have been guilty of any or no; give up the point so long contested; and acknowledge the right of parliament to d—n us whenever they please; and to add to all this, we must pay for a article unjustly forced upon us with the sole view to pick our pockets (not that I would by any means justify the destruction of that article): when that is done, where are we? Why, in much the same situation as before, without one flattering hope of relief: entirely dependent upon the will of an arbitrary Minister, who'd sacrifice the Kingdom to gratify a cursed revenge.

The first real news of the contents of the Port Act came to Boston on May 2. Many Bostonians refused to believe that Parliament would pass such a vicious bill, but the Boston Committee of Correspondence was less optimistic. Its members had probably seen Benjamin Franklin's letter advising that the town would have to pay for the tea (which allegedly prompted Sam Adams to remark that Franklin was a great philosopher but a poor politician). By May 7 the committee had invited all the surrounding towns to a joint meeting on May 12 and had begun to draft circular letters. Thus it had already taken the first steps toward resistance when the ship *Harmony* arrived on May 10 with a text of the Port Act. For moderates like John Andrews and most other merchants, the act was the worst thing that could possibly have happened. For the radicals, like Dr. Thomas Young, it presented an opportunity. Within a few days Young was writing to John Lamb in New York: "At length the perfect crisis of American politics seems arrived and a very few months must decide whether we and our posterity shall be slaves or freemen."

What the radicals wanted was a massive, united American response to the Port Act in the form of a halt to all trade with Britain and the West Indies, and a meeting of delegates from all the colonies to settle with England the question of home rule—but in that order. There is no doubt that the Boston radicals looked forward to a continental congress; Sam Adams had broadly hinted at one, to achieve independence, in his reply to Hutchinson in January 1773. John Hancock had called for such a congress in his Massacre Oration only two months before. What they did not want, however, was for suspension of trade to be held up until a congress was convened. As a tactic for dealing with England, this order of priority made much sense; but it miscalculated the reaction of the rest of America so badly that it put the whole resistance movement in jeopardy.

The Boston committee met at noon on May 12 to prepare for the joint meeting scheduled for later that afternoon. It had just received a heartening letter from John Bowler, Speaker of the Rhode Island House of Representatives. This letter, which the Boston committee ought to have read with a grain of salt, claimed that Rhode Island had been assured by every colonial assembly except Nova Scotia's that they would join in measures for "preserving the Liberties and promoting the Union of the American Colonies." The committee took this to mean that the other colonies were ready to come to Boston's aid. When the representatives of eight other towns met with them a few hours later, the Boston committee was ready with proposals for suspension of trade.

At 3:00 P.M. the committees of Boston, Newton, Lynn, Lexington, Charlestown, Cambridge, Brookline, Roxbury, and Dorchester convened in Faneuil Hall. After electing Sam Adams as moderator, the joint meeting adopted a resolution denouncing the Port Act as unjust and cruel and aimed not just at Boston and Massachusetts but at the liberties of all America. Then the meeting unanimously adopted two circular letters already drafted by the Boston committee. One prepared for the port towns and Committees of Correspondence of the other colonies specifically called for a suspension of trade. As Sam Adams explained it, "Our business is to make Britain share in the miseries which she has unrighteously brought upon us." The letter to the other towns in Massachusetts was less direct. It denied the rumor (which was at least partly true) that Colonel Isaac Barré had denounced the Bostonians and alleged that he had in fact called upon Americans to distress British manufacturers by stopping trade.

The following day, even as the *Lively* brought General Thomas Gage into the harbor, the Boston town meeting met to take up the Port Act. The radicals seemed at first to be completely in control. Sam Adams was moderator, and a committee appointed to consider ways and means to oppose the Port Act included five members of the Committee of Correspondence. John Amory's proposal that the town pay for the tea got little support. The Newburyport town meeting's offer to suspend all trade, passed the day before, was thankfully received, and a committee appointed to see if Salem and Marblehead would follow suit. When the town meeting voted a communication to the rest of America, however, it was significantly weaker than the letter adopted by the joint meeting. Instead of calling for an immediate boycott of trade with Britain, the town meeting resolved that

if the other Colonies came into the JOINT resolution to stop all importations from Great Britain and every part of the West Indies until the act for blocking up this harbor be repealed, the same will prove the salvation of

[91]

North America and her liberties. On the other hand, if they continue their exports and imports, there is high reason to fear that fraud, power, and the most odious oppression will rise triumphant over right, justice, social happiness, and freedom.

The next day Paul Revere rode off to New York and Philadelphia with this communication and the circular letters of the joint meeting.

So far, Boston had shown unanimity in its reaction to the Port Act. Within a few days, however, the Committee of Correspondence, seeking further to demonstrate that unanimity, succeeded in destroying it. On May 20 the committee began to circulate to the merchants of Boston a pledge that they would countermand the orders for goods they had already sent to England. Most of the merchants, whatever their view of British policy, were averse to any committee's telling them how to run their business. They thought it was necessary to import goods early, since Boston, the only good winter port in Massachusetts, would be closed. Besides, the town meeting had resolved to suspend trade only if the other colonies agreed to do likewise. As their grumbles rose to a crescendo, a sizable minority of merchants got together to prepare an address to the departing Governor Hutchinson praising his administration, denouncing the radicals for destroying the tea, and promising to see that the tea was paid for.

The address was presented to Hutchinson on May 28, but the Committee of Correspondence got word of it six days earlier. On May 27 the committee wrote a "counter address" that was published in the *Boston Gazette* as the "unanimous opinion" of the merchants and tradesmen of Boston, and dated it May 24! No names were attached, of course, since the "mass Meeting" of merchants and tradesmen existed only in the minds of the Committee of Correspondence. The ruse fooled no one in Boston, but it was designed to counteract the publication of the merchants' address to Hutchinson in the other colonies.

On May 30 the Boston town meeting assembled again to hear the recommendations of the ways and means committee appointed at the May 13 meeting. The committee was not yet ready to report, so the town meeting agreed to adjourn to June 17. But before adjourning, the meeting instructed the committee to draw up an agreement "to be carried to each Family in the Town, ... not to purchase any Articles of British Manufactures, that can be obtained among Ourselves." The Committee of Correspondence was then to send the resulting limited nonconsumption agreement to the other towns.

The Committee of Correspondence, however, went far beyond the town meeting's mandate. On June 5 it adopted a plan by Dr. Joseph Warren with the good Calvinist name of "Solemn League and Covenant." The covenanters pledged themselves to suspend trade with Britain, to purchase no English goods imported after August 31 and to boycott anyone who refused to sign the covenant. The Solemn League and Covenant was not circulated in Boston, but was sent to the other towns as if the Bostonians had already adopted it. Radical newspapers like the *Boston Gazette* assured their readers that thousands had already signed the covenant, and they explained that nonconsumption had been adopted because the people were impatient at the delay in starting a monimportation movement. The Boston Committee of Correspondence wrote the New Yorkers that the Solemn League and Covenant had been originated by the "two venerable orders of men," farmers and mechanics. The American revolutionaries did not eschew the "big lie" technique.

Any revolutionary tactic, however, is justified only by its success—and the Solemn League of Covenant was a resounding failure. Few towns adopted it at all, and most of those modified its wording. In Boston itself, a real mass meeting of tradesmen, some 800 strong, met on June 15 and refused to endorse the Solemn League and Covenant. The Boston Committee of Correspondence—and with it the revolutionary movement—was clearly in trouble. Joseph Warren, Sam Adams's right-hand man, was afraid that when the adjourned town meeting reconvened on June 17 there would be an attempt to censure the committee and pay for the tea. He begged Adams to hurry back from Salem, where he was attending the legislature, but Adams was engaged in an even deeper intrigue there and could not return to Boston.

Had the "party who are for paying for the tea" actually been ready on June 17, it might have been a near thing. Not only Sam Adams, but Thomas Cushing, John Hancock, and William Phillips, probably the town's most influential men, were all at Salem. Neither James Bowdoin nor John Rowe, both of them wealthy merchants, cared to preside over a town meeting potentially so explosive, so John Adams was finally picked as moderator. The first order of business was the report of the committee of ways and means that had been put off on May 30. Joseph Warren spoke for the committee. He reported that it had decided to hold off making any recommendations until it had heard from the other colonies. Obviously Warren did not want to give his opponents anything on which to base a censure motion.

He need not have worried. The town meeting voted, with only one dissent, to order the Committee of Correspondence "to write to all the other Colonies, acquainting them that we are not idle," that Boston was considering what to do, and that meanwhile the farmers were all entering into a nonconsumption agreement. The last bit of wishful thinking was as close as the town meeting came to mentioning the Solemn League and Covenant. Later in the afternoon, the meeting voted its thanks to the Committee of Correspondence and desired that it continue its "Vigilance & Activity." Both of these votes could be read, outside of Boston anyway, as endorsements of the Solemn League and Covenant. The Committee of Correspondence saw to it that the proceedings of the June 17 Boston town meeting were sent to all the other towns.

Ten days later, the town meeting convened again. This time the opposition was prepared, but the hour had passed them by. Sam Adams was back in the chair as moderator, and he was ready. So many people turned out for the meeting that it had to be moved from Faneuil Hall to Old South Meeting House. One observer said "there was nigh as many torys [sic] I believe as Whigs," and there were a good many who, like John Andrews, were enraged at the Committee of Correspondence for circulating the Solemn League and Covenant without first putting it to a vote by the town meeting.

Andrews said that he and others like him "would equally oppose and detest Tyranny exerciz'd either in England or America," and charged that "those who have govern'd the town for years past and were in a great measure the authors of all our evils, by their injudicious conduct—are grown more obstinate than ever, and seem determin'd to bring total destruction upon us." What particularly bothered merchants like Andrews was that most of them had in good faith ordered goods that could not possibly arrive before August 31; besides, they thought nonimportation was not binding since the other colonies had not agreed to it.

The meeting of June 27 was scheduled to begin with the town clerk's reading all the letters to and from the Committee of Correspondence. John Amory, probably assisted by the fact that it was the hottest day of the year so far, successfully moved that the meeting hear only the Solemn League and Covenant and its covering letter. When that was done, Amory moved that the Committee of Correspondence be censured and annihilated. Sam Adams turned the chair over to Thomas Cushing and joined the debate.

Adams was backed by other members of the Committee of Correspondence; Amory by several prominent merchants and Harrison Gray, the province treasurer. All of them had a lot to say. As the long, hot summer twilight deepened into darkness, the meeting was forced to adjourn until the next day. On June 28, when the temperature soared into the mid-eighties, "after long

[94]

Debates," the censure and annihilation motion was voted down "by a great Majority." The radicals quickly followed up their advantage; a motion of confidence in the committee of correspondence passed "by a *Vast Majority,*" at least four to one.

If the Committee of Correspondence had made a tactical error in its handling of the Solemn League and Covenant, the merchants had made a worse one in moving to censure and dismiss the committee, rather than simply to "suspend the Covenant till the Congress should meet," as John Andrews urged. Many of the merchants had put themselves in bad odor by signing the address to Hutchinson and had further weakened their position on June 8 when 127 of them wrote to Gage offering to pay for the tea. Gage thanked them, but pointed out that even if they did, the Port Act did not give him the power to reopen the port. Most of all, the merchants had given the radicals time to get out the vote and to change the situation. On June 17, the day the merchants chose not to try to censure the Committee of Correspondence, Sam Adams, abandoning his plan to push for general nonimportation before a meeting of the colonies, induced the legislature to call for a continental congress. Many of the moderates hoped that such a congress would save them from both the ministry and the Sons of Liberty.

Thomas Gage attributed the failure of the censure and annihilation motion to an excess of democracy. "The better Sort of People . . . were outvoted, by a great Majority of the lower Class," the governor told Lord Dartmouth. The day after the censure motion lost, Gage proved how little he understood American politics: he officially proclaimed that the Solemn League and Covenant was "scandalous, traiterous, and seditious," and that anyone who signed or circulated it should be arrested, presumably for treason. Gage had done the one thing that could have breathed life into the moribund Covenant. Before the summer was over, several more New England towns endorsed it.

Sam Adams, on the other hand, proved more adept than the general at beating a strategic retreat. The call for a universal nonimportation movement that Paul Revere had carried south in May met with a disappointing response. New York was torn by internal dissension. Philadelphia hinted strongly that Boston ought to pay for the tea and said the Pennsylvanians preferred that a nonimportation and nonexportation agreement come from a general congress. Providence voted to support Boston if the rest of America would cooperate, and proposed a congress for the purpose. The last thing Sam Adams wanted was a mercantile congress that would meet only to take up nonimportation, and the

[95]

Boston Committee of Correspondence replied, trying to discourage the scheme. The Rhode Island legislature, however, went ahead and elected delegates to a continental congress if one should be called.

Governor Gage had prorogued the Massachusetts legislature on May 28, to reconvene in Salem on June 7. By that time Sam Adams had become reconciled to a continental congress, and decided to have the Massachusetts House issue the call to the other colonies. He knew, however, that the House could not openly take up the matter, or Gage would dissolve it. On June 7 the House of Representatives appointed a committee to consider the state of the province. Sam Adams was its chairman, and all but one of its members were patriots. Daniel Leonard, a conservative lawyer who later wrote the Tory "Massachusettensis" papers, was probably put on the committee to lull Gage into thinking it was not up to anything. At its regular meetings, the committee seriously discussed paying for the tea. At night, without Leonard, it drew up a resolution to call a continental congress and selected five delegates to attend. Then, so the committee could make a formal resolution to the House, Robert Treat Paine, like Leonard also from Taunton, talked Leonard into going back home with him to attend a court session.

On June 17 Adams was ready. He had the doors to the House chamber locked and the doorkeeper instructed to allow no one to enter or leave. The committee presented its report. One Tory, pleading an urgent call of nature, managed to get outside and rushed off to tell Gage what was happening. The governor immediately sent the province secretary, Thomas Flucker, with an order dissolving the legislature, but Flucker could not get inside. While he was reading Gage's proclamation to the locked door, the House adopted the committee report. It invited the other colonies to a continental congress to open in Philadelphia on September 1, chose Sam and John Adams, James Bowdoin, Thomas Cushing, and Robert Treat Paine as delegates, and asked the towns to add their share of £500 to their regular tax remissions to pay the delegates' expenses. That done, the House allowed itself to be dissolved. It never met again under a royal governor.

While General Gage had been, as the Reverend William Gordon gleefully wrote in his *History*, "out-generalled" by Sam Adams, he did not seem to be unduly chagrined by it. When he reported the incident to Lord Dartmouth, Gage confided that "They will not agree to Non-Importation either at New York or Philadelphia, or even in this Province, tho' I believe a Congress of some sort may be obtained, but when or how it will be composed is yet at a Distance; and after all, Boston may get little more than fair words." Two months later, after most of the other colonies had supported the call for a congress, Gage hoped that it had been a dodge by the moderates "only to amuse those amongst themselves who have been so strangely violent in Support of Boston, and to which their own provincial Factions have not a little contributed."

Sam Adams may secretly have feared that Gage was right about the upcoming Continental Congress. Before he departed for Philadelphia, Adams and Joseph Warren worked out tactics by which the Suffolk County convention would issue a plea to Congress to come to Boston's aid. Paul Revere was alerted to gallop off to Philadelphia with the Suffolk County Resolves as soon as they were adopted by the convention. In addition, the convention was to issue a call for a provincial congress to meet in October which would effectively end royal government in Massachusetts.

Other Bostonians had plans, too, that they worked out in July and August. They were determined that Massachusetts would cut a good figure in Philadelphia. First, however, something had to be done about the acknowledged leader of the Massachusetts delegation, Sam Adams. Rumors persisted that he would be arrested and hauled off to England before Congress met. That would be most embarrassing, and it would be only slightly less embarrassing if Sam showed up in Philadelphia in his old clothes. Therefore, to impress the royal authorities that Sam "had certainly *very* many friends," as John Andrews put it, to make him look respectable in Congress, and out of genuine esteem as well, several of his wealthy friends came to his assistance. His decaying old barn, a neighborhood eyesore, was torn down and a new one built. His house was thoroughly repaired. One evening a tailor, refusing to say who had sent him, showed up at Sam's house to take his measurements. A few days later, Sam got a large package containing a new suit, cloak, cane, wig, hat, hose, and shoes. A friend "modestly enquir'd of him whether his finances want rather low than otherways. He reply'd it was true that was the case, but he was very indifferent about these matters, so that his *poor* abilities was of any service to the Publick; upon which the Gentleman oblig'd him to accept of a purse containing about 15 or 20 Johannes." Sam did not resent the gifts, their implied criticism of his providence, or the fact that the whole town knew about it. This incident alone should refute all the historians who have said Sam Adams had an inferiority complex.

On August 10 the four Massachusetts delegates (James Bowdoin stayed home because of ill health) departed for Philadelphia. "Am told they made a very respectable parade," wrote John Andrews, "in sight of five of the Regiment's encamp'd on the Common, being in a coach and four, preceded by two white servants well mounted and arm'd, with four blacks behind in livery, two on horseback and two footmen." Their journey south was a triumphal procession. Every town through which they passed gave them a welcome that would not have insulted a visiting prince. It remained to be seen if Congress would give them what they really needed, a united front against England.

CHAPTER V

Common Cause

Even the old Farmers who were So Sorry that So much Tea should be wasted Sometime Since, Now Say that they will Stand by the Bostonians and do everything in their power to Assist them.
—Wensley Hobby to Samuel Savage, Connecticut,
May 17, 1774

Resolved, unanimously, That it is the opinion of this meeting, that the town of *Boston* is now suffering in the common cause of *America,* and that it is incumbent on every Colony in *America,* to unite in effectual means to obtain a repeal of the late Act of Parliament for blocking up the harbour of *Boston.*
—Resolution of Anne Arundel County, Maryland,
June 4, 1774

Whether the people [of Boston] were warranted by justice, when they destroyed the tea, we know not; but this we know, that the Parliament, by their proceedings, have made us and all *North America,* parties in the present dispute, . . . inso-

> much, that if our sister Colony of *Massachusetts Bay* is
> enslaved, we cannot long remain free.
> —Resolution of Hanover County, Virginia, July 20, 1774

Most Americans opposed the Tea Act, but men of "sense and property" were equally strong in their conviction that Boston had gone a great deal too far in destroying the East India Company's tea. At the beginning of 1774, Boston stood in danger of being isolated, even in New England. In a very real sense, Boston was rescued by Britain's punitive measures. Americans learned about the Port Act in May and were shocked by its harshness. The other Coercive Acts and the Quebec Act added to their fears that liberty was endangered throughout America.

Everyone was concerned. As in Massachusetts, the more radical elements wanted an immediate suspension of trade with Britain and the West Indies, perhaps followed by an intercolonial congress that could present its demands from a position of strength. The moderates, however, and especially the merchants, like the idea of nonintercourse with Britain no better than they had during the Townshend Act crisis. They saw a congress as a moderating influence, as the Stamp Act Congress had been in 1765, and as a way of rescuing their business from local committees of radicals. Even some Tories favored a congress as a way of avoiding what they feared most: civil war.

By the end of August, every colony except Georgia had chosen delegates to the First Continental Congress. But each colony acted in its own way, and the process was always complicated by local issues.

I. NEW ENGLAND

New England had earned a reputation for radicalism, but early in 1774 it was divided. Boston, the largest city in the region, had always been New England's political and economic leader—but she had also won the envy and suspicion of the rest of the region. Only fear that their own liberties would be next to come under the British government's attack brought the rest of New England to Boston's rescue.

New Hampshire had always been the least radical of the New England colonies; it was ruled as a closed Wentworth family corporation. New

Hampshire was given its first royal governor in 1741, and only two men—Benning Wentworth and his nephew John Wentworth—ever held the office.

John Wentworth continued most of Benning's political practices, so that by 1774 only 46 of New Hampshire's 147 towns sent representatives to Portsmouth. Wentworth kept New Hampshire from joining the nonimportation movement against the Townshend Acts until 1770, when it was nearly dead, anyway. He probably disliked the Tea Act, but he blamed agitation against it in his province on the influence of Boston radicals.

Wentworth could ill afford a public discussion of "no taxation without representation." Nearly half of New Hampshire's population lived in towns without representation, and they paid 38 percent of the provincial taxes. In December 1773 Portsmouth, the capital and largest town, drew up a set of resolutions denouncing the Tea Act as "unjust, arbitrary and inconsistent with the fundamental principles of the British Constitution." Other towns followed Portsmouth's lead during the early weeks of 1774. Those without representation were quick to point out the parallel between their grievances and America's. Their resolutions denounced both Parliament and John Wentworth's government with equal fervor.

In January 1774 Wentworth reconvened the legislature in an effort to halt the "infectious and pestilential disorders being spread among the inhabitants, especially of Portsmouth." Instead, the Assembly voted to cooperate with the other colonial legislatures in resisting the Tea Act. Wentworth dissolved the legislature, hoping that the March elections would return a more conservative Assembly; but many of Wentworth's followers were voted out of office and replaced by radicals.

On May 27, after news of the Port Act arrived, the Assembly voted to appoint a Committee of Correspondence. Again Wentworth sent the Assembly home, but the committee stayed behind to issue a call for the former representatives to reconvene in convention on July 6. Wentworth still retained some authority. The delegates obeyed his orders to get out of the Assembly chambers; but they immediately reconvened in a local tavern, where they called upon each town, whether represented or not, to elect delegates to a provincial congress to be held at Exeter on July 21 for the purpose of electing delegates to the Continental Congress.

The First New Hampshire Provincial Congress marked the beginning of the end of Wentworth's rule. Caught up in "the spirit of enthusiasm, which generally prevails through the Colonies," the Provincial Congress asked all

[101]

towns to contribute to Boston's relief and selected two leading radicals, John Sullivan and Nathaniel Folsom, to go to Philadelphia.

In other ways, however, Wentworth was correct in reporting to Lord Dartmouth that New Hampshire "continues more moderate than any to the Southward." On June 25 the mast ship *Grosvenor* arrived with twenty-seven chests of tea, all of which were landed and entered at the customhouse before any resistance could be organized. The Portsmouth town meeting finally convened two days later, and, in Wentworth's words, "proceeded with coolness and temper beyond almost my hope." The merchant to whom the tea was consigned agreed to reship it to Halifax; however, he openly paid the duty, and a guard appointed by the town meeting stood watch while it was being reloaded, thwarting the efforts of "three overheated mariners (two of them strangers) . . . to excite a mob, to destroy the tea and vessel hired to export it."

In July the Portsmouth Committee of Correspondence issued a non-importation agreement patterned on the Boston Solemn League and Covenant. As in Massachusetts, there was considerable resistance to the covenant. The Reverend Jeremy Belknap, a moderate Whig from Dover, spoke for many when he said:

> Tyranny in one shape is as odious to me as Tyranny in another. . . . Here is no Liberty of Conscience nor right of private judgement left to any person but all . . . must implicitly adopt & subscribe a Covenant drawn up by a few men without any lawful authority or else be stigmatized as Enemies to their Country. This is a species of Tyranny . . . as dangerous in its tendency as any acts of the British Parliament.

Rhode Island differed from New Hampshire in almost every conceivable way. It was the most democratic of the colonies; in fact, its government may have been the most democratic in the eighteenth-century world. Its governor, both houses of the legislature, and superior court justices were elected annually.

But democracy did not bring stability. Every election was bitterly contested between the followers of Stephen Hopkins and those of Samuel Ward. As David S. Lovejoy has pointed out, the Ward-Hopkins rivalry "was more than a controversy; it was continuous political warfare which had reverberations throughout Rhode Island and which affected in some way most of the inhabitants."

The rivalry, however, was largely confined to internal affairs. Rhode Islanders were united as no other colony in their opposition to British policy. Only a handful of Tories, most of them in Newport, supported king and Parliament. Rhode Islanders were as given to rioting as Bostonians. By the middle of 1772, Rhode Islanders had fired on the Royal Navy vessel *St. John*, scuttled the revenue cutter *Liberty*, and burned H.M.S. *Gaspee*. No one was ever punished for these outrages.

On the other hand, Rhode Island was more dependent on trading than any other colony. For this reason, Rhode Island had joined the non-importation movement against the Townshend Acts only when other colonial ports had instituted a boycott against her ships, and she was constantly accused of failing to live up to her pledge. The tiny colony was the object of considerable suspicion in both England and America.

Almost to a man, Rhode Islanders denounced the Tea Act; and, more than any other colonists, they applauded the Boston Tea Party. Even before news of the Boston Port Act arrived, the Rhode Island House had written to the Boston Committee of Correspondence claiming that every colony except Nova Scotia was ready to unite in Boston's support. And Rhode Island took the lead in calling for a continental congress.

On May 17 the Providence town meeting called for an intercolonial congress to secure "universal stoppage of all trade" with Great Britain and her African and West Indian colonies until the Boston Port Act should be rescinded. Three days later, Newport also resolved to support Boston, though without suggesting a congress.

While the idea of a continental congress had been debated in colonial newspapers, Providence was the first to issue a formal call for one, and Rhode Island was the first to elect delegates. Obviously the colony did not want to be isolated as she had been from 1767 to 1770. Furthermore, Rhode Island had a special interest in getting the other colonies behind Massachusetts. She had long acted as if she were virtually independent and knew that her own charter was in danger of being rescinded. Other colonies, for their own reasons, rapidly adopted the idea.

In May a continental congress did not fit into Sam Adams's plans. The Boston Committee of Correspondence replied to Providence trying to squelch the idea, but Adams was forced to come around. On June 17 the Massachusetts House called for the First Continental Congress to meet in Philadelphia in September. Two days before, the Rhode Island legislature had already adopted the Providence resolution and elected Stephen Hopkins and Samuel Ward as delegates if a continental congress should be called. Perhaps the two old rivals were chosen to present a united front against Britain; perhaps it was simply that the Ward faction would not agree to send Hopkins to Congress without their own champion to keep any eye on him. In any case, they journeyed to Philadelphia in August by separate routes.

Connecticut, like Rhode Island, was a charter colony in which nearly all government officials were elected. Vastly unlike Rhode Island, Connecticut was known as "the land of steady habits," though her internal political struggles were as heated as Rhode Island's. Connecticut was the most Puritan of the colonies, and the Congregational church was the established religion in the colony. During the Great Awakening, however, the Congregationalists split into "Old Light" and "New Light" factions. Oscar Zeichner has pointed out in *Connecticut's Years of Controversy* that "It was impossible to separate religion from politics in colonial Connecticut. Consequently, the religious differences stirred up by the revival quickly assumed a political aspect." The New Lights, who were the most politically radical (though most theologically conservative), were strongest east of the Connecticut River, in Windham and New London counties. The politically more conservative Old Lights were strongest in the west, especially in New Haven, Fairfield, and Litchfield counties. Connecticut also had a growing number of Anglicans, also concentrated in the west, whose pleas for an Episcopal bishop for America were opposed by all the Congregational clergy, but whose political conservatism made them natural allies of the Old Lights.

During the 1760s and 1770s the religious split was exacerbated by other issues. Connecticut was running out of space. Her last public lands were granted in the 1750s, and her soil was rapidly wearing out. In 1774 Connecticut had a population density of thirty-nine per square mile, and it was getting heavier, despite growing emigration. So many Connecticut families, like the Allens, went to Benning Wentworth's dubious land grants in what is now Vermont, that the region was first named "New Connecticut."

In 1753 a group of land speculators incorporated themselves as the Susquehannah Company. Connecticut's 1662 charter made the colony's western boundary the Pacific Ocean. Although a slice of New York intervened, the Susquehannah Company proposed to reestablish Connecticut's claim to the land west of the Delaware River. This included nearly the whole northern third of Pennsylvania. Despite the opposition of the Penns, the Indians, Indian Superintendent Sir William Johnson, and ultimately the British government, the company pressed its claims, sold land in the Wyoming Valley of Pennsylvania, and even incorporated the town of Westmoreland in Pennsylvania as part of

[104]

Litchfield County, Connecticut. From 1769 to 1775, there was open warfare between an army raised by the Penns and the Connecticut settlers, aided by the disaffected "Paxton Boys" of Pennsylvania.

The biggest issue in Connecticut's April 1774 election was whether the colony's government should officially press for the company's claim in London. The radical New Light party, headed by Governor Jonathan Trumbull, was pro-Susquehannah. Oscar Zeichner had noted that "Most of the leaders of the more radical party were New London and Windham County merchants, lawyers, and Puritan, especially New Light, divines. And many of the very same men, notably among the merchants and lawyers, assumed the major roles in the affairs of the Susquehannah Company." These were the same men who had been leading the Sons of Liberty against British policy ever since the Stamp Act. The opposition conservatives, mostly Old Lights and Anglicans, held a convention in Middletown on March 30 to oppose the Susquehannah claim. The pro-Susquehannah faction won by a landslide. Thus the party most opposed to British policy was firmly in control in 1774.

While the debate over the Susquehannah Company was reaching a climax, the Tea Act intruded. Although the Susquehannah issue still held most of Connecticut's attention, the radicals tried to organize opposition to the Tea Act. News of the Boston Tea Party divided the colony along predictable lines: it was applauded in the New Light east and denounced in the Old Light and Anglican west. Shortly after the April election, news of the Boston Port Act arrived. The more radical towns endorsed Boston's call for immediate nonintercourse with Great Britain, but Connecticut's committee of correspondence, fearing that local nonimportation agreements would be ineffective and divisive, called for a continental congress.

News of the other Coercive Acts sent a thrill of fear throughout Connecticut. She had jealously guarded her charter ever since 1662, even hiding it in the famous "Charter Oak" when the Stuarts tried to recall it. One of the major arguments of the Middletown Convention was that supporting the Susquehannah claims under the charter would bring about a revision or annulment of the charter. But even before news arrived of the Massachusetts Government Act, towns were passing vehement resolutions. Although it lay west of the Connecticut River, Farmington had one of the earliest and strongest reactions to the Port Act. On May 19 a thousand people gathered about a forty-five-foot-high liberty pole and beneath it burned a copy of the Port Act and a tarred and feathered effigy of Thomas Hutchinson. Then they resolved, among other things,

That the present ministry, being instigated by the devil, and led on by their wicked corrupt hearts, have a design to take away our liberties and properties, and to enslave us forever.

That the late Act which their malice hath caused to be passed in Parliament, for blocking up the port of Boston, is unjust, illegal, and oppressive; and that we, and every American, are sharers in the insults offered to the town of Boston

That those pimps and parasites who dared to advise their master to such detestable measures be held in utter abhorrence by us and every American, and their names be loaded with the curses of all succeeding generations.

The more conservative town of New Haven voted to support Boston, but only by "judicious and constitutional measures," and it elected the archconservative and future Tory Joshua Chandler to the town's Committee of Correspondence. Although most of Connecticut opposed the Coercive Acts, Theophilus Morgan, a moderate from Killingworth, spoke for most of western Connecticut:

altho' we in the main concur in Sentiments with the eastern part of this Colony and the other Colonies on this Continent, respecting our Rights, Liberties and Privileges as Englishmen, yet you must be sensible the Western Part of this Colony never have concurred in Sentiments with regard to the best method to preserve them.

The lower house of the Connecticut legislature adopted a long list of resolutions that pledged loyalty to the crown, but nevertheless claimed virtual home rule for Connecticut. The Council prudently held off endorsing the resolutions for several months, but it did, in June, join the House in empowering the colony's Committee of Correspondence to choose delegates to the Continental Congress. On July 13 the committee, trying to achieve a political and geographical balance, picked Eliphalet Dyer, William Samuel Johnson, Erastus Wolcott, Silas Deane, and Richard Law, or any three of them, to go to Philadelphia. But Wolcott and Law pled ill health, and Johnson refused to attend the Continental Congress on ideological grounds. Therefore, the committee chose two arch Whigs, Roger Sherman and Joseph Trumbull, either of whom could attend Congress. The three Connecticut delegates who finally went to Philadelphia—Sherman, Dyer, and Deane—were all staunch Whigs. Thus the

[106]

four New England colonies sent delegations that were as radical as Sam Adams could have wished, and were certainly more radical than many of their constituents.

II. THE MIDDLE COLONIES

The Middle Colonies were far less committed to the American Revolution than any of the others, except for Georgia. Only in Delaware did the radicals triumph during the summer of 1774. In New York, New Jersey, and Pennsylvania conservatives remained firmly in control and only reluctantly acceded even to the idea of a continental congress.

Many years ago, Carl Becker, in one of the most quoted phrases ever written by an historian, summed up the political struggle in revolutionary New York in two questions: "The first was whether essential colonial rights should be maintained; the second was by whom and by what methods they should be maintained. The first was the question of home rule; the second was the question, if we may so put it, of who should rule at home." At the beginning of 1774 there is no doubt that conservatives ruled in New York. True, there was bitter party conflict, but it was between the conservative De Lancey faction and the only slightly less conservative Livingston faction, both dominated by merchants, lawyers, and great landholders. The Livingstons had briefly flirted with popular politics during the Stamp Act crisis, when they cooperated with the Sons of Liberty and their leaders, Isaac Sears, John Lamb, and Alexander McDougall; but they were as frightened as the De Lanceys by the violence displayed by the "triumvirate's" followers. The Livingstons helped put down the tenant farmers' revolt in 1766. The De Lanceys won control of the New York legislature in 1769, and would not have to face another election until 1776. Shunned by the Livingstons since 1769, Sears, Lamb, and McDougall saw in the Coercive Acts a chance to come back into the political limelight.

A copy of the Boston Port Act arrived in New York on May 12. The triumvirate immediately called for nonimportation, an idea anathema to the De Lanceys, who had killed a similar agreement in 1769. On May 14 Sears called for a merchants' meeting to take up nonimportation and discuss the formation of a Committee of Correspondence that would bring about a continental congress. The next day Sears and McDougall wrote the Boston Committee of Correspondence that "great numbers" of New Yorkers were ready to support nonimportation under regulations established by a "general congress."

[107]

"Great numbers" indeed had an opinion about the scheme—so great that the meeting of May 16 had to be moved from Fraunces Tavern to the Merchants' Exchange—but a majority of them were De Lancey supporters. They readily agreed to a Committee of Correspondence, so long as it was under their control. The Sons of Liberty's plan for a small, effective committee was voted down; instead, the meeting proposed a committee of fifty, packed with De Lancey men, to be submitted to a general vote of the citizens of New York City on May 19. On May 18, McDougall called a meeting of "mechanics" which drew up a slate of twenty-five, taken from the May 16 list, but which would have shifted the Committee of Correspondence to a much more radical balance. At the city meeting the next day, however, the De Lanceys again turned out in force and shouted down Isaac Sears's attempt to read letters Paul Revere had just brought from Boston. The triumvirate had to admit defeat. On May 20 they agreed to the larger committee, with the face-saving device of increasing it to fifty-one by the addition of Francis Lewis.

On May 23 the Committee of Fifty-one informed the Boston committee that, while "the cause is general, and concerns a whole continent," New York could not agree to nonintercourse unless a continental congress unanimously agreed to it; but the committee avoided suggesting where or when such a congress might meet. McDougall was sure that this was merely a trick by the De Lanceys to avoid a congress. He was soon to find out that the New York conservatives had unwitting allies in Boston, for the Boston Committee of Correspondence replied to the Committee of Fifty-one that a continental congress would take too long to assemble. Therefore, each town in America should decide for itself what it would stop importing. Then a copy of the *Boston Gazette* arrived with an edited version of the triumvirate's secret letter of May 15, in which all mention of a continental congress was deleted. With some justification, Sears and McDougall denied that they had written the letter.

Despite their whipsawing from New York conservatives and Boston radicals, the triumvirate continued to press for a congress. After Sam Adams switched his position and the Massachusetts House called for a September meeting in Philadelphia, on June 29, McDougall asked the Committee of Fifty-one to call a convention to elect delegates. The committee replied that such action should be taken only by the Assembly, knowing that Cadwallader Colden, who at eighty-four was again acting governor of New York, would refuse to call an Assembly session.

But the De Lanceys were under pressure, too. As colony after colony adopted the idea of a continental congress, New York's moderates came around to the idea and town after town outside New York City passed resolutions in favor of a congress. Besides, the Livingstons would be sure to make an issue of it in the next election. On July 14 the Committee of Fifty-one agreed to choose delegates, but it rejected Sears's slate, which included McDougall and John Morin Scott, in favor of one of Isaac Low, James Duane, Philip Livingston, John Alsop, and John Jay, all of whom could be counted upon to do nothing rash in Philadelphia. Once again the committee failed to pass a resolution denouncing the Boston Port Act.

McDougall was outraged. He called a mass meeting on July 6, at which his slate of five delegates and a number of radical resolutions were confirmed. The next evening the Committee of Fifty-one overwhelmingly rejected the mass meeting's proceedings, whereupon McDougall and ten others resigned from the committee. The remaining committeemen drew up a series of resolutions, one of which criticized Boston's destruction of the tea, and submitted them, along with their slate of delegates, to another mass meeting on July 19.

This time the tables were turned. The radicals came out in force and shouted down the conservatives' resolutions. Finally, on July 28, another mass meeting, called by the remnants of the Committee of Fifty-one, met to choose a delegation to Congress. By this time the triumvirate had decided that it was more important to get the New York delegation committed to nonimportation and support of Boston than it was to have Alexander McDougall as part of it. In return for a commitment to vote for nonimportation, the radicals agreed to support the committee's nominees. Thus New York sent one of the most conservative delegations to Philadelphia, but under instructions that went far beyond what the conservatives wanted. Joseph Warren had summed it up pretty well on June 14, when he told Sam Adams that "I fear New York will not assist us with a very good grace but she may perhaps be ashamed to desert us—at least if her merchants offer to sell us, her mechanics will forbid the auction."

New Jersey had become a single royal colony in 1692, but in many ways she was still divided into proprietaries of East Jersey and West Jersey. The eastern section, economically dominated by the Hudson and New York City, had a Dutch and Yankee population. West Jersey, drained by the Delaware, looked to Philadelphia and was still largely Quaker, with a strong mixture of Scots-Irish. The New Jersey legislature was the scene of bickering remarkable even for eighteenth-century America. L.H. Gipson has said that New Jersey "illustrates how a people may live in the midst of both economic prosperity and political conditions that border on anarchy, with a government powerless to function in

[109]

the direction of establishing even the semblance of law and order." While most Jerseymen generally opposed both the royal governor and British policy, West Jersey always took a more conservative view of what form the opposition should take.

William Franklin, who had been governor of the colony since 1763, was Benjamin Franklin's illegitimate son, but his views in 1774 were closer to the British government's than to his father's. On May 31 Franklin told the earl of Dartmouth that the merchants of New York and Philadelphia were inclined to assist Boston "in some degree, but not to carry matters so far as to enter into a general nonimportation and exportation agreement." Many of them, fearing nonimportation, were ordering extra goods from England. Franklin noted that several colonies had proposed a continental congress, but he was not sure it would ever take place. He had hoped that the New Jersey legislature would ignore Virginia's call to form a provincial Committee of Correspondence, but "the Assembly of *New York* had just before resolved to appoint such a Committee, and they did not wish to appear singular."

The committee was formed on February 8. Six of its members met in New Brunswick on May 31, where they endorsed both a continental congress and a "Non-Importation and perhaps a Non-Exportation Agreement." "Our Committee," wrote one of its members, "is well disposed in the cause of *American* freedom," because they feared that New Jersey would be "eventually in the same predicament with *Boston.*"

The committee's report touched off a series of town and county meetings. The first of these, held in Lower Freehold in East Jersey, was in many ways the most radical. Unlike subsequent meetings, Freehold passed no pious resolves pledging allegiance to the king, and it did not specifically call for a continental congress. Instead, it recommended "an entire stoppage of importation and exportation from and to *Great Britain* and the *West Indies,* until the said Port Bill and other Acts be repealed." In June and July most of the counties held meetings that called for a continental congress to establish rules for nonimportation from Britain and, for some reason, the East Indies.

On June 18, a week after Essex County had met, Governor Franklin sent its proceedings to Lord Dartmouth. Franklin said he had been requested to call a meeting of the Assembly for August, "with which I have not, nor shall not comply," but admitted he was powerless to stop the county meetings "where the chief part of the inhabitants incline to attend them." Franklin doubted that "they will agree to the general non-importation from *Great Britain,* which has been recommended—Their principal aim seems to be to bring about a Congress of Deputies from all the Colonies." On the whole, Franklin did not think that would be a bad thing. Many of the friends of government in New Jersey believed that an American Congress, authorized by the king and composed of governors and legislators from the colonies, along with "some Gentlemen of Abilities, Moderation and Candour from Great Britain," might well cool things off.

Each of the county meetings chose delegates to a colony-wide convention held at New Brunswick on July 21-23. The delegates, who included a majority of the members of the New Jersey House, unanimously adopted resolutions pledging loyalty to George III, denouncing the Declaratory Act and the Coercive Acts, and endorsing the upcoming Continental Congress to which "we do earnestly recommend a general nonimportation and non-consumption agreement." However, the five men chosen for Congress—James Kinsey, William Livingston, John DeHart, Stephen Crane, and Richard Smith—were generally more conservative than the instructions they carried.

In Pennsylvania the patriots had less success than in any other colony except Georgia. As in New York, conservatives controlled Pennsylvania's major political factions. The Proprietary party upheld the prerogatives of the Penn family. Their opponents, the Quaker party, had once tried to get Pennsylvania converted to a royal colony, but that scheme had been in abeyance ever since the Stamp Act crisis. Although the Quakers had long since become only a minority of the population, they were the wealthiest; and wealth, plus their pacifist beliefs, made them naturally conservative and opposed even to such nonviolent measures as nonimportation. The Quakers themselves had largely withdrawn from politics during the French and Indian War. In 1774 the Quaker party was led by a non-Quaker, the conservative Joseph Galloway.

Philadelphia, the largest and richest city in America, was the center of power. Philadelphia and the eastern counties held far more than their fair share of representation in Pennsylvania's unicameral legislature, but property qualifications kept large numbers of the urban population from voting. In 1774 the underrepresented west was beset by open conflicts with Indians and armies from Connecticut and Virginia.

Although Philadelphia had taken the lead in denouncing the Tea Act in October 1773, Philadelphians were shocked by the Boston Tea Party. When the first news of the Port Act arrived on May 14, Pennsylvania had not yet even formed a Committee of Correspondence. Indicative of the political situation, the moderate John Dickinson was one of the strongest voices in support of Boston.

[111]

Dickinson was joined by Joseph Reed, a friend of Lord Dartmouth, Thomas Mifflin, a wealthy Quaker merchant whose views were radical only in comparison with the rest of his class and sect, and Charles Thomson, the "Sam Adams of Philadelphia," the only one of the lot who could be considered a real radical.

The *Pennsylvania Gazette* published the text of the Boston Port Act on May 18. The next day Paul Revere rode into town with Boston's plea for a nonimportation movement. Thomson, Reed, and Mifflin called a meeting of leading citizens for the evening of May 20 in the City Tavern. Before going to the meeting, however, the three went to Dickinson's home to plan their course of action. Exactly what went on at that preliminary meeting will never be known, for the four participants have left conflicting accounts. We do know, however, that all were canny politicians. They feared that the Philadelphia merchants would oppose any vigorous action in support of Boston, and their actions at the City Tavern were well calculated to get as much as possible from the meeting.

When the four arrived, the City Tavern was jammed with perhaps three hundred men, many of them conservative merchants. Joseph Reed spoke first, "with moderation but in pathetic terms," calling upon Governor John Penn to call the Assembly to draw up a petition for redress of grievances. Then Mifflin gave a fire-eating speech in support of Boston, perhaps even to the point of nonimportation. Thomson seconded Mifflin in a dramatic speech that ended suddenly when he fainted. Whether or not the faint was staged, it set things up nicely for the cool and reasonable Dickinson. He endorsed Reed's call for an Assembly session and proposed a Committee of Correspondence of nineteen members, to serve until replaced by a larger one picked by a "more general Meeting of the Inhabitants."

The conservatives who dominated the meeting gladly accepted Dickinson's proposals. Governor Penn reported to Lord Dartmouth that he would certainly refuse (as he did, on June 7) any request to call the Assembly, adding "I have, however, been informed that the movers of this extraordinary measure had not the most distant expectation of succeeding in it, but that their real scheme was to gain time by it to see what part the other Colonies will take in so critical a juncture." Penn may have been right, but he did not note that a Committee of Correspondence was at last set up, or that even by such moderate action the conservative meeting had implicitly joined in Boston's cause.

Boston, however, must have gotten little pleasure from the first letter drawn up by the Committee of Nineteen. After assuring the Bostonians "that you are considered as suffering in the general cause," the committee's letter of May 21 observed that any concrete action "requires more mature deliberation." It hinted that Boston ought to pay for the tea. It claimed that Pennsylvanians would never agree to nonimportation and nonexportation except as "our last resource," if a petition "to his Majesty, in firm, but decent and dutiful terms," by a "Congress of Deputies from the different Colonies," should first have failed. In the meantime, Boston should conduct herself with "Firmness, Prudence, and Moderation." Daniel Dulany of Maryland summed up the letter very well for Arthur Lee: "The *Philadelphians* were very cool, indeed, upon [Boston's] application. There is a stroke of insulting pity in their answer which I am sure will raise your indignation to the highest pitch."

On May 30 the Committee of Nineteen met to consider plans for observing June 1, the day the Port Act went into effect.It could agree only to make it a day of mourning, and even this was repudiated by the Quakers and Anglicans as unsupported by Scripture. Still, many people did observe the day by closing businesses, muffling church bells, and flying ships' colors at half mast. And on June 4, the king's birthday, "scarcely, if any, notice was taken of it in this city, by way of rejoicing: not one of our bells suffered to ring, and but very few colours were shown by the shipping in the harbour; no, nor not one bonfire kindled."

After the governor refused to call the Assembly, and after the Committee of Nineteen showed no disposition to do anything about it, a meeting of nearly 1,200 mechanics from Philadelphia and its suburbs gathered at the State House to hear a letter from the mechanics of New York. The mechanics' meeting voted to establish its own Committee of Correspondence "to strengthen the hand of the merchants' committee." That stirred the Committee of Nineteen sufficiently to draw up resolutions condemning the Port Act, urging aid for Boston, and calling for a mass meeting on June 18 to form a new, larger Committee of Correspondence.

By the time the mass meeting of 8,000 people gathered at the State House on June 18, the tide had begun to turn against the conservatives. The mechanics' meeting had forced the Committee of Nineteen into more vigorous measures. Lancaster County in the west had passed resolves roundly denouncing the Port Act and calling for nonimportation and nonexportation without mentioning a continental congress. Letters and news reports rolled in from other colonies, particularly from the south, showing that Pennsylvania could safely become a little more outspoken. And many conservatives, including Joseph Galloway, Speaker of the Assembly, looked upon a continental congress as a way of preserving order and reaching an accommodation with Britain. The Committee of Forty-three, picked by the June 18 mass meeting, was chaired by John Dickinson. The meeting called for a continental congress and left to the Committee of Forty-three the method of choosing Pennsylvania's delegates.

John Dickinson was pleased with the results of the mass meeting. He wrote to Josiah Quincy, Jr., of Massachusetts, that Pennsylvania had at last joined the other colonies in desiring a congress, and that "our country people" were standing behind it. "Doubt not that every thing bears a most favourable aspect. Nothing can throw us into a pernicious confusion, but one Colony's breaking the line of opposition, by advancing too hastily before the rest." Quincy retorted, quite justifiably, that "I see no reason to apprehend our advancing before our brethren, unless the plans [congress] should adopt should very evidently be too languid and spiritless to give any rational hopes of safety to us, in our adherence to them."

Dickinson did labor prodigiously during the month after the June 18 meeting to get Pennsylvania behind Boston. He, Thomson, and Mifflin made a tour of the western counties, drumming up support for a convention to pick delegates to a continental congress. The Committee of Forty-three issued a call for representatives from each county to meet in Philadelphia on July 15, and Dickinson worked long and hard to prepare an agenda for the convention.

In the meantime, Governor Penn and the conservatives had second thoughts about a continental congress. Many colonies had already chosen delegates, and the Committee of Forty-three had insured that Pennsylvania would be represented. Furthermore, wily Joseph Galloway, Dickinson's old political enemy, thought a continental congress might be a forum in which the dispute with England could be settled on conservative terms. On June 28 Galloway and three other members of the Assembly, constituting themselves the "Committee of Correspondence," wrote to the Massachusetts committee that a congress must consist of deputies chosen by the regular houses of representatives, meeting either in formal session or in convention, which could then

establish a political union between the two countries, with the assent of both. . . . Any thing short of this will leave the Colonies in their present precarious state; disunited among themselves, unsettled in their rights, ignorant of their duties, and destitute of that connection with *Great Britain* which is indispensably necessary to the safety and happiness of both.

The Committee of Forty-three agreed that it would be best to have the formal choice of delegates made by the Assembly; therefore it proposed that at the same time the convention met, Galloway would call the members of the Assembly into informal session to ratify the convention's choices. But neither Galloway nor Governor Penn wanted the precedent of extralegal Assembly sessions. Penn had refused to call the Assembly for the purpose of electing delegates, but he was, in a sense, rescued by the real need for an Assembly session to deal with the outbreak of Indian troubles on the frontier. Thus Penn called the Assembly to convene on July 18, with the tacit understanding that it would also take up the election of delegates to the Continental Congress.

Seventy-five delegates representing all of Pennsylvania's eleven counties met in Philadelphia from July 15 to July 22. Only one was from Bedford County, as compared to thirty-four from Philadelphia, but each county had one vote. Unlike the Assembly, Philadelphia and the eastern counties could not dominate the west. John Dickinson had already drafted a long set of resolutions, instructions, and a closely reasoned constitutional argument to be taken up by the convention.

The results of the convention were far more radical than anyone could have expected from Pennsylvania. Of the sixteen resolutions, most of them denouncing the Coercive Acts, fourteen passed unanimously. The tenth resolution, passed unanimously, recommended that the Continental Congress first petition the king for a redress of grievances before taking sterner action. Nevertheless, the eleventh, passed "by a great majority," agreed to support a congressional resolution for nonimportation and nonexportation even if not preceded by a petition. The twelfth, "Resolved, by a majority," committed Pennsylvania to support "such farther steps" as Congress deemed necessary beyond nonimportation and nonexportation. Sam Adams could hardly have asked for more.

Furthermore, the convention adopted instructions to the delegates that demanded Parliament's renunciation of the Declaratory Act and repeal of all statutes regulating or taxing American trade passed since 1760, plus the Treason Act of 35 Henry VIII, with which Parliament was threatening to transport American radicals to England for trial, and the Hat Act and Iron Act, which severely restricted American manufactures. In return, the colonies would pay for the tea, settle a permanent income on the king, and ratify the Navigation Acts. The convention did not add Dickinson's constitutional arguments to the instructions, but it endorsed them by ordering them printed. It proposed that John Dickinson, James Wilson, and Thomas Willing be delegates to the Continental Congress. Finally, it appointed Dickinson, Thomson, and Reed to present the resolves and instructions to the Assembly.

Joseph Galloway, however, had no intention of allowing the Pennsylvania delegation to bear such radical instructions. The Assembly, chosen in October 1773 before revolutionary fervor began to work in Pennsylvania, was dominated by conservatives. A handbill signed "A FREEMAN" circulated in the Assembly denouncing the convention as "setting up a power to controul [sic] you, is setting up anarchy above order—IT IS THE BEGINNING OF REPUBLICANISM. . . . Nip this pernicious weed in the bud."

The Assembly seemed to agree. It contemptuously rejected the convention's recommendations and its nominations to Congress. Instead, Speaker Galloway would lead a delegation composed of members of the Assembly. Of them, only Thomas Mifflin was closely identified with the leaders of the convention. The others—Samuel Rhoads, Charles Humphreys, John Morton, George Ross, and Edward Biddle—ranged from conservative to moderate. They were not committed to support any of the actions of Congress; indeed, their only real instruction was "to avoid every thing indecent or disrespectful to the mother state."

The radicals and even the moderates were thwarted by Galloway. Pennsylvania would send a delegation as conservative as New York's. Governor Penn rightly crowed to Lord Dartmouth that "your Lordship will perceive that the steps taken by the Assembly are rather a check than an encouragment to the proceedings of the Committee, and this I was well assured would be the case." But the groundwork had been laid for a real revolution in Pennsylvania politics within a few months.

The Three Lower Counties on the Delaware, while they shared their governor, John Penn, with Pennsylvania, and were under Philadelphia's economic influence, took a far more radical course than Pennsylvania during 1774. Delaware's population had a large number of Scots-Irish and was Calvinist, rather than Quaker, although the concentration of Anglicans in the south tended to make Sussex County somewhat more conservative than either New Castle or Kent County.

Throughout the revolutionary period, Delaware politics had been led by three arch Whigs: Thomas McKean and George Read of New Castle, and Caesar Rodney of Kent County. They had been active against the Stamp Act and Townshend Acts, keeping Delaware among the most faithful observers of the nonimportation agreements in 1769-70. McKean was speaker of the Delaware House in 1773, while Rodney held the same office in 1774. Read was attorney general of the colony. Perhaps their long-time opposition to British policy

[116]

explains why Delaware, alone of the colonies, did not confine itself to resolutions against the Tea Act and Coercive Acts, but denounced all aspects of British policy since 1763.

As soon as news arrived of the Port Act, the Delaware Committee of Correspondence, Read, McKean, and John Mckinly of New Castle, wrote the Virginia Committee of Correspondence that "We consider each Colony on this Continent as parts of the same Body, and an Attack on one to affect all." The committee believed that Delaware would support nonimportation, nonexportation, and a continental congress.

On June 17 A FREEMAN—probably Read and McKean—issued a call for the "Gentlemen, Freeholders, and others" of New Castle County to meet in the town of New Castle on June 29 "to consider the most proper mode of procuring relief" for Boston, and "restoring our invaded property and expiring liberties." Five hundred citizens showed up for the meeting, chaired by McKean, where they passed resolutions that not only called for a continental congress and urged the other two counties to meet in New Castle on August 1 to pick a delegation, but also committed New Castle County to support any suspension of trade the Congress agreed upon.

The other counties were somewhat miffed by New Castle's going so far without first consulting them. Kent nevertheless held a meeting on July 20 which endorsed most of the New Castle resolutions. Caesar Rodney, as Speaker of the House, decided to call the House members into extralegal session on August 1, even without hearing from Sussex. The House was not scheduled to meet in regular session until September 30, and there was no chance that Governor Penn, who had already turned down Pennsylvania's request for a special session, would agree to call the Delaware legislature in time to elect delegates to the Continental Congress.

Sussex was further displeased by Rodney's action, and the county meeting debated whether to elect its own representative to the Continental Congress. However, at the county convention held at Lewes on July 23, Thomas McKean won the delegates over with a speech pleading for united resistance to British policy that included an impassioned catalog of everything Americans had objected to since 1763. Sussex went along. On August 1 and August 2 the Three Lower Counties on the Delaware committed themselves fully to nonimportation, nonexportation, and any other measures that Congress should approve; and they sent Caesar Rodney, Thomas McKean, and George Read to represent them in Philadelphia.

III. THE CHESAPEAKE

While Boston was the center of opposition to Great Britain in 1774, a second center—hardly less important—was the Chesapeake colonies of Maryland and Virginia. These two ancient colonies contained 30 percent of the American population, and nearly 25 percent of the white population. At first glance, the region seems unlikely to have taken a radical stance. Their governors were among the strongest in America, and their legislatures were controlled by planter aristocrats who were anything but democrats. Because of their staple crop, tobacco, both had much closer commercial and cultural ties with England than any other region. Nevertheless, they rallied to Boston's support early and vigorously.

Maryland, like Pennsylvania, was a proprietary colony whose political parties were divided into "court," or proprietary, or "country," or antiproprietary, factions. Maryland also had, in Daniel Dulany, the counterpart of Pennsylvania's John Dickinson. There the resemblance ceased. Dulany did not represent radicalism in Maryland. Such men as Thomas Johnson, Samuel Chase, William Paca, and Charles Carroll of Carrolton had long been in conflict with both Governor Robert Eden and the British government. These popular leaders, while impeccably aristocratic, already had considerable experience in organizing extralegal associations, provincial conventions, and mobs. The antiproprietary party they led had triumphed in the 1773 election, the last held in Maryland under the British empire. In April 1774 Governor Eden prorogued the Assembly and left the colony until November.

On May 18, even before news of the Port Act arrived, a mass meeting in Chestertown denounced the Tea Act as "calculated to enslave the *Americans,*" and called all who obeyed it "enemies to the liberties of *America.*" The next day the *Maryland Gazette* published the Boston Port Act. On May 25 eighty inhabitants of Annapolis adopted six resolves in support of Boston, including a recommendation "that the gentlemen of the law of this Province, bring no suit for the recovery of any debt due from any inhabitant of this Province to any inhabitant of *Great Britain,* until the said Act be repealed." That resolution aroused an immediate storm of protest, but the following day another mass meeting reaffirmed all the resolutions. Those calling for nonimportation and nonexportation passed nearly unanimously. The resolution on debt recovery passed only by 47-31.

On May 30, 161 citizens of Annapolis signed a protest against the debt-recovery resolution "because our credit as a commercial people will expire under the wound." Among the signers was Daniel Dulany, who had denounced Pennsylvania's weak response to the Port Act, but who feared the resolution carried "so much injustice and partiality, that I am afraid it will give a handle to our enemies to hurt the general cause." Writing to Arthur Lee, Dulany said "I would have agreed to it if it had extended to merchants in this country as well as foreign merchants." That was the only resolution that ran into trouble; as William Eddis told a London correspondent, the others were "of too popular a nature to admit of opposition." However, none of the resolutions was to go into effect until a majority of the colonies and of Maryland's counties agreed.

Other counties held their own meetings during May and June. Some ignored the Annapolis resolution on debt recovery, and Caroline County unanimously resolved "that the Courts of Justice be kept open; but should a non-exportation agreement be generally come into, . . . the Courts of Justice be shut up." Harford County repeated the Annapolis resolution, while Anne Arundel and Frederick counties followed Dulany's sentiments and called for suspension of debt-recovery suits by Maryland as well as British merchants.

On June 22, little more than a month after they first heard of the Boston Port Act, representatives of all sixteen Maryland counties met in Annapolis. During the next four days they approved resolutions supporting Boston, calling for a continental congress to decide restrictions on imports and exports, and electing Matthew Tilghman, Thomas Johnson, Robert Goldsborough, William Paca, and Samuel Chase as representatives to the congress. The Maryland convention did not make any resolution on suspension of debt recovery, and it stipulated that nonexportation of tobacco was to go into effect only if Virginia and North Carolina agreed to do so. However, the relative conservatism of the convention's resolutions, compared to the earlier statements by some of the counties, should not be misleading. Maryland acted very early, long before her nearest neighbors in Virginia, Pennsylvania, and Delaware. Her example helped to turn the others into a more radical course.

Virginia was the oldest, the most populous, and the most politically stable of the thirteen colonies, which perhaps accounts for the deliberation with which she moved. In the end, however, Virginia took the most radical measures and was the most united of all the colonies in support of Massachusetts.

Everything about Virginia seemed to militate against radicalism. Her government had been dominated by a planter oligarchy throughout the eighteenth century. Her governor already had many of the powers Thomas Gage received only in the Massachusetts Government Act. Virginia had the strongest trade and cultural ties to England of any of the colonies. Most Virginians were flattered by the fact that John Murray, earl of Dunmore, was both a peer and an authentic royal governor, not, as so often in the past, a lieutenant governor serving as surrogate for some more exalted personage in England. True, Dunmore was a Scot, and Virginians generally disliked Scots. His official portrait, in windblown kilt, elicited a good deal of crude humor from his constituents. Still, he was convivial, and he had established friendships with such planters as George Washington. Dunmore had swallowed his disappointment at being transferred from New York to Virginia, and he further flattered the Virginians by bringing his family to the colony early in 1774.

On the other hand, while Virginians had no single major grievance against royal government, they had a number of smaller ones that came to fruition in 1774. The low price of tobacco, combined with the restrictions of the Navigation Acts and the planters' penchant for stylish living, had put most of the planter class in perpetual debt to British mercantile houses. Parliament's restrictions on paper currency exacerbated the money shortage in the colony. In February 1774 Lord Dunmore received instructions to sell Virginia's western lands only at public auction, and with the minimum price increased fourfold and quitrents doubled. Finally, although the Church of England was the established religion in Virginia and the faith of most of the planters, they had no greater desire to see an Anglican bishop in America than did Calvinist New England. However, none of these issues by itself—and possibly not in combination—really accounts for Virginia's revolutionary attitude, and scholars continue to debate the matter.

The Virginia gentry did not approve of the Boston Tea Party, and they were further worried by the false report that New York Governor Tryon's house was burned by the Sons of Liberty because he threatened to land tea "under the mouths of the Cannon!" That was quickly forgotten, however, when news of the Boston Port Act arrived in Virginia about May 19.

The House of Burgesses was in session in Williamsburg. Regular business ground on until May 24, but behind the scenes some of the younger members, including Patrick Henry, Richard Henry Lee, Francis Lightfoot Lee, and Thomas Jefferson, assisted by George Mason who was in town on business, were preparing a bombshell. It took the form of a resolution by the Burgesses that

[120]

June 1—the day the Port Act was to take effect—should be set aside as "a day of fasting, humiliation and prayer . . . to give us one heart and one mind firmly to oppose, by all just and proper means, every injury to American rights." As Jefferson later recounted it, they "cooked up a resolution" with the aid of John Rushworth's *Historical Collections.* Significantly, Rushworth had been secretary to Oliver Cromwell and was the chronicler of the execution of Charles I. Since none of the "cooks" had any great reputation for seeking divine guidance, they decided to persuade Robert Carter Nicholas, treasurer of the colony and a man of immense respectability and piety, to introduce the resolution.

Nicholas's resolution passed with little debate and no division. The framers, while they knew Governor Dunmore would consider it an affront, nevertheless expected him to let the session to run another week because many important matters were still to be considered. On May 26, however, Dunmore ordered the House to attend him in the Council chamber. There he tersely announced: "Mr. Speaker and Gentlemen of the House of Burgesses, I have in my hand a paper published by order of your House, conceived in such terms as reflect highly upon his Majesty and the Parliament of Great Britain; which makes it necessary for me to dissolve you; and you are dissolved accordingly."

Five years previously, another governor had dissolved the House when it passed some unpalatable resolves; then the former Burgesses repaired to the Raleigh Tavern to adopt a nonimportation agreement. So it was in 1774. On May 27 most of the former House met again in the Raleigh Tavern, elected Speaker Peyton Randolph as moderator, and adopted an "Association . . . in support of the constitutional liberties of *America,* against the late oppressive Acts of the *British* Parliament, respecting the town of *Boston,* which, in the end, must affect all the other Colonies."

The Association denounced Parliament's taxing America and the Port Act. It further called for a boycott not only of tea but of all other East India goods except saltpeter (an ingredient of gunpowder) and spices. It called for a continental congress to meet annually. Finally, it noted that only "a tender regard for the interest of our fellow-subjects, the merchants and manufacturers of *Great Britain,* prevents us from going further at this time," but if the unconstitutional taxation persisted, they would be compelled "to avoid all commercial intercourse with *Britain.* " Ironically, the same evening most of the former Burgesses attended a ball in honor of Lady Dunmore.

The following day, most of the Burgesses left for home. The provincial Committee of Correspondence, however, stayed behind to draft a letter to the other colonies calling for a continental congress; then they, too, departed. But on

Sunday, May 29, Peyton Randolph received Sam Adams's letters and the Boston Town Meeting resolution for suspension of trade with Great Britain. Randolph immediately sent out a call for all the former Burgesses living near Williamsburg to reconvene on Monday morning. Twenty-five of them showed up to hear the resolutions from Boston and the resolutions from other cities and colonies north of the Potomac.

The meeting was in a quandary. Most of them recognized the need for nonimportation, but disagreed about nonexportation; and they were frightened by the Annapolis resolution to block suits for recovery of debts. Finally they agreed that the matter should be left up to the whole colony, so they unanimously resolved that the members of the dissolved House of Burgesses should return to Williamsburg on August 1 to discuss the matter.

So far, the Burgesses had taken very little concrete action. Their constituents, however, were not so cool. Philip Vickers Fithian, a young tutor on Robert Carter's plantation, recorded in his diary for May 31: "the lower Class of People here are in a tumult on the account of Reports from Boston, many of them expect to be press'd & compell'd to go and fight the Britains!" Nicholas Cresswell, an Englishman who was markedly unsympathetic to revolutionary activities, observed that "the people seem much exasperated at the proceedings of the Ministry and talk as if they were determined to dispute the matter with the sword." John Harrower, an indentured servant, wrote to his wife in England that "if the Parliament do not give over it will cause a total revolt." Robert Carter ordered that no one from Nomini Hall was to attend fast-day services on June 1, but most Virginians were in church that day. His kinsman, Landon Carter, heartily approved his rector's modification of the Anglican service from "God save the King" to "God preserve all the just rights and liberties of America." On May 20 Landon Carter had noted that "Ld. Dunmore wants 1,200 men to fight the Pennsylvanians. I'd rather raise them for Boston a great deal." Richard Henry Lee asked his brother Arthur to keep him posted on events in England, because "when the dirty Ministerial Stomach is daily ejecting its foul contents upon us, it is quite necessary that the friendly streams of information and advice should be frequently applied to wash away the impurity." The Virginians were in a decidedly truculent mood as they gathered in county meetings during June and July.

Virginia did not have the New England tradition of town meetings in which questions of the day were threshed out. Nevertheless, during the two months before the Burgesses reconvened on August 1, more than half of Virginia's counties held public meetings. Unlike the usual county election meetings, these welcomed not only "gentlemen freeholders" but all male inhabitants over twenty-one. Aristocratic Virginia had its first taste of participatory democracy. Lord Dunmore rightly predicted that the conservatism "which is publicly declared by many of the families of distinction here, will avail little against the turbulence and prejudice which prevails throughout the country."

Considering that over thirty counties held meetings, there is remarkable unanimity in their resolves. Most agreed that Boston was suffering in the common cause of all America; that parliamentary taxation and the Coercive Acts were illegal; that trade with Great Britain and the West Indies should be suspended; and that a continental congress was the proper body to seek a redress of grievances. Middlesex County in the Tidewater was by far the most conservative; its resolutions denounced the Boston Tea Party, acknowledged Parliament's power to regulate trade, and observed "that an unlimited non-exportation and non-importation scheme is impracticable; and were it not so, would be irreconcilable with every principle of justice and honesty, injurious to the commerce, and fatal to the credit of this Colony." But even Middlesex denounced parliamentary taxation and the Coercive Acts. Several counties, including Richard Henry Lee's seat of Westmoreland, resolved that lawyers should not "bring any writ for the recovery of debt, or push to conclusion any such suit already brought," as long as nonexportation remained in effect. A few counties called for an end to the slave trade.

The most important meeting was held in Alexandria, Fairfax County, on July 18. George Washington was in the chair, prepared with a lengthy set of resolutions drawn up by his friend, the philosopher George Mason. The resolutions began with the statement that "*Virginia* cannot be considered as a conquered country, and, if it was, that the present inhabitants are the descendents, not of the conquered, but of the conquerers." The first ten resolutions were statements of principle and denunciations of acts of Parliament. The remaining fourteen called for specific actions. While Virginians would gladly have helped pay for the Boston Tea Party, if the tea were private property, since the East India Company was simply "the tools and instruments of oppression in the hands of Government, and the cause of the present distress," Americans should have no "further dealings with them." Debt payment should be suspended.

Most important, Mason's resolves called for a Continental Association to enforce nonimportation and nonexportation through local committees of inspection. Here at last was a practical proposal in answer to Boston's call, and the genesis of the action subsequently taken by the First Continental Congress.

George Washington may not have agreed with all of Mason's resolutions, particularly the one for suspension of debt payments; but he refrained from presenting a set of counterproposals drawn up by another friend, Brian Fairfax, that called for reconciliation with Britain. All of Mason's resolutions passed.

In the meantime, Governor Dunmore had another problem. His dissolution of the House of Burgesses left unresolved Virginia's conflict with Indians and Pennsylvanians in the Ohio Valley, and had allowed the law setting fees in debt-recovery cases to lapse. On June 17 Dunmore issued writs for a new election for a House of Burgesses to meet on August 11. Most counties returned the incumbents. George Washington was reelected from Fairfax County. Nicholas Cresswell attended Washington's victory party, at which there was "Coffee and Chocolate, but no Tea. This Herb is in disgrace amongst them at present."

But on July 8 Dunmore, faced with the fact that the August 11 session would probably endorse the actions that would be taken by the extralegal session still scheduled for August 1, decided that there was "no urgent occasion for their meeting at that time," and prorogued the opening of the session to the first Thursday in November. On July 10 Dunmore went off to the Ohio Valley to conduct "Lord Dunmore's War" and did not come back to Williamsburg until December. Thus the Virginia Convention met August 1-6 with no interference from the governor.

Sixty of Virginia's sixty-one counties sent delegations to the convention. In everything but name it was a regular meeting of the House of Burgesses, with more members present than George Washington had ever seen at any one time. Illness prevented Thomas Jefferson from attending, but he sent along a draft of one of his most famous writings, "A Summary View of the Rights of British America, Set Forth in some Resolutions Intended for the Inspection of the Present Delegates of the People of Virginia, now in Convention."

The resolutions of the Virginia Convention were, in large part, a somewhat duller version of George Mason's Fairfax County Resolves. They included an association not to import any British goods after November 1; and, if American grievances were not resolved, to export no goods after August 10, 1775. They did not include a ban on suits for debt recovery, but that was partly because the statute regulating such cases had lapsed. They appointed Peyton Randolph, Richard Henry Lee, George Washington, Patrick Henry, Richard Bland, Benjamin Harrison, and Edmund Pendleton as Virginia's delegates to the Continental Congress. With the exception of Lee and Henry, all were moderates; but the instructions they carried were among the most radical in America.

[124]

IV. THE CAROLINAS AND GEORGIA

The three remaining provinces had little in common except their location at the southernmost end of the chain of intercolonial communications, which helps to explain why all of them acted late. North Carolina, with no major port or towns and with a population mostly of farmers, was nearly as radical as Virginia. South Carolina, dominated by Charleston merchants and tidewater rice planters, was inclined to be conservative. Still little more than a colonial outpost, Georgia alone refused to send a delegation to the First Continental Congress.

North Carolina was, as John Pownall reported in April 1774, in a state "of the greatest anarchy and confusion." She still felt the effects of the Regulator protest of 1768 to 1771, which pitted the tidewater against the back country in open civil war. Governor Josiah Martin attempted to placate the back country, but he was constantly at odds with his legislature over a host of problems, including currency, taxes to sink the public debt, fees, a boundary dispute with South Carolina, and his attempt to change the Court Law of 1768. Martin, a former army officer, felt himself to be absolutely bound by his instructions. Among the results of this executive-legislative conflict was the lapsing of the Court Law, so that North Carolina had no courts of justice from March 1773 until long after Independence. Martin dissolved the Assembly on March 30, 1774, and never called another.

The first leader of the North Carolina radicals was William Hooper of Wilmington, a former Bostonian who had studied law in James Otis's office. In April 1774 Hooper was already predicting American independence. On July 21 Hooper chaired a meeting of delegates from the six counties nearest to Wilmington that agreed to a circular letter calling for a general meeting of county delegates in August. Governor Martin responded with an injunction to "all and every his Majesty's subjects to forbear to attend at any such illegal Meetings." Most of the counties, however, ignored Martin, held their own mass meetings, passed resolves supporting Boston, and elected delegates to the provincial convention. Significantly, the Regulator counties swallowed their suspicion of the tidewater Whigs and gratitude to Martin; their resolutions were the most radical of all.

With representatives from all but six of North Carolina's thirty-eight counties, the convention assembled in Newbern on August 25-27. Governor

Martin summed up their actions nicely for Lord Dartmouth: "The readiness with which the intemperate declarations of the *Virginia* Assembly were adopted and re-echoed here, will have shown your Lordship, that this people are of but too congenial disposition." Martin himself remained in Newbern to observe the convention, but he took the precaution of sending his family to New York, "as the only chance of preserving it from destruction." North Carolina's resolutions were among the most radical of all; not only did they adopt an association and agree to boycott any province, town, or individual that did not agree to follow any general plan of the Continental Congress, they further resolved that they were completely independent of the British Parliament. The convention elected William Hooper and Joseph Hewes, later signers of the Declaration of Independence, and Richard Caswell, first governor of the state of North Carolina, to the Continental Congress.

South Carolina was economically and politically dominated by Charleston, the only real city in the south. It was the residence not only of merchants, lawyers, and government officials, but also of many planters; and South Carolina's rice nabobs were probably the most affluent group in America in 1774. Like North Carolina and Pennsylvania, South Carolina was torn by conflict between the tidewater and the underrepresented back country, although it did not, as in those colonies, erupt into open civil war. The South Carolina Assembly had for years engaged in a running fight with the acting governor, William Bull, and British customs officials. Nevertheless, South Carolina was hardly radical. In marked contrast to Boston, Philadelphia, and New York, Charleston allowed East India Company tea to be landed and stored, and Charlestonians were generally horrified by the Boston Tea Party.

News of the Boston Port Act did not get to Charleston until the end of May. Almost at once Peter Timothy's *South Carolina Gazette,* which had hitherto largely ignored revolutionary issues, became distinctly radical in tone. No colony was more generous than South Carolina in sending aid to the Bostonians, and Christopher Gadsden paid for storing and shipping relief goods out of his own pocket.

Governor Bull was surprised at the reaction. On July 31 he wrote to Lord Dartmouth:

I had expectations that the measures taken by the Parliament relative to *Boston* would have had some happy effect towards composing the disturbances in this Province, which seemed to have subsided a little last winter, but it has taken a contrary turn. Their own apprehensions and thoughts, confirmed by the resolutions and correspondence from other Colonies, have raised an universal spirit of jealousy against *Great Britain,* and of unanimity towards each other; I say universal, my Lord, for few who think otherwise are hardy enough to avow it publickly.

But if the South Carolina establishment was genuinely distressed at the Coercive Acts, it was equally disturbed at the idea of nonimportation and nonexportation, particularly if enforced by committees of radicals. While Timothy's *Gazette* pleaded for action, the Charleston Chamber of Commerce worked behind the scenes to keep the action as moderate as possible. On June 13 Charleston's Committee of Correspondence sent out a call for a meeting "of the inhabitants of this Colony" in Charleston on July 6. In the meantime, the Chamber of Commerce drew up a slate of candidates who could be counted upon to oppose nonintercourse in the Continental Congress.

One hundred four delegates showed up for the Charleston meeting of July 6-8. Forty-five of them were from Charleston, and everyone who attended had a vote. Thus the back country, with nearly 80 percent of the free population, was once again badly underrepresented. At first the meeting went exactly as the conservatives had planned. It passed several resolutions denouncing the Coercive Acts, but made the actions of the Continental Congress binding on the colony only if the South Carolina delegation voted for them; and the candidates already picked by the Chamber of Commerce—Henry Middleton, John Rutledge, Charles Pinckney, Miles Brewton, and Rawlins Lowndes—opposed nonimportation and nonexportation. The more radical members of the meeting were willing to accept Middleton and John Rutledge, but insisted on replacing the others with Christopher Gadsden, Thomas Lynch, and Gadsden's son-in-law, Edward Rutledge.

The vote on allowing the South Carolina delegation to bind the colony to Congress's measures was so close that the conservatives feared the Chamber of Commerce slate might be defeated; therefore they tried a clever stategem. The meeting agreed that on that very afternoon, between 2:00 and 6:00, every free white in South Carolina could come in to vote for the congressional delegation. This seeming venture into democracy was in reality a plot by the merchants to march their clerks and employees to the poll to be voted in favor of the merchants' slate. It must have been a rude shock to them when Gadsden and Timothy turned out the mechanics in such numbers that the Chamber of Commerce slate lost by nearly 400 votes.

Governor Bull had called a meeting of the Assembly for August 2. All but five of its members had been at the Charleston meeting. The governor was still in bed when messengers from the Assembly arrived to tell him that the body was sitting ready to do business at the unwontedly early hour of 8:00 A.M. Before Bull could arrive, the Assembly officially endorsed the delegation elected at Charleston, and voted £1,500 for their expenses.

Even with Gadsden and Lynch as members, the South Carolina delegation to Philadelphia was hardly radical, and their instructions did not even mention nonimportation and nonexportation. Nevertheless, the radicals had achieved a significant victory at the Charleston meeting, and popular opinion in South Carolina was certainly in favor of supporting Boston. Many merchants thought it wise to volunteer to cease imports even before the Continental Congress met.

Georgia alone refused to send delegates to the Continental Congress, but Georgia was a special case. Founded half a century after any of the other twelve colonies, Georgia was far more dependent upon Britain than any of the others. She had only 33,000 people, nearly half of them black slaves, which lent to a feeling of insecurity on the part of many Georgians. Her frontiers were constantly threatened by Indians, who in the spring of 1774 were on the warpath again. Parliament contributed far more to Georgia's budget than her taxpayers did, and the Navigation Acts worked to her economic advantage. Finally, Sir James Wright, son of a chief justice of South Carolina and grandson of a lord chief justice of England, was perhaps the ablest, toughest, and most popular governor in America.

Nevertheless, Georgia had a significant revolutionary movement, and it took all of Wright's efforts to keep her from joining the other colonies in the Continental Congress. On July 14, after news arrived of the South Carolina Convention in Charleston, a group of prominent Savannah men—Noble Wimberly Jones, Archibald Bulloch, John Houston, and George Walton—called for a mass meeting on July 27. Over a hundred persons attended the meeting, chaired by John Glen, but postponed final agreement on resolutions for another meeting to be held August 10. On August 5 Governor Wright forbade the meeting and threatened punishment for all who should attend. Although a considerable number ignored Wright's warning, the August 10 meeting of "Liberty people," as Wright called them, did little to cause the governor concern. While the meeting passed resolves against the Coercive Acts and created a Committee of Correspondence, it did not adopt an association and defeated an attempt to elect delegates to the Continental Congress.

Four of Georgia's parishes held a subsequent meeting at Midway on August 30 and actually nominated a delegate to attend the Continental Congress "if the other Parishes agree." But they did not, so Georgia was unrepresented at Philadelphia. However, Georgia was not important enough for the patriots to consider this a serious setback or for Britain to consider it a significant victory. And Georgia at least had the beginnings of a revolutionary movement that ultimately brough her into the patriot camp.

The Coercive Acts touched off a real political revolution. At the beginning of 1774, few informed persons either in England or in America would have believed that twelve American colonies could unite on anything important; yet in little more than three months after news of the Boston Port Act arrived, an American congress was a reality. The union created at the First Continental Congress has survived for two centuries.

The delegates who converged on Philadelphia around the end of August were a diverse lot, chosen by several different methods, and strongly affected by the local issues and prejudices of their provinces. Most probably hoped that the Continental Congress would effect a reconciliation with Britain. A few recognized that America would be satisfied with nothing less than home rule, but they kept these sentiments to themselves.

While each colony was different from all the others, certain similarities run throughout. All except a few British officials and archconservatives were horrified by the Coercive Acts, fearing that if Massachusetts were forced to submit, their turn would not be long in coming. Significantly, this attitude emerged as soon as the text of the Boston Port Act was made public; it did not wait for news of the Massachusetts Government or Administration of Justice acts, which simply added fuel to an already raging fire.

In almost every colony, the common people supported more radical measures than did their leaders—and this is true even where the traditional leadership was staunchly Whig. "Democracy" was still something of a scare word in the eighteenth century, but the summer of 1774 saw an unprecedented exercise in participatory democracy. Town, county, and urban mass meetings threw open their doors to people who either could not or chose not to participate in the political process before. In the colonies with a revolutionary tradition, such as Connecticut and Virginia, these meetings encouraged the Whig leadership to take a more radical stand. In others, such as New York and Pennsylvania, they forced the conservatives to go further than they wanted to. In 1774, at least, the American Revolution was decidely a popular movement.

[129]

Another similarity is the demand for a continental congress. While Providence, Rhode Island, was the first to issue a call, others—such as New York and Virginia's dissolved House of Burgesses—called for a congress even before they heard of the Providence resolutions. At first both the extreme radicals and the extreme conservatives opposed a congress, but public opinion forced them to come around.

As the delegates gathered in Philadelphia, the most pressing question was whether the things that brought them together could overbalance their old suspicions, prejudices, and rivalries.

CHAPTER VI

The First Continental Congress

The measures of the late Continental Congress, have
occasioned much warmth and discord in this country. . . .
Adams, with his crew, and the haughty Sultans of the South,
juggled the whole conclave of the Delegates. Fie on't, Oh fie!
—A Merchant at Annapolis, January 28, 1775

The Proceedings of the Continental Congress astonish and
terrify all considerate Men.
—General Gage to Lord Dartmouth, November 15, 1774

John Adams accurately described the delegates who gathered in Philadelphia
during September and October 1774 as "Fifty gentlemen meeting together,
[who] are all strangers, not acquainted with each other's language, ideas, views,
designs. They are therefore jealous of each other—fearful, timid, skittish." They
thought of themselves not as representatives to the first session of an American
legislature, but as ambassadors of separate nations. Those from New Hampshire,

[131]

New York, Connecticut, Pennsylvania, and Virginia represented provinces literally at war with one or more of their neighbors. Each colony, each region, had its own special interests to protect, while small colonies feared their larger neighbors in every region. The delegates themselves had been chosen by almost every conceivable method. Furthermore, they represented widely divergent views as to the proper course to take toward Britain.

Nevertheless, these evident differences should not blind us to what the delegates shared. All of them—from the radical Sam Adams to the conservative Joseph Galloway—were on record as opposing Parliament's attempts to tax Americans. All feared that if Massachusetts, however outrageous her behavior had been, were forced to submit to the Coercive Acts, their own colonies' liberties would be put in jeopardy. And nearly all of them were canny, experienced politicians. Even the most conservative knew that the people back home expected them to stand up to Parliament's challenge; and even the most radical realized that unity was far more important than ideology.

The First Continental Congress formally began its proceedings on Monday, September 5; but its business had begun weeks earlier, even before any of the delegates had reached Philadelphia. The Massachusetts delegation, for example, spent nearly three weeks on its southward journey, pausing frequently to be warmly greeted, wined, dined, and shown the local sights. During the festivities, however, the delegates constantly sought the kind of information upon which their mission depended. By the time he arrived in Philadelphia, on August 29, John Adams had a file on the social, economic, religious, and political situation of each colony through which he passed; and he had a fairly good notion about what to expect from the delegates of the other northern colonies, either from personal interviews or from local supporters of the Massachusetts cause, like Alexander McDougall, the Reverend Doctor John Witherspoon, and Jonathan Dickinson Sergeant.

Philadelphia welcomed the delegates with open arms, larders, and wine cellars; and her hospitality continued unabated to the end of the First Congress. John Adams reported to his wife:

> I shall be killed with kindness in this place. We go to Congress at nine, and there we stay, most earnestly engaged in debates upon the most abstruse mysteries of state, until three in the afternoon; then we adjourn, and go to dine with some of the nobles of Pennsylvania at four o'clock, and feast upon ten thousand delicacies, and sit drinking Madeira, Claret, and Burgundy, till six or seven, and then go home fatigued to death with business, company, and care. Yet I hold out suprisingly.

John Adams

But these festivities played an important role, especially in the week before Congress opened. Few of the delegates had met before, though many had known each other through letters or by reputation. One wonders what the ascetic Sam Adams and the convivial Richard Henry Lee, who had been corresponding for years, thought of each other when they finally met. And while the Adamses got together with Lee and Patrick Henry, Joseph Galloway was seeking out kindred souls like James Duane of New York and John Rutledge of South Carolina. By the time Congress met, several matters had been settled "out of doors."

On Monday, September 5, forty-three delegates from eleven colonies assembled at the City Tavern to take up the first order of business—where to meet. Joseph Galloway, as speaker of the Pennsylvania House, offered the State House. The Philadelphia mechanics countered with the local labor temple, Carpenters' Hall. The delegates walked first to Carpenters' Hall, where Thomas Lynch of South Carolina opined that the hall was so obviously suitable that there was no need to look further. James Duane protested that the body must at least visit the State House out of simple politeness to Galloway. However, a "great majority" voted to stay where they were. This seemingly spontaneous choice had really been made by the previous Saturday, when Silas Deane of Connecticut wrote that the State House "is evidently the best place, but as *he* [Galloway] offers, the other party oppose."

Lynch, who was evidently picked as the temporary spokesman for the radicals, then proposed Peyton Randolph, a large man of commanding presence who was Speaker of the Virginia House of Burgesses, as president of Congress. The conservatives certainly had no quarrel with this choice. But then Lynch rose a third time to nominate Charles Thomson as permanent secretary. Thomson, described by John Adams as "the Sam Adams of Philadelphia," was Galloway's bitter enemy, and his choice was, Silas Deane reported, "mortifying in the last degree to Mr. Galloway and his party." Galloway and the New Yorkers, realizing that the matter had already been decided "out of doors," made only a perfunctory attempt to argue that the secretary should be a member of Congress; Thomson held the post for the next fifteen years.

After receiving the delegates' credentials, Congress took up an issue that had not been settled, though it certainly must have been debated, out of doors—voting procedure. Here the party lines broke down. Virginia, Massachusetts, and Pennsylvania, containing nearly half the people in the colonies, called for representation by population. South Carolina, home of the rice and indigo nabobs, countered with the proposition that property value be the basis for voting. The small colonies, noting that they had as much to lose as the large ones, demanded equality.

[134]

Everyone easily saw through Patrick Henry's assertion that "the distinctions between Virginians, Pennsylvanians, New Yorkers, and New Englanders are no more. I am not a Virginian, but an American." Samuel Ward of Rhode Island reminded Henry that his own House of Burgesses paid no attention to population. Some American congresses might have debated such an issue for weeks, but in 1774 time was too important. There was no census, and no colony was willing to accept the others' estimates of their size or wealth. Congress ended its first day with the matter unresolved; but on Tuesday, September 6, it quickly defeated a motion to refer rules and voting to a committee and agreed that "each Colony or Province shall have one Vote," with the added notation that Congress was not "possess'd of, or at present able to procure proper materials for ascertaining the importance of each Colony," so that it would not be considered a precedent for future congresses. But precedent it was—for at least one house of Congress—ever after.

The rules of procedure agreed upon were few and simple: no member could speak more than twice on the same point; any colony could delay a vote for one day; the proceedings of Congress were to be kept strictly secret. This last provision was, of course, absolutely necessary. The First Continental Congress was a revolutionary body quite outside the laws of England, and no one appreciated this more than the conservatives. Furthermore, because of the unit rule for each colony's voting, and Charles Thomson's natural caution, many votes are recorded as "unanimous" which must have come after very bitter debate. The members of the 1774 Congress, unlike those of 1974, were not given to leaking information; but, of course, they had a lot more to lose. Historians may regret their adherence to the rules; except for a few diaries and some later—usually self-serving—accounts, we have very little to indicate what passions were released in that hot meeting room.

But even the sketchy reports of the first two days' debates reveal a certain amount of truculence. Perhaps for this reason, Thomas Cushing of Massachusetts suggested that thereafter, in the interest of harmony, Congress should open with prayer. At once objections were raised: it would be "considered as Enthusiasm and Cant"; the "Efficacy of private Devotion"; and especially the fact that the members represented a multitude of sects. Then Sam Adams arose to state (not completely candidly) that "he was no bigot." He could hear a prayer from any minister of piety and virtue, and he had heard that the Reverend Jacob Duché, an Anglican clergyman, was such a man. He therefore moved that Mr. Duché be asked to open Congress the next day with prayers. Adams, who had no more use for the Church of England than for the North government, and had often said so, explained to Joseph Warren that since "many of our warmest friends are members of the Church of England, I thought it prudent, as well on that as some other accounts, to move that the service be performed by a clergyman of that denomination." Joseph Reed, an ally of Charles Thomson's later said that the Adamses "never were guilty of a more Masterly Stroke of Policy, than in moving that Mr. Duché might read Prayers."

When Congress assembled at nine o'clock the next morning, September 7, its members were in a somber mood. The previous afternoon had brought a report that fighting had broken out in Boston, the town had been shelled, and six townspeople had been killed. All during the evening Philadelphia's bells tolled sorrowfully. In this charged atmosphere, Mr. Duché read the Morning Service from the *Book of Common Prayer,* including the psalter for the seventh day, the Thirty-fifth Psalm:

> Plead thou my cause, O LORD, with them that strive with me, and fight thou against them that fight against me.
> Lay hand upon the shield and buckler, and stand up to help me. . . .
> Let them be confounded, and put to shame, that seek after my soul; let them be turned back, and brought to confusion, that imagine mischief for me. . . .
> For they have privily laid their net to destroy me without a cause; . . .
> Awake, and stand up to judge my quarrel; avenge thou my cause, my God and my Lord. . . .

The delegates were stunned; why, it was as if King David had written the psalm for them alone. Here indeed was a sign from on high. Silas Deane told his wife to look up the Thirty-fifth Psalm which, he noted, was "accidentally extremely applicable." John Adams said " the collect for the day, the 7th of the month was most admirably adapted, though this was accidental, or rather providential." And perhaps it was. Sam Adams, after all, was not familiar with the *Book of Common Prayer.* His allies from the south, however, were mostly Anglicans. One wonders if they had told Sam that the seventh would be an excellent day to hear the Anglican morning prayer service.

Primed by the psalm and by Duché's extemporaneous prayer—"worth riding one hundred miles to hear," reported Silas Deane—Congress buckled down to work. Before the day was over, it created two committees. The first, consisting of two delegates from each colony, was to draw up a statement of the rights of the colonies, a list of the infringements of those rights, and "the means most proper to be pursued for obtaining a restoration of them." The second, with one from each colony, was to report on the several statutes that affected the colonies' trade and manufacturing. For the next ten days, while the committees were meeting, the whole Congress assembled only to receive the credentials of delegates who arrived late.

The Committee on Rights became the scene of heated debate. Perhaps the immediacy of its task seemed less apparent when, on September 8, news came that Boston had not, after all, been shelled nor any of her citizens shot down. Now Philadelphia's bells rang out again, this time for joy. The Massachusetts delegates were relieved, of course, but their relief was tempered by the growing deadlock in the Committee on Rights.

The problem was that Congress, while willing to support Boston with "fine words," was divided both on the basis of American rights and upon the action to be taken against Britain. The conservatives wished to make their stand upon the English Constitution. John Adams spoke for many of the radicals when he said that the law of nature was "a resource to which we might be driven by Parliament much sooner than we were aware." The committee tentatively agreed to base American rights "upon the laws of nature, the principles of the English Constitution, and the charters and compacts," but that did not solve the issue. On the concrete question of Parliament's power over the colonies, the debate was just as heated. By this time the radicals were unwilling to concede that Parliament had any legislative powers whatsoever over America. Even the conservatives had to admit the logic of this argument, but they wanted to concede at least Parliament's power to set trade regulations for the whole empire. During the debate little was said about the real problem: what measures to take to defeat the Coercive Acts.

But Sam Adams had prepared a trump card. Before he left for Philadelphia, he had worked out with Joseph Warren a series of resolves to be considered by the Suffolk County convention. Suffolk County included Boston and the other towns affected by the Port Act. On September 14 Adams wrote to the Boston Committee of Correspondence that "I have been waiting with great Impatience for a Letter" from the committee, "upon whose Wisdom and Judgement I very much rely." As he wrote, Paul Revere was already galloping toward Philadelphia with the letter Adams wanted.

The Suffolk County Convention met in Milton on September 9, in an atmosphere of crisis. Boston was virtually in a state of siege, with four cannon guarding her only land approach, the narrow Boston Neck, while H.M.S. *Lively*'s guns covered the ferry way between Boston and Charlestown. Only a week before, hostilities had nearly broken out when General Gage sent a

[137]

detachment to secure the colony's powder supply in Charlestown. Thousands of men from all over New England had marched on Boston, and only the Boston Committee of Correspondence's assurance that fighting had not, in fact, begun kept them from an assault on Gage's forces. Gage was hurriedly throwing up fortifications on Boston Neck, while many of those who supported his government were already seeking sanctuary in Boston. Composed of delegates from Boston and surrounding towns, the convention quickly adopted a series of resolves whose content certainly owed much to Sam Adams, but whose words came from the passionate pen of Dr. Joseph Warren. Paul Revere rode into Philadelphia with a copy of these "Suffolk Resolves" on September 16. The next morning the Massachusetts delegation presented them to Congress. First came Warren's moving preamble, which John Adams said brought tears gushing into the eyes of even the "old grave pacific Quakers of Pennsylvania."

> Whereas, the power, but not the justice; the vengeance, but not the wisdom of Great Britain . . . which scourged and exiled our fugitive parents from their native shores, now pursues us, their guiltless children, with unrelenting severity. . . . If a boundless extent of continent, swarming with millions, will tamely submit to live, move, and have their being at the arbitrary will of a licentious minister, they will basely yield to voluntary slavery, and future generations shall load their memories with incessant execrations. On the other hand, if we arrest the hand which would ransack our pockets, if we disarm the parricide who points the dagger to our bosoms, if we nobly defeat that fatal edict, which proclaims a power to frame laws for us in all cases whatsoever, . . . posterity will acknowledge that virtue which preserved them free and happy.

Then came nineteen specific resolutions. The first "cheerfully acknowl-edge[d]" George III as rightful sovereign, "agreeable to compact, of the English colonies in America," but the rest were an open avowal of rebellion against his government. No obedience was owed to any of the Coercive Acts, and those who did support them were deemed "obstinate and incorrigible enemies," who in some cases should be held in custody as hostages for any patriots who were arrested. No courts should sit, taxes be paid into the official treasury, or goods imported from Britain until the Coercive Acts were suspended. The militia should be reorganized under new officers "who have evidenced themselves to be inflexible friends to the rights of the people," and should be ready "to act merely upon the defensive, so long as such conduct may be vindicated by reason and the principles of self-preservation, but no longer."

The Suffolk meeting even proposed an extralegal provincial congress—in effect a revolutionary government for the province—to meet at Concord on October 11. Then Suffolk County tossed this revolutionary document into Congress's lap by promising to "pay all due respect and submission to such measures as may be recommended by them." Appended to the Suffolk Resolves was a letter to General Gage protesting his fortification of Boston Neck as a further attempt to starve Boston into submission, and clearly warning him that while the people of Massachusetts "have no inclination to commence a war with his majesty's troops," they were resolved "never to submit" to "the late acts of Parliament."

The Suffolk Resolves must have presented a terible dilemma to all the congressional moderates. Suffolk had asked for guidance, yet in such terms that Congress must either endorse a virtual declaration of independence or else abandon Boston to General Gage. It is true that all the delegates—even Joseph Galloway—disapproved of British policy toward Boston, but a vote for the Resolves meant endorsing everything the moderates and conservatives had been trying to avoid: an appeal to the law of nature, suspension of civil government, and a declaration of armed resistance. Yet Congress resolved unanimously its approval of the Suffolk Resolves and ordered them to be printed in the newspapers, along with a call for continued contributions to alleviate "the distresses of our brethren at Boston."

In neither the journal of the Congress nor letters and diaries written at the time is there any indication of opposition to the Suffolk Resolves. John Adams's diary says, "This was one of the happiest days of my life. In Congress we had generous, noble sentiments, and manly eloquence. This day convinced me that America will support the Massachusetts or perish with her." Samuel Ward, Caesar Rodney, Silas Deane, George Read, and Sam Adams all reported that Congress acted with unanimity, and that both Congress and the people of Philadelphia supported the resolves enthusiastically.

The only dissenting view came from Joseph Galloway, and that was written in 1780 as an apologia for his own role in the First Continental Congress. Part of Galloway's statement rings true: Sam Adams certainly did make full use of expresses from Boston to help sway Congress, and it is unlikely that so revolutionary a document as the Suffolk Resolves could have been endorsed by Congress without "long and warm debates." On the other hand, neither logic

[139]

nor evidence supports Galloway's charge that a mob ready with tar and feathers intimidated the conservatives into endorsing the Suffolk Resolves. Sam Adams was far too cagey a politician to use tactics that would discredit the whole proceedings.

In any case, the vote on the Suffolk Resolves broke the logjam that had for two weeks kept the radicals from securing any concrete action in support of Boston. On September 22 Congress unanimously requested merchants to order no more goods from Great Britain and to delay or suspend any orders already sent, pending "the sense of the Congress, on the means to be taken for the preservation of the liberties of America." Five days later, again by unanimous vote, Congress forbade any imports from Great Britain or Ireland after December 1. The much more explosive question of nonexportation, however, was put off to a later day.

In the meantime, Joseph Galloway made a dramatic attempt to steer Congress back to a more conservative course. Galloway believed, with considerable justification, that the dispute between Britain and America was basically constitutional. He certainly opposed Parliament's claim of power to legislate for the colonies "in all cases whatsoever"; but he was equally certain that Congress, by its support of the Suffolk Resolves, was headed toward disunion—and disunion meant civil war. Galloway therefore proposed a "Plan of Union" between Great Britain and the colonies. Parliament would renounce the Declaratory Act, and each colony would be guaranteed control over its own internal affairs. On matters that affected all the colonies, however, power would be exercised by a new American government, with a president general appointed by the king and a legislature, modeled after the House of Commons, chosen by the people of the colonies. On any matters which affected both Britain and America, such as trade regulation, Parliament and the American government should each have veto power over the other's legislation.

Galloway's plan was imaginative, statesmanlike—and too late. It would not solve the immediate issue of the Coercive Acts. Nevertheless, the plan had considerable support, particularly from James Duane (who seconded it) and John Jay of New York, and young Edward Rutledge of South Carolina. The radicals succeeded in delaying consideration of the plan, but only by a vote of 6-5, with one delegation evenly divided. Three weeks later, Congress sank Galloway's plan literally without a trace, for all mention of it and the votes upon it were left out of the published journal of the First Continental Congress. Thus ended the only real effort to reach a compromise with Great Britain.

With Galloway's plan out of the way, on September 30, Congress returned to

[140]

the sticky problem of nonexportation. Here regional differences threw Congress into turmoil. Massachusetts wanted total nonexportation to Great Britain, Ireland, and the West Indies to start immediately; one of her delegates, probably John Adams, introduced a resolution to the effect that "hostilities" had already commenced against Massachusetts. If these hostilities "should be further pursued" against Massachusetts, all exports should stop immediately. If any patriots were arrested and sent to England for trial, this should be "considered as a declaration of war ... against all the colonies," and nonexportation begin immediately.

This was far too strong for most of the delegates; they voted it down and, like Galloway's plan, omitted all mention of it from the published journal of Congress. Virginia refused to go along with nonexportation until she could market her 1774 tobacco crop. South Carolina demanded that her main crop, rice, be exempted from the ban. Then it was noted that the resolution of September 27 banned imports only from Great Britain and Ireland; nothing had been said about the West Indies. When Thomas Mifflin proposed that all goods subject to duties ought to be placed on the nonimportation list, southern delegates raised the embarrassing point that northern shippers had found a way around such bans in the past. Congress did resolve to start nonexportation on September 10, 1775, and to add molasses, coffee, and pimento from the British West Indies and wines from Madeira and the Western Islands to the nonimportation due to start on December 1, 1774. The details for enforcing nonimportation, nonexportation, and nonconsumption were left to a committee of Thomas Cushing, Isaac Low, Thomas Mifflin, Richard Henry Lee, and Thomas Johnson.

As yet, however, nothing had really been done to assist Massachusetts, and her delegates fumed at the interminable debates. Then, on October 6, Paul Revere rode into town with another bombshell. This was a letter from the Boston Committee of Correspondence, noting that General Gage had continued to fortify the approaches to Boston. What would Congress advise? Should the townspeople be evacuated? Should all law and government continue to be suspended? Boston would do whatever Congress advised.

The debate over how to instruct Boston raged from Friday, October 7, until Tuesday, October 11. Richard Henry Lee moved that "it is inconsistent with the honour and safety of a free people" to live under military control; therefore they should evacuate the town "and find an asylum among their hospitable countrymen." Christopher Gadsden would go further: he wanted Congress to authorize an attack on Gage's forces before he received reinforcements. George

Ross and Joseph Galloway countered with a proposal that Massachusetts be left to her own devices respecting government, justice, and defense—in effect, that Congress should wash its hands of her.

None of these extreme proposals had a chance of passing, as John Adams had already reported on October 7. "Their opinions are fixed against hostilities and rupture, except as they should become absolutely necessary; and this necessity they do not see." Instead, Congress responded to Boston's plea with a series of ambivalent resolutions. It approved Massachusetts's opposition to the Coercive Acts, and "if the same shall be attempted to be carried into execution by force, in such case, all America ought to support them in their opposition." It advised that Boston ought not to be evacuated without "the utmost deliberation," and unless the Massachusetts Provincial Congress "should judge it absolutely necessary." The people of Massachusetts should "submit to a suspension of the administration of justice, where it cannot be procured in a legal and peaceable manner." Congress rejected a hard-hitting letter to General Gage drafted by Sam Adams and replaced it with a much milder one. The only really firm stand it took was in saying that all who supported the Massachusetts Government Act "ought to be held in detestation and abhorrence by all good men, and considered as the wicked tools of . . . despotism." On the other hand, the people of Boston were advised "still to conduct themselves peaceably towards his excellency General Gage, and his majesty's troops now stationed in the town."

But Congress was not abandoning Massachusetts. Once it got the advice to Boston out of the way, it settled down to the matters for which it had been convened: a declaration of rights and grievances, and an association to put into effect nonimportation, nonexportation, and nonconsumption. The product in both cases was the result of compromise, but on the whole it represented a triumph for the radicals.

In the declaration of rights and grievances adopted on October 14, Congress boldly based the rights of the colonists upon "the immutable laws of nature" as well as the English constitution and the colonial charters and compacts. Those rights were spelled out in ten resolutions, beginning with the assertion "That they are entitled to life, liberty and property, and they have never ceded to any sovereign power whatever, a right to dispose of either without their consent."

Nine articles of this "bill of rights" passed without opposition, but the fourth, which spelled out the exact relationship between Parliament and America, produced a deadlock on the issue of Parliament's power to regulate the trade of the empire. After two days of debate, five colonies voted to concede Parliament that power, five against, and both Rhode Island and Massachusetts were split.

Finally John Adams, using some of James Duane's words, came up with a resolution that a majority could reluctantly support. Since the colonies were not and could not be represented in Parliament, it followed that each had exclusive power in its own legislature, subject only to the king's veto; "But, from the necessity of the case, we cheerfully consent" to *bona fide* trade regulations passed by the British Parliament for the good of the whole empire, "excluding every idea of taxation, internal or external, for raising a revenue on the subjects in America, without their consent." In reality, this was a victory for the radicals, for it conceded no "right" to Parliament at all, it simply consented to the Trade and Navigation Acts so long as it was in the colonists' interest to do so.

Following the list of rights came the list of grievances, including virtually every law Parliament had made for America since 1763. "To these grievous acts and measures," Congress declared, "Americans cannot submit"; but in hopes that Britain would speedily see the light, "we have for the present only resolved to pursue the following peaceable measures." Two of these measures were mild enough: an address to the people of Great Britain and (a sop to the conservatives) a "loyal address to his Majesty." To draft these addresses, Congress entrusted two fire-eating Virginians, Richard Henry Lee and Patrick Henry, who had been called the "Cicero and Demosthenes of America." Alas, Cicero and Demosthenes proved to have more facile tongues than pens. When Lee's address to the English people was presented, "every countenance fell and a dead silence ensued for many minutes." But John Jay had prepared an address of his own, and Congress gladly adopted it. Henry's address to the king had no better luck. Congress then turned to John Dickinson, who had taken a seat in Congress only on October 17, after a radical triumph in the Pennsylvania House elections. The "Pennsylvania Farmer" lived up to his reputation.

On October 15, Congress began to debate the most important—and most controversial—of the three "peaceable measures," a "nonimportation, noncomsumption, and nonexportation agreement or association." The Association, as it was called, had in one way or another occupied the Congress from the beginning, and had several times brought open clashes between economic interest groups.

After a preamble which once again stated America's grievances, the Association began with a restatement of the resolution of September 27 banning all imports from Great Britain and Ireland after December 1. It added tea "from any part of the world," British West Indian products such as molasses, wines from Madeira and the Western Islands, foreign indigo, and slaves. To back up nonimportation, the Association agreed not to consume any of the banned goods.

[143]

Furthermore, the Association promoted "endeavours to improve the breed of sheep," and asked Americans to forgo eating mutton in the interest of increasing the domestic wool supply. It discountenanced and discouraged "every species of extravagance and dissipation," especially singling out horse racing, gaming, cock-fighting, shows, plays, and excessive manifestations of mourning.

The most controversial point, as always, was nonexportation. The Association stated: "The earnest desire we have not to injure our fellow-subjects in Great Britain, Ireland, or the West Indies, induces us to suspend a non-exportation until the tenth day of September, 1775." This was not completely candid; the real inducement was the fact that Virginia would not agree to nonexportation until she had marketed her tobacco. Even then, the South Carolina delegates refused to sign and walked out because rice and indigo were not excepted. They finally returned when the words "except rice to Europe" were added.

The muscle behind the Association was in its call to create revolutionary committees in "every county, city, and town . . . whose business it shall be attentively to observe the conduct of all persons touching this Association." These committees should publish the names of all who violated the Association's provisions, by importing, exporting, or consuming the banned goods, profiting from the scarcity it would produce, or even failing to accede to it. Publishing of names may seem like a mild enough punishment, but everyone knew that much more was implied, including the "modern punishment" of tar and feathers. Merrill Jensen has noted that these committees "took control of the economic life of the colonies and became centers of political power as well." The Association forever stamps the First Continental Congress as a truly revolutionary body.

Congress adopted the Association on October 20. Its main task was over. Before it dissolved on Wednesday, October 26, its members cleaned up a few loose ends, such as signing the Association, the addresses to the king and the English people, as well as further addresses to the American people and the inhabitants of Quebec and the other British colonies that had not sent delegations to Congress. By that time, some members had already gone home, so that—for example—George Washington and Richard Henry Lee signed for all the members of the Virginia delegation. And everyone did sign, though Joseph Galloway later claimed that he did so only through fear for his own safety. Ironically, Galloway was on the committee "to revise the minutes of the Congress" for publication—in other words, to delete anything that might cause trouble. One of the items left out was Galloway's own plan of union. But in the midst of all this housekeeping, Congress added two more important resolutions.

[144]

The first said that any attempt to seize an American for trial beyond the sea "will justify, and ought to meet with resistance and reprisal." And finally, if Great Britain did not bow to the First Continental Congress's demands, a Second Congress should convene in Philadelphia on May 10, 1775.

The First Continental Congress contained few philosophical radicals; but, given its membership, it did everything that Massachusetts could reasonably have expected. She now had eleven other colonies committed to her support, not just with "fine words" (although there were plenty of them), but with a tough Association.

Why did a group of basically moderate men produce so radical a result? Part of the answer must surely be that they all thought that a show of unity and the threat of economic reprisal would bring England to her senses, that by taking a hard line they were actually avoiding a split and war. There is much to suggest that even Galloway felt this way, in spite of his later claim that he was coerced into going along with the actions of Congress. John Adams departed "the happy, the peaceful, the elegant, the hospitable, and polite city of Philadelphia," with the feeling: "It is not likely that I shall ever see this part of the world again." He obviously hoped and expected that a Second Continental Congress would be unnecessary.

Beyond that, however, the members of the First Continental Congress really did represent the mood of their constituents. Whatever sober second thoughts Americans may have had six months later, when hostilities began, in the fall of 1774 they were in a defiant mood. In this sense, the Declaration of Rights and Grievances and the Association were the product of American democracy.

CHAPTER VII

The Revolution Within

Will you be instrumental in bringing the most abject slavery
on yourselves? Will you choose such Committees? Will you
submit to them, should they be chosen by the weak, foolish,
turbulant part of the country people?—Do as you please but,
by HIM that made me, I will not—No, if I must be enslaved,
let it be by a King at least, and not by a parcel of upstart,
lawless Committee-men. If I must be devoured, let me be
devoured by the Jaws of a lion, and not *gnawed* to death by
rats and vermin.

—The Reverend Samuel Seabury, *Free Thoughts on the
Proceedings of Congress*

We read now and then, it is true, of a good king; so we read
likewise of a prophet escaping unhurt from a lion's den, and
of three men walking in a fiery furnace without having even
their garments singed. The order of nature is as much
inverted in the first as it was in the last two cases. A good
king is a miracle. ... The American Congress derives all its
power, wisdom and justice, not from scrolls of parchment

> signed by kings, but from the people. ... A freeman in
> honouring and obeying the Congress, honours and obeys
> himself. The man who refuses to do both is a slave.
> —Anonymous, *Political Observations, Without Order*

As its participants fully realized, the American Revolution was a civil war. It involved not only a violent parting from a formerly loved mother country, but also a conflict of neighbor against neighbor, relative against relative. By the time shots were exchanged at Lexington, most of the other aspects of civil war were already apparent: Americans were excoriating each other with words, fists, and the tar brush, while by the end of 1774 effective government in nearly every colony was in the hands of revolutionaries. While we Americans might prefer to forget it, the fact is that our revolution included terrorism, ruthless suppression of dissent, and forced exile. The Tory exodus that later swelled to a torrent was, by the end of 1774, already a sizable freshet, including not only a hated royal governor, Thomas Hutchinson, but the brilliant young painter John Singleton Copley, and some fifty others.

I. THE WAR OF WORDS

The struggle for Americans' minds that had smoldered for at least a decade flared up with the Tea Act and blazed ever more brightly with fuel from the Coercive Acts, the First Continental Congress, and the Association. Broadsides, pamphlets, newspapers, pulpits, speakers' platforms, and mass meetings all helped to crystallize opinion on both sides.

The war of words never lacked for ammunition. There were approximately 500,000 literate adults in America in 1774. They were bombarded with hundreds of pamphlets, at least two thousand newspaper essays, and countless broadsides and handbills. Joseph Reed of Pennsylvania claimed that America was "a country where people more generally read, discuss, and judge for themselves, than perhaps any other in the world."

The patriot forces had a great advantage in numbers. Most printers were on their side, perhaps because they remembered that the abortive Stamp Act had been especially damaging to them. A majority of the Calvinist clergy in all regions, plus many of the Anglican clergy in the south, used their pulpits to support the patriot cause. Finally, the patriots seemed to have far greater numbers of eager pamphleteers, essayists, and speakers—possibly because Tories by their nature were not activists.

Nevertheless, the Tories had considerable resources. James Rivington's *New-York Gazetteer* had the biggest circulation of any American newspaper, and several Tory writers—especially a group of New York Anglican clergymen—were as able polemicists as any on the patriot side.

As literature, few if any of the propaganda pieces of 1774 bear comparison with such British writers as Swift and Defoe, who raised polemic to a high art, nor even with Tom Paine, who came to America in 1774 but did not begin his British-trained essay writing until after Lexington and Concord. Even the better known writers were not at the top of their literary form. John Adams's *Novanglus* is a lawyer's answer to another lawyer (Daniel Leonard's *Massachusettensis)*, and sounds like it. Thomas Jefferson's *Summary View* is, as Bernard Bailyn has pointed out, a very important political position paper; but it was got up in a hurry because Jefferson was too ill to attend the Virginia Convention and it lacks the polish of Jefferson's other pieces. Alexander Hamilton's *Farmer Refuted,* an answer to the Reverend Samuel Seabury's *Letters of a Westchester Farmer,* seems (not surprisingly, since Hamilton was about seventeen) slightly sophomoric.

The ventures into poetry were even worse. "A Poor Man's Advice to his Poor Neighbors" is amusing in small doses:

> Isn't it now a pretty story,
> One smells it in a trice,
> If I send wheat, I am a Tory,
> But Charles-town may send RICE.

Few, however, would care to plow through all eighty-two stanzas of this anti-Association doggerel.

The theme dominating both patriot and Tory writings is conspiracy: the patriots view with alarm the attempts of the ministry and Parliament to enslave them, while the Tories charge that the revolution is a plot for the advancement of a few avaricious men. Both sides were undoubtedly sincere, but neither paid too much attention to facts. General Gage did not exaggerate in the following report to Lord Dartmouth: "The People are told that the present Acts only lead to others which are to divide their Lands into Lordships, and tax them at so much Pr Acre; and the Quebec Bill has been made use of to perswade them that their Religion is to be changed, and they cannot be made to believe the contrary."

Both sides defended the legitimacy of their cause while attacking that of the other side. The patriots, appealing to nearly a century of Whiggish justifications of the Glorious Revolution, constantly pointed out that their rights as Englishmen were in jeopardy. Tories replied not only with their own interpretations of the same Whiggish doctrine, but with embarrassing reports of tar and feathers, smashed Tory printing presses, suspended courts, and repudiated debts.

One of the most common types of written propaganda was the "extract of a letter" printed in newspapers. These extracts were sometimes genuine, but obviously written to put across a particular point of view. Throughout 1774 the papers were filled with "letters from England" counseling the Americans to remain firm, for English public opinion was on their side and a show of unanimity was bound to force the ministry to its knees. Americans who believed this must have suffered a rude shock when they learned the results of the Parliamentary elections in the fall of 1774. Another theme common to essayists and letter writers was the military prowess of England and America. Tory writers, of course, stressed England's power. Some Tory writers took obvious relish in speculating about the fate awaiting any colonist who took arms against England. Patriot writers, on the other hand, stressed America's vast resources, military traditions, and marksmanship, along with England's distance from American shores.

The war of words did not confine itself to print; public speeches and sermons were just as ubiquitous. Unfortunately, most of these were not written down. For instance, we know that on March 23, 1775, Patrick Henry gave perhaps the most important and famous speech of his career, in support of his motion that Virginia "be immediately put into a state of defense." Over forty years later, Henry's biographer, William Wirt, reconstructed the speech with this magnificent peroration: "Is life so dear or peace so sweet as to be purchased at the price of chains and slavery? Forbid it, Almighty God—I know not what course others may take; but as for me, give me liberty or give me death!"

Henry may well have said something of the sort, but we will never know for certain; the only contemporary account is by James Parker, a Tory who was not the most accurate of observers: "You never heard anything more infamously insolent than P. Henry's speech: He called the K——a Tyrant, a fool, a puppet and a tool to the ministry. . . ."

We do, however, have a transcript of Dr. Joseph Warren's famous Massacre Day address (given on March 6 in 1775 because March 5 fell on a Sunday). The following excerpt will give some idea of the oratory of the time:

... bring in each hand thy infant children to bewail their father's fate—take heed, ye orphan babes, lest, whilst your streaming eyes are fixed upon the ghastly corpse, *your feet slide on the stones bespattered with your father's brains.* Enough! this tragedy need not be heightened by an infant weltering in the blood of him that gave it birth. ...

Sermons were perhaps more important than public addresses. Daniel Leonard observed in his *Massachusettensis* papers that

All our dissenting ministers were not inactive on this occasion. When the clergy engage in political warfare, religion becomes a most powerful engine, either to support or overthrow the state. What effect it must have had upon the audience to hear the same sentiments and principles, which they had before read in a newspaper, delivered on Sundays from the sacred desk, with religious awe, and the most solemn appeals to heaven, from lips which they had been taught, from their cradles, to believe could utter nothing but eternal truths?

Nicholas Cresswell, an Englishman recently come to Virginia to seek a fortune, testily recorded in his diary for November 6, 1774: "Went to a Presbyterian meeting. These are a set of rebellious scoundrels, nothing but political discourses instead of Religious Lectures." A week later, Cresswell again "Went to Church, but won't go any more to hear their Political Sermons."

Not all the political preachers were on the patriot side, however. The Reverend Jonathan Boucher, an Anglican minister in Maryland, delivered sermons that have been called "some of the finest propaganda of the period." Boucher, who was so conservative that he even eschewed Locke, preferring the divine right doctrine of the seventeenth century, was a very tough customer. He preached with a pair of loaded pistols beside him in the pulpit and once knocked out a blacksmith with his bare fists. Boucher later commented: "In America, as in the Grand Rebellion in England, much execution was done by sermons."

During the last half of 1774 and beginning of 1775, the war of words centered around the First Continental Congress. First, as we have seen, came the debate over whether to have a congress. Then, during the late summer, came a rash of advice to the delegates. The most famous of these was Thomas Jefferson's *Summary View of the Rights of British America,* which anticipated most of the charges he later brought in the Declaration of Independence. Other letters, essays and pamphlets promoted whatever their authors desired from the

Congress. Some called for immediate nonintercourse with Britain, while others counseled moderation. Thomas Mason, in the *Virginia Gazette,* proposed that the Continental Congress meet not in Philadelphia but in Frederick, Maryland, or Winchester, Virginia, "as no ships of war could bombard either of those towns, and the number of expert riflemen in those parts would be able to prevent any unwelcome visitors from interupting the Congress." After Congress met, it allowed selected resolutions, such as those supporting the Suffolk Resolves, to be published. But the biggest battles in the war of words came after Congress published its final resolutions, including the Continental Association.

The Association itself depended heavily upon the press. Article Eleven called for committees to be chosen "to observe the conduct of all persons touching this Association." Whenever a majority of a committee found a person in violation of the Association, it should "cause the truth of the case to be published in the Gazette, to the end that all such foes to the rights of *British America* may be publickly known, and universally contemned as the enemies of *American* Liberty; and thenceforth we respectively will break off all dealings with him or her."

The Association brough forth the most concerted—and probably most effective—efforts of the Tory pamphleteers. A common tactic was to question the very legitimacy of the Continental Congress, as Thomas Bradbury Chandler did in his *American Querist.* Chandler's one hundred questions (which Bernard Bailyn has noted "will exhaust the patience of any reader") stressed both constitutional and religious reasons for obedience to the mother country. Others used derision to attack Congress; for instance, many Tory essayists and versifiers referred to it as the "Congo." One of the more amusing pictures of Congress as a collection of bumpkins was the verse play, *A Dialogue, Between a Southern Delegate and his Spouse on his Return from the Grand Continental Congress.* The ablest Tory pamphleteer of all was Samuel Seabury, later to become the first Episcopal bishop of the United States. Seabury seemed to write with a perpetual sneer, as witness the well-known passage from *Free Thoughts on the Proceedings of the Congress* quoted at the beginning of this chapter.

The patriot writers were more than ready to spring to the defense of Congress and the Association. Writing as *Novanglus,* John Adams appealed to history and the English Constitution and threw the odium of change upon the Tories. Young Alexander Hamilton, answering Samuel Seabury, took both the conservative position that there was nothing "novel" about the actions of Congress, and the radical one that "the sacred rights of mankind are not to be rummaged for among old parchments or musty records. They are written, as with a sunbeam, in the whole *volume* of human nature, by the hand of divinity itself, and can never be erased or obscured by mortal power."

Perhaps few minds were changed by the plethora of words churned out by writers and speechmakers; but certainly all who read or listened were exposed to a very sophisticated knowledge of what the controversy was all about. In this sense, the American Revolution was both a popular and an intellectual movement, probably more so than any other event in our history.

But perhaps the most important function of the press was not in its presentation of the ideological debate, but simply in providing information. Everyone could read—or have read to him—the Boston Port Act; and in case he missed the point, it was usually printed with black borders. Resolutions of both Congress and local committees received wide circulation in newspapers, broadsides, and handbills. The patriots' version of important events, such as the battles of Lexington and Concord, always seemed to get into print long before the Tories'. Finally, the publication of Tories' names and misdeeds led to a kind of reign of terror that drove many of them underground or into exile even before warfare broke out in April 1775.

II. ENFORCING THE ASSOCIATION

The most revolutionary action taken by the First Continental Congress was its adoption of the Association. A body of no legal standing had acted as an American national legislature, not only setting up rules governing the economy, but providing enforcement machinery. From December 1, only a little over a month after Congress finished its work, no goods could be imported from Great Britain or Ireland, nor could the items taxed by the Sugar Act be imported from the British West Indies, Madeira, or the Western Isles. No slaves or tea could be brought in from anywhere. If any ships arrived in America with such goods between December 1, 1774, and February 1, 1775, they must be either reshipped immediately, stored for the duration of nonimportation, or sold at auction with all profits going to the relief of Boston. After February 1 they could not be brought in at all. Sheep were not to be exported, and slaughtered "as seldom as may be," in order to increase wool production. The people were to eschew "every species of extravagance and dissipation," including plays, gambling, horse racing, and excessive displays of mourning. Merchants with British goods already on hand were ordered not to raise their prices.

Congress put enforcement of the Continental Association in the hands of committees chosen by the eligible voters "of every county, city, and town."

The Alternative of Williams-Burg

Significantly, there was no provision requiring that the Association be ratified by the colonial legislatures. Some localities formed committees almost at once. Others waited for the endorsement of the legislature or provincial congress, while a few adopted the Association only after they were threatened with boycott by other localities. Committee members were chosen by regular elections, by mass meetings, and by conventions. In a sense, however, the enforcement machinery was not an innovation. Local committees had enforced nonimportation agreements during the Stamp Act, Townshend Act, and Tea Act crises. Indeed, many of the committees of "safety," "observation," or "inspection" set up to enforce the Association were simply the old Committees of Correspondence. As in the past, conservatives often sought election to the committees in order to control them; but the radicals had learned their lessons, and in several hitherto conservative localities, notably New York and Philadelphia, they succeeded in electing men committed to revolutionary measures.

As might be expected, acceptance of the Association followed much the same pattern as had resistance to the Port Act earlier in the year. New England, New Jersey, Delaware, Maryland, and Virginia, despite pockets of opposition, tended to adopt the Association early and enthusiastically. Georgia rejected it, leading radical St. John's Parish to try to secede and join South Carolina. South Carolina quickly approved and vigorously enforced the nonimportation sections of the Association; but there was a serious split between radicals and moderates over the nonexportation rules supposed to go into effect September 10, 1775. The radicals narrowly lost a vote to decline Congress's exemption of "rice to Europe," put in after the South Carolina delegation threatened to walk out of Congress. North Carolina was divided, with the tidewater accepting the Association and the old Regulator counties in the back country usually rejecting it. Pennsylvania generally supported the Association, in spite of opposition from the Society of Friends, conservative merchants, and the redoubtable Joseph Galloway, as well as private misgivings on the part of such patriots as John Dickinson and Joseph Reed. New York City enforced the Association, but most of the rest of the colony did not, and the New York legislature refused even to elect delegates to the Second Continental Congress.

Despite the widely varying degrees of acceptance, the Association proved to be quite effective. The key to its effectiveness was the fact that the cities controlled imports and distribution—and opposition to British policy had always been concentrated in the cities. Thus it made little difference that most of upstate New York and western Connecticut rejected the Association; as long as

New York City's mechanics supported it, it would be effective throughout the region. Philadelphia's and Charleston's mechanics played a similar role.

The enforcement procedures set up by Congress seem mild enough, on paper. If a majority of a local committee found anyone had violated the Association, it was to "cause the truth of the case to be published in the gazette; to the end that all such foes to the rights of British America may be publicly known, and universally condemned as the enemies of American liberty; and thenceforth we respectively will break off all dealings with him or her." As the anonymous author of *Political Observations, Without Order* put it, punishment did "not consist of the gallows, the rack, and the stake ... but INFAMY." Most localities drew up a covenant pledging obedience to the Association to be signed by all inhabitants. Significantly, the roster of those who refused to sign was often called the "rebel list."

Getting on this list, however, usually proved to be a very serious matter. One Maryland merchant who refused to sign found not only that he lost his customers, but that no one would even sell him food. Most merchants signed in order to keep their business, but those who stood on principle found they were in danger of losing more than their customers.

Most committees conducted their investigations of alleged violations in a quasi-judicial manner, often finding in favor of the accused. But the committees did not have a completely free hand, as witness the case of Robert Smyth, who returned to Charleston from England in March 1775. Could he land his furniture and two horses? The committee decided that he could by a vote of 17-16. But within a few days the committee received a petition, with more than 250 signatures, asking that it reconsider. It reconvened, this time with all seventy members present, and proceeded to debate the matter before a large crowd. Christopher Gadsden moved that the vote to allow landing the horses be rescinded. Thomas Lynch and both Rutledges argued that the spirit of the Association was not violated, and that the committee would bring itself into disrepute if it reversed its earlier ruling. William Drayton, hitherto a conservative, supported the radical Gadsden on the grounds that George III might just as logically refuse to alter Britain's course. Gadsden's motion passed by 35-34, and the horses presumably were banished. Drayton called this "the first instance of a point of importance and controversy being carried against those by whose opinion the people had been long governed."

Most cases taken up by the committees seem of very minor importance. Merchants were chastised for trying to sell a few pounds of tea; flocks of sheep were rescued just before being shipped off to the West Indies; a Maryland committee solemnly ruled that an imported tombstone must be broken up; salt carried as ballast had to be dumped overboard, rather than sold. The great and powerful had to conform, along with lesser men. Henry Laurens of Charleston reported that his daughter's "little Wax Toys were sentenced to the Ceremony" of being auctioned for the benefit of the Boston relief fund. The sumptuary regulations of the Association forced cancellation of horse races, a puppet show, and at least one gala ball. The fact that so much committee action was concerned with such trivial transgressions points up the fact that the Association was a decided success.

The most concerted effort to evade the Association's ban on imports came in New York, which had previously been controlled by conservatives. In November the old Committee of Fifty-one called for the election of ward committees, which would have insured that the Association would be lightly enforced indeed in parts of the city. The mechanics, however, forced a citywide election; and the new Committee of Sixty was thoroughly radical. By February 1, the committee had forced the auction of twenty-one cargoes, and the profit of £347 was by far the largest any committee turned over to the Boston relief fund. After February 1, the committee and its supporters forced three large vessels—the *Lady Gage,* the *Beulah,* and the *James*—to leave without breaking bulk. The *Beulah*'s owners then smuggled part of their cargo ashore, but were forced to round it up again and to subscribe £200 to a local hospital. Thus we have a mob defeating an attempt to smuggle on the part of supporters of the king, who were assisted by the Royal Navy vessel *Kings Fisher.* It was indeed "The World Turned Upside Down."

Lord Dunmore's report on the Association in Virginia would likely hold true for most of the other colonies as well: "the Laws of Congress . . . they talk of in a style of respect, and treat with marks of reverence, which they never bestowed on their legal Government, or the Laws proceeding from it." Dunmore complained that every county had its committee, which could "inspect the books, invoices, and all other secrets" of the merchants, "watch the conduct of every inhabitant," and "stigmatize" transgressors, "which stigmatizing is no other than inviting the vengeance of an outrageous and lawless mob." In Virginia, as in many other colonies, the mere threat of mob action was usually enough to make a merchant open his books. The patriots had ways of dealing with those who proved recalcitrant.

III. DEALING WITH THE TORIES

Throughout the Revolutionary period, Americans were ready to resort to terrorism when persuasion of a gentler nature did not work. Indeed, as scholars like Pauline Maier and George Rudé have shown, mob action was a political fact of life in both England and America throughout the eighteenth century. A mob destroyed Thomas Hutchinson's house during the Stamp Act crisis. Another man, who imprudently did business on stamped paper, found himself the object of the following resolutions by a mass meeting:

Vote 1. That this Man is not a Christian.
Vote 2. That he ought to be of some Religion.
Therefore, 3dly, Voted, That he be a Jew.
Whereupon, Resolved, That he be circumcised.

These resolutions had the desired effect: the culprit begged forgiveness, "upon which the Sentence was remitted." Other instances of mob action include the *Liberty* riot, the burning of the *Gaspee,* and, of course, the Boston Tea Party. And we have already seen how a Boston mob dealt with Captain John Malcom, a customs officer, in January 1774.

It is true that action against Tories more often took the form of humiliation than of violence, and that there was remarkably little bloodshed. Except for one customs informer, the only deaths in prewar colonial uprisings were of rioters themselves. (Pauline Maier, George Rudé, and G. Kitson Clark have all noted "the tendency of crowds in England and America to avoid bloodshed.") Some Tories, of course, escaped death or serious injury only through sheer luck; but the major reason for their relative safety from serious physical harm is that, at least through 1774, they were so small and discredited a minority that they could offer little resistance. Many of those who had second thoughts after Lexington and Concord or after the Declaration of Independence were, in 1774, at least passive supporters of resistance to the Coercive Acts.

Even before the First Continental Congress published the Association, local committees and less official bodies were in action, especially against tea importers and users. In January 1774 the students of Princeton confiscated all their masters' tea and burned it. In New Hampshire, a tea importer was allowed to reship his cargo in June, even though he had paid the duty on it; but when he tried it again in September, a mob assaulted his house. The most serious pre-Association incident took place in Annapolis in October.

The brig *Peggy Stewart* arrived in Annapolis on October 14 with more than a ton of tea consigned to the firm of T.C. Williams and Company. Her chief owner, Anthony Stewart, paid the duty on the tea after local customs officers refused to let him make a partial entry of the rest of *Peggy Stewart*'s cargo. The Anne Arundel County committee quickly called a public meeting, which unanimously resolved that the tea not be landed. Stewart agreed that he would either reship the tea or destroy it himself, and explained that he had paid the duty only because the ship was leaky and had to be entered before she could be repaired. This satisfied the committee, but on Wednesday, October 19, Stewart and the Williamses had to appear before a mass meeting to repeat their offer. The meeting, attended by people from all over eastern Maryland, voted that it would be satisfied if the tea were burned under the public gallows. A vociferous minority, however, would settle for nothing less than burning the ship with all her tackle and cargo. Stewart and his fellow owners were so frightened that, in spite of the vote in their favor, they acknowledged their "most daring insult" and personally put the torch to the *Peggy Stewart*. Not even a Boston mob had ever forced such a concession. A shaken Joseph Galloway wrote: "I think Sir I went to Annapolis yesterday to see my Liberty destroyed."

By the time the Association officially went into effect on December 1, those who had contemplated disobeying it already had a fair idea of the consequences. Nicholas Cresswell reported in October that merchants who sold tea or bought British goods had already been subjected to arson and tar and feathers. On November 1 Cresswell went to a tavern in Alexandria, Virginia, to hear the resolves of the Continental Congress. He thought them "insults to the understanding and dignity of the British Sovereign and people," but admitted to his diary that "I am obliged to act the hypocrit [sic] and extol these proceedings as the wisest productions of any assembly on Earth." Even in Philadelphia, in October merchants already predicted that Congress would adopt nonimportation, and "the mob here may enforce these measures among us peaceable folk." One merchant reported that "the language among some of the Heroes are, let any Man dare oppose or counteract the Decrees of the Congress, he ought to be forthwith say they treated as a Traitor and hang'd without Judge or Jury on the first high Tree."

Terrorism, of course, was only the last resort for enforcing the Association. Most people signed and obeyed it because they sincerely believed that it was an effective, peaceable means to make England change her policies, and a vast majority of Americans of every ideology wanted those policies changed. The group most immediately affected by the Association—the merchants—undoubtedly disliked having radical committees nosing into their business; but most of them signed it to avoid losing their customers. Furthermore, they had anticipated nonimportation and increased their orders for the summer of 1774. Imports of British goods during 1774 were higher than they had been for several years.

Peddlers—especially if they were also Scottish—were suspect everywhere. Many communities required that they have a certificate showing the origin of all their goods, while others banned them outright. Epsom, New Hampshire, resolved "That no Pedlars, Hawkers, or Petty-Chapmen shall be tolerated . . . upon no less penalty than receiving a new suit, agreeable to the modern mode, and a forfeiture of their Goods."

In some localities—especially in northern New York and western Connecticut—a Tory majority felt enough safety in numbers to ignore or reject outright the Association. A few of them even adopted the "Tory Association," drawn up by Brigadier Timothy Ruggles of Hardwick, Massachusetts. This "Association" bound its signers to mutual assistance against attack or harassment, rejected the authority of Congress and Committees of Correspondence, pledged loyalty to the king, threatened resistance and retaliation against all who should injure one of their number, and promised "That we will, upon all occasions, mutually support each other in the free exercise and enjoyment of our undoubted right to liberty, in eating, drinking, buying, selling, communing, and acting what, with whom, and as we please, consistent with the laws of *God* and the King." Richard Henry Lee wrote to Sam Adams: "I think a certain Mr. Ruggles with you, whose Body itches so much for the stroke of Knighthood, should be first stricken with rods, and then find his fate on the Tree where Traitors to their Country should all hang." Ruggles escaped the fate suggested by the fiery Virginian, but he did not get off unscathed. Long before he composed his "Tory Association," Ruggles's valuable stallion was poisoned and his house attacked. He was forced to flee to Boston, riding on a horse whose mane and tail had been bobbed and body covered with paint.

A number of inhabitants of Dutchess County, New York, actually adopted Ruggles's "Association," while Marshfield, Massachusetts, sought and received a detachment of a hundred redcoats in January 1775. In April General Gage had to pull his soldiers back to Boston, along with those inhabitants of Marshfield who did not dare stay behind. Barnstable, Massachusetts, and Ridgefield,

Connecticut, denounced the Association. In February 1775 two inhabitants of Ridgefield made the mistake of supporting their town's stand in a Wethersfield tavern. "A number of gentlemen present" voted that they be escorted back to Ridgefield in the manner "as by law is provided, in cases of strolling ideots, lunaticks, &c." Soon after April 19, Ridgefield and the other Tory towns of western Connecticut were disarmed.

Actual violence seems to have been little used to enforce the Association. Many violators found their names on "rebel lists," and some found their doorways smeared with excrement, called "Hillsborough paint" by the patriots. In most cases that was enough to bring a quick apology because, outside of a few communities, the Tories were literally defenseless. Almost all of the British Army was tied up in Boston, and local peace officers were either on the patriot side or as helpless, in the face of overwhelming public opinion, as the Tories they might have protected.

Specific instances of terrorism are hard to find. The patriots' near-monopoly of the press kept them from being publicized, and American historians have so far shown little inclination to dig deeply into this unsavory aspect of our revolution. Probably rumors of violence and the fear of what *might* happen were enough to keep most Tories from being openly defiant. But there are enough recorded instances of actual terrorism to prove that the Tories were not unnaturally timid.

The most serious cases of anti-Tory violence had little to do with enforcing the Association. Indeed, many of them took place in August and September, long before it was even written. Most of them occurred in Massachusetts and Connecticut, the two colonies most immediately threatened by British rule. Their purpose was to silence known supporters of the Coercive Acts, especially the Massachusetts Government Act.

By Parliamentary fiat, the Government Act changed the whole system of government and justice in Massachusetts. Every part of Massachusetts was affected by the act, whether or not it had previously opposed British authority. Connecticut was not covered by the act but, as General Gage reported, it was as opposed to it as Massachusetts was, because its citizens knew the precedent of parliamentary tampering could easily be applied to the Connecticut charter, as well. The two colonies were virtually in a state of rebellion from August 1 on. They simply could not allow courts to open, the new Mandamus Council to function, or militia officers to exercise their commissions from the governor.

The first moves against the courts came in western Massachusetts, hitherto relatively quiet. On August 2 the Berkshire County Court attempted to hold its regular session in Great Barrington. But a crowd that included 1,200 Massachusetts men, plus 300 more from Litchfield County, Connecticut, halted the proceedings. Although the judges assured them that they had not been instructed "to act under the new regulations appointed by the Parliament of *Great Britain,*" the crowd "required they quitted the town immediately, which was complied with." The Connecticut men discovered an old enemy, David Ingersoll, who had moved to Great Barrington. They hauled him back to Canaan and kept him prisoner for twelve hours.

On August 30 a crowd of "about three thousand" not only forced the county court in Springfield, Massachusetts, to close, it also made all the judges sign a promise never to act under the authority of the Massachusetts Government Act. On the same day, the Superior Court opened in Boston, under the protection of Gage's troops; but as no juror would take the oath, no business could be done.

General Gage considered sending troops to protect the courts in Worcester and other counties, but quickly reconsidered when he realized that such a move would bring open warfare. Nearly 5,000 men, many of them armed, showed up for the scheduled September session of the Worcester County court. They forced all the judges, sheriffs, and lawyers to pass between two files of grim-faced patriots, hats in hand, reading over and over their "disavowal of holding Courts under the new Acts of Parliament." As General Gage told Lord Dartmouth on September 2, the courts were "expiring one after another." They did not open again under British rule.

Mobs paid special attention to the "mandamus councilors," the cream of Massachusetts loyalism. Under the Massachusetts Government Act, the old elected Council was dissolved on August 1, to be replaced by thirty-six royal appointees that Gage called "as respectable Persons as any in the Province." Twenty-four of them accepted and were sworn in on August 8 and August 16. Of the other twelve, one was dead, two had left the province, and eight were wise enough to refuse, though several of them, including Israel Williams, William Vassal, and John Worthington, were encouraged in their refusal by visits from large numbers of outraged patriots.

Those who had accepted appointment to the Council felt the full brunt of the patriots' fury. Ten of them resigned, and all the rest who lived outside of Boston had to flee to the protection of Gage's troops in the city, for Gage knew that any soldiers he sent to support them would probably be massacred. Abijah Willard found that even being outside Massachusetts was no protection. He went to Union, Connecticut, to attend to a lawsuit; but his attorneys dropped his case, a mob seized him, and he was condemned to imprisonment in Simsbury's notorious salt mine. This moved Willard to sign a confession that he had taken the councilor's oath "without due consideration." He promised never to "sit or act in the said Council," and asked "the forgiveness of all honest, worthy gentlemen I have offended" by taking the oath. The mob let Willard go, but one of his supporters, a Captain Davis, was not so lucky. For "treating the people with bad language," Davis "was stripped, and honoured with the new fashion dress of tar and feathers; a proof this, *that the Act for tarring and feathering is not repealed!*"

The day after Willard's ordeal, another mob warned Brigadier Timothy Ruggles to leave Bristol County. Ruggles promised to do so, but he did not resign from the Council, and later raised a loyalist regiment, the King's American Dragoons. On August 27, 2,000 armed men, led by militia officers, assembled on Worcester Common. After extracting a resignation and apology from Timothy Paine, they marched off to Rutland and repeated the performance with John Murray. Israel Williams never accepted his appointment to the Council, but he continued to support royal government. In February 1775 a number of his Hatfield neighbors locked him in a room, covered the chimney, and smoked him all night.

Gage reported, with little exaggeration, that the councilors suffered "daily Threats of Plunder, Devastation, and Ruin, and even of Assassination." No councilor, however, suffered much physical harm, possibly because the mob retained a subconscious awe of men who had been community leaders for so long, but more likely because most of the councilors either resigned or fled to Boston with little resistance. Still, many of them had shots fired into their houses, their animals poisoned, their families terrorized. And the mob was not so tender with those of a less exalted rank who, like Captain Davis, supported the councilors. Even doing business with a councilor was dangerous. One Jesse Dunbar of Halifax purchased some beef cattle from Councilor Nathaniel Rae Thomas. A Plymouth mob stuffed Dunbar into the belly of one of the slaughtered steers and carted him to Kingston and Duxbury before they let him go. Thomas resigned.

One of the favored punishments for Tories made use of the rail fences that were until this century common to the American landscape. Split rails are both sharp-edged and splintery. Daniel Dunbar, a militia officer who refused to resign his commission from the governor, was attended to by a mob that included some of the Halifax selectmen. "They broke into his house, took him out, forced him upon a rail, and was held on it by his hands and legs, and tossed up with violence; in resisting, when they attempted to put him on the rail, they seized him by his

The Bostonian's Paying the Excise-Man

private parts to drag him on it, then beat him." A Dr. Clarke of Reading, Connecticut, "whose only crime was speaking in terms of respect of the king, and of his government," was seized by a Hartford mob. While the local authorities ignored the spectacle, he was "carried upon a rail about the parish, · under which cruelty he several times fainted. When dismissed by his tormentors, and examined by Dr. Tidmarsh, he was found to be injured in a manner unfit for description. The doctor was menaced with the same treatment for his humanity to the sufferer."

Considering the barbarity of riding on a rail, one may wonder why Tories feared even more the "modern punishment," tar and feathers. According to the staunch Tory Peter Oliver, the victim was stripped, coated with pine tar, rolled in feathers, then a candle applied to the feathers; and if they caught fire, "so much the better." One can well imagine why such an incendiary mixture would strike fear into Tories' hearts, although there is no recorded case of one of them actually being immolated.

Nor were women exempt from the tar brush. A Concord woman was warned out of town under pain of tarring and feathering for the "crime" of giving directions to two British officers in March 1775. There was a great deal of curiosity about the practice in England. Even King George III mentioned it. He said to Thomas Hutchinson, "I see they threatened to pitch and feather you." "Tar and feather, may it please Your Majesty," Hutchinson replied, "but I don't remember that ever I was threatened with it."

Most of the cases mentioned here were published in the *Boston News-Letter* in February 1775. Peter Oliver copied them for his *Origin & Progress of the American Rebellion*, with the comment that they all took place well before Lexington, "when the Rebels say that the War began." Little wonder that by the end of 1774 many Tories, such as the tea consignee Richard Clark and Essex County Sheriff Richard Saltonstall, had abandoned their estates and fled to Boston, or that John Singleton Copley had already left for England. Nor is it any wonder that General Gage could get replacements for his Council only after promising the nominees that he would keep the honor secret.

IV. THE END OF BRITISH GOVERNMENT

By the end of 1774, only three lawful British governments remained in control of their provinces—and two of these, the charter colonies of Connecticut and Rhode Island—were among the most radical of all. Only in Georgia was royal government functioning with a semblance of normality. In New York, Acting Governor Cadwallader Colden and a conservative legislature appeared to be in control, but the appearance was misleading, for New York City was in radical hands, and a few days after Lexington New York's royal government simply collapsed. In the other nine colonies, hardly a semblance of legal government remained. The legislatures were either dissolved or acting at the direction of extralegal provincial congresses. But America was not in a state of anarchy; revolutionary governments were already functioning in most colonies.

The most revolutionary activity was, of course, in Massachusetts. As governor, General Thomas Gage tried to carry out his instructions. In June he removed the seat of government from Boston to Salem. After he finally received instructions on August 6, Gage implemented the Massachusetts Government Act by forbidding town meetings and appointing a new Council. But Gage had already effectively ceased to be governor when he dissolved the Massachusetts legislature on June 17, the day it chose delegates to the Continental Congress.

The new Mandamus Council, which was supposed to restore "the peace and good order" of the province, proved to be a very weak reed. Its members refused to convene in Salem, for fear "they shou'd be watched, stopped, and insulted on the Road." They begged Gage not to send any of his troops outside of Boston, for fear that they would not be safe even there. When Gage warned the Boston selectmen not to call a town meeting, they replied that they did not have to, since the town could simply meet by adjournment of the last town meeting before the Government Act went into effect. When Gage presented this bit of Yankee legalism to his councilors, they refused to advise him,"terming it a Point of Law which ought to be referred to the Crown Lawyers." And Thomas Gage was never a man to take independent action.

In the meantime, Gage found that not even a show of military force could prevent a town meeting. The Salem Committee of Correspondence called a town meeting for August 24 to elect delegates to the Essex County Convention. Gage threatened to send troops to break it up, and a detachment of eighty redcoats with loaded muskets actually advanced to within a furlong of the Salem town house. But the meeting called Gage's bluff, and elected six delegates before it adjourned. Meanwhile, Marblehead sent word to her sister town that she would send armed men to her aid "at a minute's warning" if the troops used force.

Gage himself left Salem for the last time on August 27, and on September 10 all the troops he had stationed there marched back to Boston, leaving high and dry all the local Tories who had so effusively welcomed Gage in early June. Less than four months after Gage became Governor in Chief of Massachusetts Bay, his effective control of the colony extended no farther than Boston Neck.

While Gage was losing control, revolutionary bodies were assuming it. The first county convention met in Stockbridge, Berkshire County, on July 6 to adopt a covenant not to use British imports. Other county meetings held in late August and September were far more radical. On August 26 and August 27 the Committees of Correspondence of Worcester, Middlesex, Essex, and Suffolk counties met in Boston to draw up an agenda for future county conventions. This meeting warned that the courts must be closed, and any court officer trying to exercise authority under the Massachusetts Government Act would be considered a traitor. It implicitly sanctioned violence against the mandamus councilors. It encouraged the people to study "the Military Art according to the Norfolk Plan" of drill, and asked all towns to withhold their taxes from the provincial treasurer. Finally, it called for a provincial congress to meet at Concord in October.

Although only four counties were represented at the Boston meeting, the nine county conventions held subsequently all adopted most of its recommendations. We have seen their effect on the courts. In addition, several county conventions "took notice of" individuals who had pledged their support of Governor Gage. Most of these found it wise to ask forgiveness. The most important county convention, of course, was in Suffolk, whose resolves forced the Continental Congress to take a radical stance.

The last act in the ending of British rule in Massachusetts came when the First Provincial Congress convened. General Gage had issued precepts for a meeting of the legislature in Salem on October 5, but then changed his mind and called it off. Upon the slender legal pretext that the governor could not dissolve the legislature before it sat, ninety representatives assembled at the appointed time in Salem. When Gage did not appear to open the session, they resolved themselves into a provincial congress and adjourned to Concord on October 12. From that time until the 1691 Charter was resumed in July 1775, the three successive provincial congresses were the de facto government of all Massachusetts outside of Boston. By this coup d'etat Massachusetts, in effect, completed her revolution. The War for Independence came when Gage tried to reestablish British rule.

CHAPTER VIII

The Coming of the War

Your Lordship's Idea of disarming certain Provinces would
doubtless be consistent with Prudence and Safety, but it
neither is nor has been practicable without having Recourse
to Force, and being Masters of the Country.
                    —Gage to Dartmouth, December 15, 1774

The King's Dignity, & the Honour and Safety of the
Empire, require, that, in such a Situation, Force should be
repelled by Force.
                    —Dartmouth to Gage, January 27, 1775

We are at our wit's end—which was no great journey.
                    —Horace Walpole, December 15, 1774

The first battles of the War for American Independence took place on April
19, 1775, but who can say when the war actually began? For more than seven
months, both British and American troops had been in action, capturing each
other's war materiel. On February 9 Parliament resolved that "a rebellion at this

[167]

time actually exists," an opinion already long held by both King George III and General Thomas Gage. Like most other civil wars, our own War for Independence was well under way before the participants realized it.

I. THE VIEW FROM ENGLAND

During the summer of 1774, the British government entertained fond hopes that the Coercive Acts and a minimum show of military force in Boston would solve the American problem, and the optimistic letters Thomas Gage wrote during the first two months of his governorship reinforced this confident mood. Even news that a continental congress would meet to consider a united response to the Coercive Acts did little to disturb England's euphoria. Colonial Secretary Lord Dartmouth said the Congress was "undoubtedly illegal," but "some good may arise out of it." If Congress should help cool things off, said Dartmouth, "I should in my own opinion think it wise to overlook the irregularity of the proceedings." Thomas Hutchinson, now in England, wrote to his son that "nobody seems to give themselves the least concern about the consequences of the projected Congress, supposing it can do no hurt to the Kingdom." Even that indefatigable gossip Horace Walpole complained in September that "This season has been singularly barren," and rather hoped for gloomy news from America to liven things up.

Only George III seemed immune to the languid mood. On September 11, in a heated reaction to a letter from some American Quakers suggesting British concessions, the king told Lord North: "The dye is now cast, and the colonies must either submit or triumph; I do not wish to come to severer measures but we must not retreat; by coolness and an unremitted pursuit of the measures that have been adopted I trust they will come to submit." The king did not object to telling the colonists that "for the present" no new taxes would be levied on them, but "there must always be one tax to keep up the right, and as such I approve of the tea duty."

On June 22, the day he signed the Quebec Act, the king prorogued Parliament for the summer. Parliamentary elections were not due until March 1775, but in August, partly to take advantage of favorable public reaction to the Coercive Acts, the king decided to dissolve Parliament and hold elections six months early. Both his own ministry and the opposition were taken by surprise, although news of the move leaked out well before Parliament was formally dissolved. The timorous North was sure the government would lose seats, but the king proved to be the wiser politician. The opposition, never united, was in a shambles. Neither the Rockinghamites nor Lord Chatham's followers could begin to compete with the £50,000 in campaign funds the government distributed to its friends. The Coercive Acts were not a major issue, for opposition to them was concentrated in the cities, where most of the lower classes could not vote. The supporters of America, derisively called "patriots," had little success, although John Wilkes did win a seat. By the middle of November, North could tell the king that the government had a safe majority.

In the middle of the election campaign, news from America turned decidedly sour. On October 1 the ministry received two letters from General Gage. The first, from Salem, dated August 27, told of defiance of his orders not to hold town meetings, terrorism against the mandamus councilors, and the spread of rebellion to Connecticut and western Massachusetts, where there were open preparations for war and threats to attack Gage's troops. The second, written from Boston on September 2, said that "Tho' I saw Things were bad when I wrote from Salem, I found them much worse than I expected when I arrived here." Those councilors who had not resigned and would still give him advice told Gage "that the whole was now at Stake, Connecticut, and they add Rhode Island, are as furious as they are in this Province, and that the first and only Step now to take was to secure the Friends of Government in Boston, and to reinforce the Troops here with as many more as cou'd possibly be collected." Civil government was near an end, courts closing. Gage faced not a "Boston Rabble" but an armed and angry countryside. Letters from Admiral Samuel Graves were just as somber. Both Gage and Graves begged for reinforcements.

The cabinet ministers seemed more irritated with Gage for sending bad news than ready to send him aid. They took time off from the election campaign to decide that no troops could be sent so late in the year, but they did order three ships of the line—the *Scarborough*, the *Asia*, and the *Boyne*—"with as many Marines from the several quarters as can possibly be spared," to depart for Boston forthwith.

On October 28 England learned that Congress had adopted the Suffolk Resolves, and ten days later came news that Congress had asked merchants to suspend orders of English goods. Clearly, the ministry's hopes that Congress would be a moderating influence were for naught. Yet it did nothing, waiting to learn the final resolves, probably because a spy within Congress was sending reports of dissension in its secret debates.

In the meantime, Gage was becoming more and more desperate. On September 25 he told Dartmouth that the New Englanders were drilling and collecting arms and ammunition; "Nothing less than the Conquest of almost all

[169]

the New England Provinces will procure Obedience to the late Acts of Parliament." Furthermore, New England had "warm friends" in New York and Philadelphia, and "the People of Charles Town are as mad as they are here." On the same day, Gage wrote privately to his predecessor, Thomas Hutchinson, that the wisest policy would be to suspend the Coercive Acts for a while, and in the meantime to hire Hessians and Hanoverians for a "powerful force" that could totally subdue the rebellious provinces.

Gage's accurate estimate of the situation made him no friends in the British government. North insisted that "the Acts must and should be carried into execution," and the king called Gage's idea of suspending the acts "the most absurd that can be suggested. . . . We must either master them or totally leave them to themselves and treat them as aliens." Even the news of Congress's radical resolutions, which finally arrived in the middle of December, did little to make the ministry realize that Gage was right. Horace Walpole sardonically commented, "We are at our wit's end—which was no great journey. . . . We have thrown a pebble at a mastiff, and are surprised it was not frightened." At first the ministers tried to replace Gage with Sir Jeffrey Amherst, who flatly turned them down. Gage demanded 20,000 troops; the government finally sent him, late in April, only 2,000. But it did provide him with three major generals—John Burgoyne, Sir Henry Clinton, and William Howe—who were supposed to prod him into action.

Meanwhile Lord Dartmouth clung to the hope that he might negotiate peace without giving in to the colonists' demands. He turned to the discredited Benjamin Franklin, whom the ministry still thought to be the prime mover of the rebellion. Dartmouth could not approach Franklin directly, but through an extremely involved process he arranged for two of his Quaker friends, Dr. John Fothergill and David Barclay, to ask Franklin what the Americans would settle for. They thought Franklin might already have terms to present. Franklin had not yet seen the resolves of Congress, but he knew things had gone too far for any compromise acceptable to either side. Nevertheless, he agreed to draw up "Hints for Conversations upon the Subject of Terms that may probably produce a *Durable* union between Great Britain and her Colonies."

Franklin's "Hints" virtually demanded recognition of home rule for the colonies. The one concession he made was that the East India Company should be paid for its lost tea, since "the dignity of Britain required it." But the Tea Act must be repealed and all duties previously collected on tea repaid to the colonies. The Trade and Navigation Laws would be valid only if reenacted by the colonial legislatures, and the duties from them must go into the colonial

[170]

treasuries. Customs officers must be appointed by the colonial governors. America would maintain her own military establishment, while Britain would return Castle William to Massachusetts and build no more fortresses in the province without her legislature's consent. No requisitions could be made on the colonies in peacetime, and in wartime only by an established formula. Governors' and judges' salaries must be paid by their colonial legislatures. Judges must serve during good behavior, not during the king's pleasure. Vice-admiralty courts in America were to lose their jurisdiction over revenue cases. The threat to try American radicals under the treason act of Henry VIII must be "formally disowned by Parliament." All the Coercive Acts and, in effect, the Declaratory Act must be repealed. Parliament must disclaim all powers of internal legislation for the colonies.

Franklin certainly knew that the ministry would find his "Hints" utterly unacceptable, especially when they turned out to be quite similar to the demands made by Congress. The old man must have felt bitter amusement when Barclay and Fothergill, later joined by Admiral Lord Howe, revealed their continuing delusion that Franklin controlled the revolutionary movement by trying to bribe him into lowering his terms.

Negotiation was, in fact, impossible. Already, on November 18, the king had told Lord North that "the New England Governments are in a State of Rebellion, blows must decide whether they are to be subject to this Country or independent." Dartmouth's idea of sending commissioners to bargain with the Americans got short shrift from both his fellow cabinet ministers and the king. And in Parliament, all attempts to conciliate the Americans lost by huge majorities.

The king opened Parliament on November 30 with a speech noting "fresh violences of a very criminal nature" in Massachusetts and promising continued vigorous enforcement of the Coercive Acts. The House of Commons overwhelmingly promised to support the king in any action he chose to take in the colonies. The only concession the opposition could wring from Lord North was his promise to present American papers when Parliament returned from the Christmas holiday. North laid 149 documents before Parliament on January 19, but he left out most of Gage's pessimistic reports. The papers included Congress's "Petition to the King," but Commons denied the colonial agents' requests to speak in its favor.

While the Commons considered the American papers, the House of Lords heard an impassioned plea for reconciliation from Lord Chatham. On January 20 Chatham presented a motion to withdraw all British troops from Boston. The

The Council of the Rulers, and the Elders against the Tribe of yᵉ Americanites

earl of Suffolk, answering for the cabinet, declared "the ministerial resolution of enforcing obedience by arms." Chatham's motion lost 68-18, but on February 1 he presented ten additional proposals under the title of "A Provisional Act for settling the troubles in America."

Chatham's plan bore some resemblance to Benjamin Franklin's "Hints." The earl of Sandwich, in fact, told the House of Lords that Franklin was the author. But although Chatham had talked to Franklin, the plan was undoubtedly his own. While it made many concessions to the Americans, including repeal of the Sugar Act, the tea tax, and the Coercive Acts, it still left the Americans a great deal less than equal partners in the empire. Dartmouth thought the plan ought at least to be considered, but his fellow cabinet ministers roundly denounced it. The plan was rejected 61-32, the most votes the friends of America ever managed to muster in Lords, but still an overwhelming defeat for Chatham and conciliation. It is doubtful that even Chatham thought it had a serious chance of passing; and, given the resolves of Congress, it is almost as unlikely that the Americans would have accepted it, either.

America's friends had no better luck in the House of Commons, in spite of valient efforts by Charles James Fox, David Hartley, Colonel Isaac Barre, and John Wilkes. And on March 22 Edmund Burke pleaded for conciliation in perhaps the greatest speech of his illustrious career. For nearly three hours, while all sides listened appreciatively to his masterful performance, Burke argued that the government's measures would harm the whole empire. He presented thirteen resolutions that answered many—though by no means all—of America's demands. Burke sat down to "the loudest, the most unanimous and highest strains of applause." Then the House defeated his proposals, 270-78.

The North ministry probably had most English public opinion on its side. It is true that a number of shipping and manufacturing centers—including London, Bristol, Norwich, Wolverhampton, Liverpool, Manchester, and eight towns of Staffordshire—all petitioned for a quick settlement with the Americans because nonimportation had already caused massive unemployment. Many other towns and country districts, however, demanded that America be punished. Horace Walpole told Sir Horace Mann that "the town of Birmingham has petitioned the Parliament to enforce the American Acts, that is, make war; for they have a manufacture of swords and muskets. I believe the Dutch will petition too, for much such a reason!"

Lord North helped mold public opinion by financing a formidable propaganda effort. Among his hired pens was Boston's old enemy, John Mein, who, as "Sagittarius," titlilated British readers with descriptions of Benjamin Franklin as an "old factious agent, who vomits out his venom in the newspapers," and John Hancock as both lecherous and impotent. Dr. Samuel Johnson rented his famous pen to the government in a pamphlet, *Taxation No Tyranny*. Johnson argued, among other things, that the colonists' claim that they could not be taxed because they were not represented in Parliament was patently ridiculous. If they were serious, said Johnson, they would have purchased seats in Parliament like the West Indians did! Horace Walpole, on February 15, marveled that "The war with our colonies, which is now declared, is a proof how much influence jargon has on human actions. A war on our own trade is *popular!* Both Houses are as eager for it as they were for conquering the Indies."

The government made only one gesture toward conciliation, and that was transparently fraudulent. On February 20, North offered to exempt from parliamentary taxation any colony whose legislature would agree to pay for civil government and meet *any* demands from Parliament for money for the common defense. Futhermore, he offered a royal pardon to all Massachusetts rebels who would, within a month, take an oath to obey all the acts of Parliament. North's "conciliation" offered American terms little short of unconditional surrender.

By overwhelming majorities, Parliament endorsed the ministry's decision to force the Americans into submission. On February 9 both houses presented an address to the king that declared "that a rebellion at this time actually exists" in Massachusetts, "countenanced and encouraged by unlawful combinations entered into by your Majesty's subjects in several of the other Colonies." Within the next week, North presented bills to increase the size of the army and navy and "to Restrain the Trade and Commerce" of all New England.

The Restraining Act was Britain's reply to the Continental Association. The Association sought to end all trade with Great Britain, Ireland, and the West Indies. The Restraining Act forbade the colonies of Massachusetts, New Hampshire, Connecticut, and Rhode Island to trade with anyone *but* Great Britain, Ireland, and the West Indies—not even with each other or the other British colonies. Furthermore, the act forbade ships of the four colonies to fish anywhere in North American waters. In vain did the opposition denounce this "attempt to coerce by famine the whole body of great and populous Provinces . . . without precedent in the history of this, or perhaps of any civilized nation." A month later, a second Restraining Act extended the same trade prohibition to New Jersey, Pennsylvania (including Delaware), Maryland, Virginia, and South Carolina. Only New York and North Carolina were exempted, in recognition of the considerable opposition to the Association in those colonies.

[174]

Parliament adjourned for Easter on April 13. When it returned twelve days later, England and America were openly at war.

II. MILITARY BACKGROUND

A major reason for the British government's willingness for armed confrontation with the colonists, while at the same time denying General Gage anything like enough troops to insure success, is that it had a very low opinion of the Americans' fighting qualities. And, in truth, during the past three decades the Americans had done very little to give any other impression.

During the first century of settlement, every colonist had to be a part-time soldier. During the first three French and Indian Wars, the colonists had to do most of the North American fighting. Amateur American armies twice captured the French citadel at Port Royal, and in 1745, against seemingly impossible odds, a New England expedition took the "Gibraltar of North America," Louisbourg.

Americans cherished the memory of such exploits, but, as the country became more settled and the frontier more distant, they began to take military training far less seriously. The last of the French and Indian Wars began in 1754 when Virginia militiamen under twenty-two year old Major George Washington defeated a French and Indian force at Great Meadows, near the forks of the Ohio River, but then surrendered to a much larger one at Fort Necessity. Thereafter, most of the French and Indian War was fought by professional soldiers from Great Britain.

At least 7,500 Americans served in the French and Indian War, but they were a far different lot than their countrymen in the earlier wars. The American armies in those wars were made up of men drafted from the regular militia. Fighting, as John Shy has pointed out, was a "community function." But the Americans who served in the French and Indian War were volunteers, recruited largely from the very classes that were excluded from regular militia drill: servants and apprentices, free Negroes and mulattoes, vagabonds and adventurers with no community ties. They were attracted by large bounties paid by England, escape, and "the assurance of easy discipline." Shy has said that "the colonial volunteers of the eighteenth century had more in common with the pitiable recruits of the contemporary European armies than with the militia levies of an earlier period."

British officers were almost universally disgusted with the quality of American

Lord Sandwich

soldiers. General James Abercromby called them "the rif-raf of the continent." A colonel described an American camp at Lake George in 1756 as "nastier than anything I could conceive, their necessary houses, kitchens, graves and places for slaughtering cattle, all mixed through their encampment." General James Wolfe called the provincial troops "the dirtiest, most contemptible, cowardly dogs you can conceive. There is no depending on them in action."

Stories like this still prevailed when Parliament debated America's fate in 1775. A Colonel Grant, who had served in the colonies, told the Commons that Americans "would never dare to face an *English* Army, and did not possess any of the qualifications necessary to make a good soldier." During the debate over the Restraining Act, when Lord Camden claimed that a military conquest of America was impossible, Lord Sandwich replied:

> I cannot think the noble Lord can be serious on this matter. Suppose the Colonies do abound in men, what does that signify? . . . Believe me, my Lords, the very sound of a cannon would carry them off . . . as fast as their feet could carry them.

Not everyone who had served in America agreed with this view. Colonel Isaac Barré had been warning that Americans would fight ever since 1765. Another officer who never disparaged the Americans' fighting qualities was General Thomas Gage, who knew he owed his own life to the bravery of the Virginia militia during Braddock's Defeat. But even Gage underestimated American leadership and discipline. In March 1775 he told Dartmouth that "there is not a man amongst [them] capable of taking command or directing the motions of any Army. A regular encampment seems abhorrent to the genius and inclination of the People, much more is to be apprehended from their patience and cunning, in forming ambushments." Three months later, after Bunker Hill, Gage remarked that "In all their Wars against the French, they never Shewed so much Conduct Attention and Perseverance as they do now."

All the colonies still had militia laws which required all able-bodied men to keep arms and attend drills; but in many towns the requirement was simply ignored. By the late 1760s, the militia in most of the settled areas was more a social than a military institution. One of the status symbols of colonial America was a militia commission, and an enormous number of colonial politicians preferred to be addressed by their military title. Young blades who liked to dress up in uniform eagerly sought membership in elite companies, such as Colonel John Hancock's Boston Corps of Cadets, the governor's honor guard. But most militia drills were pretty disgraceful, and regimental Muster Day was commonly the scene of a good deal of horseplay. A favorite prank was to fire a blank charge at an officer's feet or at spectators, especially ladies. A bit of tangle-footed drill, interrupted by a long lunch, was usually followed by a good drunk.

But while Americans never cared much for formal drill, most of them fancied themselves as experts with guns. In a population that was 90 percent rural, most families had a real need for a gun, and hunting was a common pastime. So was bragging about marksmanship. John Andrews told his bother-in-law in Philadelphia about how a "countryman" watched with amused scorn while a whole regiment of British soldiers missed a floating target in the Back Bay. Irritated, they challenged him to do better; and with a borrowed musket, he hit the mark three times running. "I'll tell you *naow,*" he told the astonished redcoats, "I have got a boy at home that will toss up an apple and shoot out all the seeds as it's coming down."

Richard Henry Lee boasted that Virginia's frontier counties could supply 6,000 experts with the "rifle gun," not one of whom would "wish a distance of less than 200 yards or a larger object than an orange. Every shot is fatal." John Harrower, an indentured servant in Virginia, told of Washington's trying to pare down to 500 a huge number of volunteers by holding a shooting contest at 150 yards; but nearly everyone hit the mark, "the shape of a moderate nose." James Madison, then in his ascetic period, was far more modest: he claimed only that he could hit a man's face at a hundred yards.

Even General Gage was not immune to inflated claims of American marksmanship. On March 4, 1775, he told Lord Dartmouth: "The most natural and most eligible mode of attack on the part of the people is that of detached parties of Bushmen who from their adroitness in the habitual use of the Firelock suppose themselves sure of their mark at a distance of 200 rods." One assumes he meant "yards" rather than "rods," but even if he meant to say "200 feet," he was giving the New Englanders the benefit of the doubt.

The standard weapon of both Gage's army and the New England militia was the .75 caliber, flintlock, smoothbore musket. Major George Hanger, who served with the British army during the War for Independence, claimed that "A soldier's musket, if not exceedingly ill-bored (as many of them are)" could hit a man at eighty yards and sometimes a hundred, but "I do maintain and will prove, whenever called on, that no man was ever killed at 200 yards, by a common soldier's musket, by the person who aimed at him."

Of course, Virginia and Pennsylvania frontiersmen armed with the "Kentucky" long rifle could hit a stationary man (though not an orange or a moderate nose) at 200 yards. But rifles were too slow loading, threw too light a ball, and could not mount a bayonet. During the revolution neither side used them for much except snipers' weapons. Besides, there is no indication that the New Englanders possessed a single rifle in 1775. The Yankee farmers with their smoothbores took a fearful toll of the British troops retreating from Concord; but, considering the number of rounds they fired at a massed column, if they had been half as good shots as they claimed, no redcoat would have survived.

Americans' familiarity with firearms was a decided asset, and after news of the Boston Port Act arrived, they took military training far more seriously. Many of their officers and noncoms had served in the French and Indian Wars. In addition, dozens of British soldiers deserted Gage's army, and they lent their military know-how to their adopted country. By midsummer of 1774, many companies were drilling at least twice a week. Even Lord Percy, who thought the New Englanders "the most designing artful villains in the world," who were never known to behave decently in the field, had to admit they "do not make a despicable *appearance* as soldiers."

Above all, the Americans had enthusiasm. In fact, not only in New England but in the south, the revolutionary leadership had a real problem in keeping the common folk from marching off to Boston to do battle before they were ready. Several times before Lexington, thousands of New Englanders took up arms because of false alarms. Gage's letters, considered hysterical by his government, were, if anything, understated. His aide, General Frederick Haldimand, believed the New England colonies could put 30,000 men in the field without seriously hurting the economy, and at least two-thirds that number besieged Boston the day after Lexington and Concord. At the time, the whole British army numbered fewer than 50,000 men. With little exaggeration, Horace Walpole said America "can find a troop as easily as we a trooper."

Against these huge numbers of half-trained but dedicated citizen-soldiers, Gage had but 4,000 well-trained professionals. They were not, however, combat veterans. Only the 43rd Regiment had served in America during the last French war, and many of the others had seen no action in any theatre of the Seven Years' War. Many of the men were collected from the jails and slums of the British Isles, and a good part of their officers got their rank by purchasing it. Life for Tommy Atkins was no more pleasant in the eighteenth century than it was when Kipling immortalized him, and it was especially hard in Boston during the winter of 1774-75.

The Americans, through appeals to patriotism, threats, tar and feathers, and sabotage, made it nearly impossible to supply Gage's troops from local sources.

Rations, which had to be sent from England, were often short, and the army suffered along with Boston's civilians from the lack of firewood. Soldiers could always get rum, though, which Major John Pitcairn of the Royal Marines told Lord Sandwich "is so cheap that it debauches both navy and army and kills many of them. Depend on it my Lord, it will destroy more of us than the Yankies [sic] will." No local workmen would construct barracks, and Gage's attempt to import carpenters from New York was thwarted by the New York mechanics. The housing pressed under the Quartering Act was inadequate. One troop, quartered in a vacant rum distillery, used the mash fermenting vats for a latrine. The combination of urine and old lees produced a noxious gas from which many sickened and died. In fact, sickness was rife; more than a hundred soldiers and dependents died during the winter of 1774-75. Dozens of others deserted, some of them enticed by offers of cash or lands to settle on.

Boston was occupied, but not quite under martial law. The local magistrates still held court, and woe betide the British soldier—whether officer or enlisted man—who appeared before them. Both officers and men bitterly resented the fact that "Tommy," or "the old Woman," as they unfondly dubbed Gage, seldom took their side but constantly tried to placate the civilians. Gage's troops were not happy and yet, in a battle fought under European conditions, the superior discipline of this discontented little army would have made it a match for at least double its numbers of American militia. Thomas Gage understood— as his superiors in London did not—that he was never likely to fight under European conditions or against odds of only two to one.

III. PREPARATIONS FOR WAR

As soon as news of the Coercive Acts arrived, Americans had to face up to the possibility—even the probability—of war. John Adams carried to the Continental Congress some "Broken Hints" by Major Joseph Hawley, surely no fire-eater, that opened with the statement "We must fight," if England refused to back down. "A certain clear plan, for a constant, adequate and lasting supply of arms and military stores, must be devised and fully contemplated. . . . Men, in that case, will not be wanting." Adams showed the "Broken Hints" to Patrick Henry, who exclaimed, "By God, I am of that man's mind!"

It is impossible to say just when or where the patriots first began to make serious preparations for war, but by August there were reports of them from all parts of America. Militia companies took their drills seriously for the first time in years, and volunteer companies began assembling outside the regular militia organization. Gunsmiths and importers quickly sold out their stocks of arms and ammunition; during the month of August more than 5,000 small arms were sold in Boston alone. Whether from patriotism or hope of profit, merchants began placing large orders for war materiel. On August 28, Admiral Samuel Graves heard that an American ship was bound from Germany with firearms and 400 barrels of gunpowder. Her master reportedly said "it was indifferent to him on what part of the Coast he came, for, upon hoisting his Flag, Boats would immediately crowd to him." The day before, General Gage had reported to Lord Dartmouth: "In Worcester they keep no terms, openly threaten Resistance by Arms, have been purchasing Arms, preparing them, casting Ball, and providing Powder, and threaten to attack any Troops who dare to oppose them."

Prepared or not, the war very nearly began on September 1. Most of the towns around Boston stored their powder in a government powderhouse on Quarry Hill in Charlestown. During the summer, they had removed all that they owned. On August 26 or August 27, General William Brattle of Cambridge, a Tory who was the ranking officer in the Massachusetts militia, warned Gage that the patriots intended to appropriate the 200 or so half-barrels of government-owned powder that remained. At sunrise on September 1, a picked force of 260 men under Colonel Maddison of the 4th Regiment rowed across the Back Bay to Charlestown. One detachment quickly removed the powder while another marched to Cambridge, where Brattle turned over two brass fieldpieces. Everything went perfectly. By the time the people knew what was happening, soldiers, powder, and cannon were on their way to Castle William.

But as the soldiers, glowing with success, returned to their quarters, the news of their "raid" spread like wildfire, becoming more and more exaggerated with every mile. The troops had disarmed the Bostonians; they had fired on them; there was fighting in the streets; Graves's naval squadron had shelled the city. All over New England, men took up their muskets and headed for Boston. By 8:00 A.M. September 2, 3000 angry, armed men were gathered on Cambridge Common. Another thousand would join them by noon, and observers estimated that anywhere from 30,000 to 50,000 New Englanders began to march toward Boston before they were assured it was a false alarm. We have seen the effect of the rumor in Philadelphia, where Congress was sitting. It was just as great in Maryland and Virginia. Joseph Reed told Lord Dartmouth that if the rumor had been true, 40,000 men from Pennsylvania and her neighbors would have gone to avenge Boston.

Dr. Joseph Warren learned about the approaching militia at 6:00 A.M. Aghast at the chance of starting a war before the rest of the continent was committed, Warren and the rest of the Boston Committee of Correspondence rushed off to stop the militia. By the time they got to Cambridge, Judge Samuel Danforth had already convinced the militia that no one had been harmed. They returned to their homes, but not before forcing Lieutenant Governor Thomas Oliver to resign from the Council and extracting pledges from several officials, Danforth among them, not to comply with the Massachusetts Government Act.

The alarm had a sobering effect on both sides. From then on, Boston was distinctly more moderate than the countryside. On September 2 Gage admitted that "Tho' the People are not held in high Estimation by the Troops, yet they are numerous, worked up to a Fury, and not a Boston Rabble but the Freeholders and Farmers of the Country." He abandoned his plans to send troops to protect the county courts and mandamus councilors. But he also tried to repeat, a week later, his successful powderhouse raid.

On the night of September 8, another detachment of redcoats rowed to Charlestown, this time to secure the cannon mounted in the Charlestown battery. Again the operation went without a hitch—until the troops reached the battery and found neither guns nor ammunition. Gage could not repeat the surprise he achieved on September 1. The sight of an officer inspecting the Charlestown battery was enough to send out a call for every team and timber wagon in the locality. Even as Gage's detachment was embarking, the battery was stripped. Gage was so shaken by the incident that on September 15 he ordered all the guns in Boston's north battery to be spiked, lest they, too, be stolen. That may have been a wise precaustion, for two days later four cannon stored in the armory near Boston Commom disappeared from under the very noses of Gage's troops.

On Sunday, September 18, Gage got another demonstration of the patriots' alarm system. The 38th Regiment, with full equipment, marched to a parade ground near the point where the two previous expeditions had embarked. Within minutes, dispatch riders were galloping off, crying the alarm to every congregation. Soon the militiamen, dressed in their Sunday best, were again marching toward Boston. As it happened, the 38th was turning out only for inspection. The soldiers got a good laugh out of the incident, but Gage was less amused. Soon he was writing privately to the secretary of war, Lord Barrington, that "From Appearances no People are more determined for a Civil War, the whole Country from hence to New York armed, training and providing Military Stores."

No central command had ordered the militia out for these alarms, nor sent

[182]

them home when they were over. Each company had acted independently. During the summer of 1774, apparently without any outside direction, quite a number of militia companies revived an old concept, the minutemen. During the French and Indian Wars, a portion of each militia company always kept their arms with them, ready to go into action "at a minute's warning."

General William Brattle, in the same letter that touched off the powder-house raid, informed Gage that many captains had warned their troops to be ready "to meet at one minute's warning, equipped with arms and ammunition," and others were being pressured to do the same. Brattle suggested that Gage rescind all militia commissions, so that patriot officers would have no legal authority to call out their troops. Gage managed to lose Brattle's letter. The patriots published it, with three results: Brattle had to flee to Boston; the idea of minuteman companies received wide publicity; patriots realized that Brattle's suggestion cut both ways, for if every militia officer resigned, it would effectively remove Tory officers like Brattle, too. Then the militia could be reorganized under patriot control.

The Worcester County Convention, which had been meeting since August 9, was the first to take up militia reorganization. On August 31 it debated a motion that if Gage sent troops to open the county court on September 6, the county's inhabitants should "attend, properly armed, in order to repel any hostile force which may be employed for that purpose." The motion was finally watered down to a resolution that the inhabitants "all come properly armed and accoutered to protect and defend" any town in the county threatened with invasion. Nevertheless, the county militia did turn out, 6,000 strong, on September 6. By this time Gage had reconsidered his plan to send troops to Worcester, or we might be celebrating September 6 instead of April 19. But the presence of so many militiamen reemphasized the need to reorganize the militia.

On the afternoon of September 6, the Worcester Convention asked all militia officers to resign, with field-grade officers publishing their resignations in the Boston newspapers. Then the militiamen should elect new company officers, who should in turn assemble on October 10 to pick regimental officers. The convention further recommended that the company officers "enlist one third of the men of their respective towns, between sixteen and sixty years of age, to be ready to act at a minute's warning." Within a few weeks, Suffolk, Essex and Middlesex Counties had adopted the Worcester plan, and the term "minute-men" was already in popular use.

The First Provincial Congress of Massachusetts assembled in Concord on October 11 with more than 300 delegates present. At first it did little, while it waited for Paul Revere to return from Philadelphia with the Continental Congress's reply to the Suffolk Resolves, except to ask tax collectors to withhold money from Gage's treasurer and to exchange acrimonious letters with the general over his fortification of Boston Neck. But after the Provincial Congress moved to Cambridge on October 17, it began to consider the militia problem. By this time many officers had resigned their commissions willingly or under duress, and their companies had elected new officers. Towns and individuals were supplying themselves with arms. Three alarms had already taken place, putting thousands of militiamen in the field. And General Gage, despite protests from both the Provincial Congress and Continental Congress, continued to fortify Boston Neck and bring troops to Boston from all over his command.

On the afternoon of October 26 the Provincial Congress, reflecting the newfound radicalism of its western members, created a militia organization. It set up a Committee of Safety to take command of the province's militia, consisting of three members elected from Boston and eight "of the country." Any five of them—including not more than one from Boston—could call the militia into action. Congress then chose three field commanders; Jedediah Preble from Maine, Seth Pomeroy from Hampshire County, and Artemas Ward from Worcester County. Five commissaries—none of whom were from Boston—were authorized to procure twenty fieldpieces, carriages for twelve siege guns, four mortars, and five thousand small arms. With ammunition, the whole would cost £20,837. All militia companies who had not yet done so were urged to elect new officers and form minuteman companies.

The First Provincial Congress did little more to build an army. It continued to remind towns to procure supplies, especially for the minutemen, who should have "an effective fire arm, bayonet, pouch, knapsack, thirty rounds of cartridges and balls," and should drill at least three times a week. It asked the towns to encourage men to volunteer for minuteman duty by paying them for their services, and promised that the province would pay them an "adequate allowance" if the Committee of Safety called them out. But despite rumors to the contrary, the First Provincial Congress dissolved itself on December 10 without trying to create a standing army.

While the Provincial Congress was out of session, the Committees of Safety and Supplies acted as if they would soon have an army in the field. Meeting jointly, the committees labored mightily to provide not only arms and ammunition but beef, pork, flour, rice, peas, tents, axes, spades, candles, and the thousand and one other things an army needs, and to create supply dumps, especially in Concord and Worcester.

[184]

The Second Provincial Congress met from February 1 to February 16, then adjourned until March 22. During the first session, after hot debates, the members considered the need to create a standing army. It allowed the Committee of Safety to appoint a commissary to take charge of supplies, elected John Thomas and William Heath to join Preble, Ward, and Pomeroy as generals, and, on February 10, appointed a committee to draw up articles of war to govern a "constitutional army," if one should be created.

During the interim between sessions of the Second Provincial Congress, the Committee of Safety voted to buy supplies for an army of 15,000 and to assume the authority to call the Provincial Congress back into session if Gage should receive reinforcements. It also organized artillery companies and drafted orders for one-quarter of the militia to assemble for provincial duty. Some began to fear that the Committee of Safety was going too far. Major Joseph Hawley, who the previous August had said, "We must fight," now feared that if the Committee of Safety ever called out the minutemen, they would fight even if the time was not ripe. Gage, who was receiving accurate intelligence from Dr. Benjamin Church, a member of the Provincial Congress and the Committee of Safety, began to hope that dissension would keep the Americans from creating an effective military force.

The second session of the Second Provincial Congress sat from March 22 to April 15. After a long debate it adopted the articles of war, but it also voted that the Committee of Safety should not call out the minutemen unless Gage's troops marched out of Boston with baggage and artillery. On April 8, after news of the New England Restraining Act arrived, the Congress finally agreed to ask cooperation from the other New England colonies in creating a standing army. But when Congress adjourned, four days before Lexington and Concord, the defense of Massachusetts still depended upon minutemen and militia.

Massachusetts was not the only colony to prepare for hostilities, although the need was less pressing in the others. Connecticut, whose government was firmly in patriot hands, already had a formidable militia establishment. In early 1774 Governor Trumbull reported to the colonial secretary that his province had 20,000 men organized in eighteen regiments. Many of them began to march toward Boston at the news of the powderhouse raid. A few days later, a Norwich meeting of representatives from Windham and New London counties recommended that every town increase its ammunition supply and that at least 5,000 more men be added to the Connecticut militia. Gage had already reported that Connecticut's farmers were "exercising in arms." On October 13 the Connecticut Assembly voted to require the militia to drill at least twelve half-days by May, and for militia officers to see that all weapons were ready for use. Subsequently the Assembly doubled the amount of ammunition each town was required to have on hand and ordered carriages built to convert New London's cannon into fieldpieces. Oscar Zeichner has written that "Connecticut was practically in a state of war in the first months of 1775, even before the skirmishes at Lexington and Concord."

Despite the misgivings of Governor Joseph Wanton, Rhode Island was as militant as Connecticut. When the Assembly met in October, it was flooded with requests for charters to set up independent military companies. In December it revised the militia laws and authorized Rhode Island troops to go to the aid of any neighboring province that came under attack. Most important, on December 8 the Assembly ordered all cannon and ammunition removed from Fort George in Newport Harbor and stored in Providence, where it would be safe from the Royal Navy. Captain James Wallace and H.M.S. *Rose* arrived too late to prevent the loss of forty-four of "the King's Cannon." Governor Wanton told Wallace, "frankly . . . they had done it to prevent their falling into the hands of the King, or any of his Servants."

On the surface, New Hampshire did not seem to have much of a militia system or to be nearly as radical as the other New England colonies. Its people claimed they could not afford a sizable military establishment. In May 1774 Governor John Wentworth had great difficulty in getting his legislature to appropriate funds for an officer and five privates to garrison Fort William and Mary in Portsmouth. But on December 13, Governor Wentworth reported, "One Paul Rivere arrived in [Portsmouth] Express from a Committee in Boston to another Committee in this Town." At noon the next day, about 400 men overpowered the fort's few defenders and took nearly a hundred barrels of powder. On December 15, reinforced by people from the outlying towns, the raiders returned to take away sixteen cannon and sixty muskets. Only the arrival of two Royal Navy ships kept them from capturing the twenty remaining cannon. In January the New Hampshire Provincial Congress mildly urged the towns to have more militia drills, but New Hampshire proportionately made one of the largest contributions of men to the army that besieged Boston after Lexington and Concord.

There was yet another military force in New England, though it was recognized by no government. The Green Mountain Boys, led by a Connecticut land speculator named Ethan Allen, had for several years been fighting New York sheriffs' posses in the "Hampshire Grants," now Vermont. New York raised the price on Allen's head to £100 in 1774, and if it had not been for the situation in Boston, Gage would have sent troops to the region. Early in 1775 the Boston Committee of Correspondence sent John Brown to Montreal to drum up support. On March 29 Brown wrote from Montreal that Canada could give Massachusetts no help; however, Brown had not wasted his time. On his way to Montreal, Brown had decided that "the Fort at Tyconderoga [sic] must be seised [sic] as soon as possible should hostilities be committed by the Kings Troops. The People on N Hampshire grants have ingaged to do this Business and in my opinion they are the most proper Persons for this Jobb." Three weeks after Lexington, the "Jobb" was done.

The colonies south of New England made fewer official preparations for war, though they were full of unofficial ones. New York was in the process of revising its militia laws, but to meet the threat of the Green Mountain Boys, not the British army. Within a few hours after news arrived of Lexington and Concord, New York City's Sons of Liberty seized the armory and distributed guns and ammunition to the populace. A hundred redcoats and the regular militia could do nothing about it.

Pennsylvania held a convention in January. It avoided all mention of military preparations, but did recommend that powder-mill owners increase their production because it might soon be needed, "especially in the Indian trade." In December the Maryland Convention called for all men between sixteen and fifty to form militia companies, and it authorized the county committees of inspection to raise £10,000 to buy armaments.

South Carolina's Provincial Congress called for military training for all inhabitants, but the Assembly never got around to appropriating money to buy arms. However, a secret committee of the Provincial Congress, led by William Henry Drayton, endeavored to steal South Carolina's entire supply of guns and ammunition, much of it stored in the State House in Charleston. The Assembly blandly told Governor Bull that they supposed it was "in consequence of the late alarming accounts from Great Britain."

As might be expected, Virginia did more to prepare for war than any other colony outside New England. During the summer of 1774, most Virginia counties formed volunteer companies. Under the tutelage of George Washington and George Mason, Fairfax County formed a company of a hundred men in September. In January, Mason presented a plan to organize all men from eighteen to fifty in companies of sixty-eight men. The county Committee of Safety voted to assess each tithable three shillings for ammunition and to publish the names of all who refused to pay.

Along with Governor Dunmore, part of Virginia's regular militia was off in

[187]

the Ohio Valley fighting "Lord Dunmore's War" against the Indians. On November 5 Dunmore's officers gathered at a wilderness fort and there voted that the obligation to defend American liberty must take precedence over their allegiance to the king. On December 24 Governor Dunmore, lately returned to Williamsburg, reported to Lord Dartmouth that the independent companies, acting under the direction of the county committees, had nearly complete control of the province.

Still, much of Virginia's old, conservative leadership did not want preparations to go any further. In March, Patrick Henry shocked the Virginia Convention with a motion "that this colony be immediately put into a state of defense," and that a committee be appointed to plan for arming and training "such a number of men as may be sufficient for that purpose." Henry's "liberty or death" speech helped pull the motion through by the bare margin of 65-60.

Perhaps little would have come of it—even after it passed—had Dunmore not pulled his own version of the powderhouse raid. On April 21, on Dunmore's orders, the captain and crew of H.M.S. *Fowey* removed the colony's powder from the Williamsburg armory. Within a few days, the independent companies of the northern counties were marching toward Williamsburg. Dunmore sent his family to the *Fowey* and armed his servants and slaves for defense of his palace. Dunmore finally paid the province £330 for the powder. The incident also cost him his brief popularity, and Virginians were already under arms when news of the Lexington clash arrived. George Washington rode off to the Second Continental Congress wearing his colonel's uniform.

In addition to the revival of the militia, America spent the last nine months before Lexington gathering war materiel. This had to be done in secret, of course. The Massachusetts Archives are full of letters from as far away as Holland and Spain, arranging arms deliveries and enjoining strict secrecy. In spite of the Tory sympathy of the province, much of New York's powder and cannon found its way to Massachusetts. On October 19 the king issued an order in council prohibiting arms imports into the colonies. Royal Navy vessels virtually blockaded Holland, stopping any American ships suspected of carrying arms. Admiral Graves constantly received consular reports of arms shipments headed for America, but he had too few ships to look for them without easing his blockade of Boston. The Bostonians sent most of their small arms and ammunition out of the city, often concealed in manure wagons. Carpenters built carriages to convert old ship guns into field artillery. Women and children folded paper cartridges. In one way or another, the supplies were found. By April 19, 1775, the Americans were about as well prepared for war as was Gage's army.

IV. THE EVE OF LEXINGTON

While the Americans prepared for war, Thomas Gage did the best he could in an impossible situation. He knew he was expected to keep order in his province, yet he had hardly enough troops to control Boston alone. During September and October he brought troops to Boston from all over his command, even from the recently conquered province of Quebec, which "Nothing but Extremity of Affairs" could make him think of doing. Gage even asked the governor of Canada, Sir Guy Carleton, if he could recruit French Canadians and Indians for service in Boston. One way or another, Gage managed to more than double the size of his forces in Boston, but they still numbered only 4,000 men.

Gage made his strongest demands for men in his private letters to the secretary of war, Lord Barrington. On October 3 he told Barrington he had

Nothing good to send your Lordship from this Continent, there is Nothing going on but Preparations for War, and Threats to take Arms, & to overwhelm us with forty or fifty Thousand Men. . . . If you wou'd get the better of America in all your Disputes, you must conquer her, and to do that effectually, . . . you should have an Army near twenty thousand strong.

A month later, Gage advised

if you will resist and not yield, that Resistance should be effectual at the Beginning. If you think ten Thousand Men sufficient, send Twenty; if one Million is thought enough, give two; you will save both Blood and Treasure in the End. A large force will terrify, and engage many to join you, a middling one will encourage Resistance, and gain no Friends.

Gage's advice, in retrospect, was dead right, but it got him no reinforcements. A gambler might have hit the American forces before they were organized—and might have won. But Gage was no gambler. He would not move against his better judgment until London left him no alternative.

During the winter of 1774-75, while he waited for the orders he knew must come, Gage did his best to turn his little army into an effective fighting machine. He paid particular attention to light infantry tactics and the use of flankers. Lieutenant General Gage did not intend to repeat the mistake of Lieutenant

Colonel Gage on the banks of the Monongahela twenty years before. He also took advantage of the unusually mild winter by constantly sending his troops on short training marches, none farther than eight miles out of Boston. By April his army was in good physical shape. This training and Gage's stress on putting out flankers may well have kept the retreat from Concord from turning into an even bigger disaster.

While Gage exercised his troops, he also exercised the minutemen, who turned out whenever Gage's soldiers left Boston. Gage may have hoped the constant false alarms would dampen their ardor and lessen their vigilance. If so, he failed. His troops were seldom out of sight of the minutemen, who gained fresh confidence as the redcoats made no hostile move.

The last training march on March 30 caused a real alarm. Lord Percy's brigade, nearly 1,200 men, marched out of Boston in full battle gear. Fearing that Percy was headed for Concord, where the Provincial Congress was in session, minutemen tore up the planking of the Charles River bridge at Cambridge. Three miles farther upstream, another unit of minutemen with two cannon guarded the bridge at Watertown. But Percy stuck to the south bank of the Charles and turned back at Jamaica Plain. Each side thought it had intimidated the other.

Gage's greatest concern was that the Americans would develop artillery capability. Nearly every move he made, from the powderhouse raid to the march to Concord, was aimed at denying cannon to the rebels. The only offensive action Gage took during the winter was another attempt to capture American artillery. Gage's spies told him that twenty pieces had been stored in Salem and were being made ready for service. Assuming that they were brass fieldpieces, Gage ordered Colonel Alexander Leslie of the Sixty-fourth Regiment to seize them. Gage's information was correct except for one thing: the cannon which Captain David Mason was fitting with carriages were not brass fieldpieces but old iron twelve-pounders that had been used on merchant ships.

After dark on Saturday, February 25, Colonel Leslie and 240 men boarded a transport vessel. At nine o'clock on Sunday morning they arrived off Homan's Cove near Marblehead, a five-mile march from Salem. With Leslie's men hidden below deck, the vessel lay off the cove until two in the afternoon, waiting for the local people to return to church for afternoon services. The Marbleheaders, however, were quick to spot the strange ship, and many of them were on hand to watch the redcoats debark. Leslie's hope of achieving surprise was gone, but he marched his troops to Salem so fast that he got there just after the messengers who were spreading the alarm.

[190]

Salem Village lay between two rivers. Leslie was delayed for a few minutes at the South River because half a dozen local patriots were tearing up the bridge's planking. Others hurried to roll the new gun carriages away and to throw hay and leaves over the cannon. The cannon, as Leslie knew, were stored near Foster's blacksmith shop near the bridge on the north side of the North River. Leslie's men rushed through the village to the North Bridge—really a 750-foot causeway with a drawbridge in the middle. No militia defended the bridge, but the draw was up, and the local people were staving in the bottoms of all the boats on the south bank. The troops halted, shivering in the February wind after a five-mile quick march, while a crowd hurled insults at them, such as "I should think you were all fiddlers, you shake so!"

Exactly what happened next depends on whether you believe the Tory or the patriot account. The draw was lowered and Leslie's troops marched across, but they quickly marched back again and returned to their ship in Marblehead without disturbing any of the cannon. Leslie claimed that the locals backed down when he declared his intention to reach his objective—Foster's forge—and that he returned only after ascertaining that there were no brass fieldpieces there, but only some old iron ship guns. The patriot version said Leslie was warned that thousands of militiamen were on the march. He accepted the patriots' offer of a face-saving device: his troops would be allowed to cross the bridge if Leslie would give his word to march them right back again.

There is probably some truth in both stories. The locals were impressed with Leslie's determination to carry out the letter of his orders, while Leslie did not care to risk his troops for some old ship guns. The patriots, however, were the big gainers. They kept their makeshift field artillery, and they had evidence that the British army could be intimidated by a show of force. Two days later, Beverly, which had been dragging its feet, voted to raise two companies of minutemen.

Meanwhile Gage knew from spies like Benjamin Church that the Committee of Safety had established two large supply dumps at Worcester and Concord. These would have to be his primary objectives, especially since they contained large numbers of the field guns he feared so much. But Gage needed the kind of information that only trained soldiers could get: marching routes, sites for encampments and fortifications, availability of supplies and, above all, locations of possible ambushes. Early in January, Gage asked for volunteers "capable of taking sketches of a country."

Most of his junior officers came forward, and from them Gage chose Captain William Browne of the 52nd and Ensign Henry De Birniere of the 10th. As military observers and mapmakers, both were first-rate. As secret agents, they were among the most inept in the history of espionage.

The two set out for Worcester on February 23, dressed in what they thought was country clothing and, at Gage's suggestion, posing as surveyors. Within a few hours their cover was blown (for one thing, they "walked like soldiers") , and only an intelligent batman, a fortuitous snowstorm, and the god who watches over fools enabled them to get to Worcester and back without receiving a coat of tar and feathers—or worse. Possibly their sketches of the route and hair-raising account of their encounters with hostile patriots helped convince Gage that he could not send an expedition to Worcester—forty-seven miles away—until he got reinforcements.

Gage sent Browne and De Birniere on a second mission on March 20—this time to Concord, only eighteen miles from Boston. Again they aroused suspicion, but returned with accurate intelligence about cannon and military supplies stored there, plus an all-too-prophetic description of "one very bad place" on the road between Lexington and Concord.

On April 3, Gage received information from Dr. Church that must have made him decide that he would have to take the offensive within a few weeks. The Provincial Congress had started negotiations with the other New England provinces to raise a standing army of 30,000 men, half from Massachusetts. Worse yet, the Congress had voted to equip six companies of artillery. Church added a suggestion: "A sudden blow struck now or immediately on the arrival of the reinforcements from England should they come within a fortnight would overset all their plans."

The *Nautilus* dropped anchor in Boston Harbor on April 14, bringing Gage's long-awaited orders from Lord Dartmouth. Written on January 27, they had not left England until early March. Gage could hardly have considered them anything but a reprimand. Dartmouth sneered at Gage's reports of American preparations, saying he had presented no facts that showed them "other than merely the Acts of a tumultuous Rabble." As for Gage's estimation that the situation could be retrieved only by conquering Massachusetts, Connecticut, and Rhode Island, and that it would take at least 20,000 men, Dartmouth reminded Gage that "such a Force cannot be collected" without full mobilization, and "I am unwilling to believe that matters are as yet come to that Issue." On the contrary, said Dartmouth, "a smaller Force now, if put to the Test, would be able to encounter them with greater probability of Success than might be expected from a greater Army." The first step toward reestablishing control "would be to arrest and imprison the principal actors & abettors in the

Provincial Congress." If this should, as Gage had warned, be "a Signal for Hostilities," so much the better; the chances would be more favorable than when the colonies were "in a riper state of Rebellion." But Dartmouth closed with this disclaimer: "It must be understood, however, after all I have said, that this is a matter which must be left to your own Discretion to be executed or not as you shall . . . think most advisable."

The intent of the letter is clear, even if Dartmouth tried to put the responsibility for any action back on Gage: Gage must achieve a military victory over the rebels in a hurry.

Gage had already made preliminary plans. The objective would be the cannon and supply dump in Concord. He would rely on speed and surprise—rather than numbers and firepower—to achieve it. On April 16 Gage drafted two companies of light infantry and grenadiers from each of his regiments to make a provisional expeditionary force of 700 men, commanded by his senior regimental commander, Lieutenant Colonel Francis Smith, seconded by Major John Pitcairn of the Royal Marines. The force would take no baggage or artillery, and only thirty-six rounds of ammunition per man.

Gage thought the expedition could accomplish its mission and be back in Boston in twenty hours. Speed and surprise were everything. Speed he certainly got, but surprise was impossible. Gage knew from Dr. Church that the Committee of Safety was not supposed to call out the minutemen unless the Redcoats carried baggage and artillery. He hoped that the expedition would be well on the way to Concord before anyone realized it was not just another training march. But three days of assembling the composite force and mustering 700 men at night on April 18 could not be carried out without dozens of watchers knowing something was afoot. And if the soldiers were rowed across the Back Bay to Charlestown, it was a dead giveaway that their objective was Concord.

The patriots' messengers were ready. Then—in the belfry of Old North Church—two lanterns told them all they had to know.

Notes on the Sources

A GENERAL NOTE ON SOURCES

The sources for the year 1774 are almost embarrassingly rich. Everything that was printed during that year in America and could still be found has been put on microcard by the American Antiquarian Society and the Readex Corporation as part of their *Early American Imprints* series. Twenty of the thirty-five newspapers published during 1774 are available on microcard or microfilm. It is very nearly possible to read everything that was printed in 1774, and I have spent several years doing just that.

In addition, several of the participants in the American Revolution wrote histories of it, and they gave due attention to the year. On the patriot side are the histories by David Ramsay, Mercy Otis Warren, and the Reverend William Gordon; on the Tory side, those by Thomas Hutchinson, Peter Oliver, and the Reverend Jonathan Boucher. The letters and diaries of many other participants have been printed as well, including not only the famous—like John Adams and George Washington—but the obscure—like Christopher Marshall, Philip Fithian, and Nicholas Cresswell.

Because of the wealth of material in print or in microform, I have used few manuscript sources. However, it was while I was working in the manuscript records of the Admiralty, Treasury, and Colonial Office in the British Public Record Office that I learned about American preparations for war during 1774 and decided that I would one day write a book about the year. Other manuscript collections I have used for this study include the Massachusetts Archives in the State House, Boston; the Samuel Adams Papers in the New York Public Library; and the photostats of the records of the Boston Committee of Correspondence in the Massachusetts Historical Society.

The most important single source for this study has been the first two volumes of the fourth series (there were no first, second, or third series) of Peter Force's *American Archives* (Washington, D.C., 1837). These huge, unwieldy volumes are as rich as a Yukon gold field—and about as easy to extract treasure from. The material in Force through April 20, 1775, takes up more than 2,200 long columns of tiny print. It is a bewildering hodgepodge of official documents, proceedings of everything from backwoods committees to the British Parliament, letters, pamphlets, sermons, and newspaper clippings. They are imperfectly indexed, their sources are seldom given, and their organization can be described only as more chronological than anything else. Force's *American Archives* is utterly fascinating.

In addition to these sources, I have used many secondary works, which will be cited in the chapter notes. The following deserve special notice: Merrill Jensen, *The Founding of a Nation* (New York, 1968) goes from 1763 to 1776, but gives more attention to 1774 than any previous one-volume history of the American Revolution. A useful supplement to it is Volume IX of *English Historical Documents,* edited by Jensen (New York, 1955), which contains not only documents but excellent bibliographies. Volume XII of Lawrence Henry Gipson's monumental *British Empire Before the American Revolution* (New York, 1965) is mostly about 1774 and is enormously detailed. Volumes XIV-XV (New York, 1969-70) are devoted to bibliographies of both manuscript and printed sources. Finally, Benjamin Woods Labaree's *Boston Tea Party* (New York, 1964) has been both a mine of imformation and an example of how history should be written.

CHAPTER I

Everything I have ever read about 1774 has in some way influenced this chapter. The references I used most often are David Hawke, *The Colonial Experience* (Indianapolis, 1966), chs. 11-12; Evarts B. Greene, *The Revolutionary Generation 1763-1790* (New York, 1943), Chs. 1-9; and the first chapter of Jensen, *Founding of a Nation.* Richard Hofstadter, *America at 1750* (New York, 1971) has more about 1774 than the title would indicate; Arthur M. Schlesinger, *The Birth of the Nation: A Portrait of the American People on the Eve of Independence* (New York, 1968) has rather less. Jensen's *English Historical Documents,* IX, 480, has a convenient population table. Modern demographic views of colonial America are in J. Potter, "The Growth of Population in America, 1700-1860," in *Population in History,* ed. D.V. Glass and D.E.C. Eversley (Chicago, 1965). An especially good description of the south and back country is Carl

Bridenbaugh's *Myths and Realities* (Baton Rouge, 1952). Harry J. Carman edited a reissue of *America Husbandry* (New York, 1939). The most important work on colonial cities is Carl Bridenbaugh, *Cities in Revolt* (New York, 1955). Information on newspapers comes from Clarence S. Brigham, *History and Bibliography of American Newspapers, 1690-1820* (2 vols., Worcester, Mass., 1947); from Arthur M. Schlesinger, *Prelude to Independence: The Newspaper War on Britain* (New York, 1958). and from the newspapers themselves. I read the *Royal American Magazine* and the *Pennsylvania Magazine* in the Boston Atheneum, but they are now available on microfilm. Other information came from Frank L. Mott, *A History of American Magazines,* Vol. I (Cambridge, Mass., 1938), 83-7. David Hawke has a very useful list of all the colonial governors in *Colonial Experience,* 687-98. There are sketches of all the 1774 governors in the *Dictionary of American Biography* except, oddly, of Georgia's James Wright, who is in the *Dictionary of National Biography.* Information on Virginia politics is from Charles Sydnor's delightful *Gentlemen Freeholders* (Chapel Hill, 1952). The indispensable book on social classes is Jackson Turner Main, *The Social Structure of Revolutionary America* (Princeton, 1965). Sutton's quote is in *The Last Journals of Horace Walpole,* ed. A. Francis Steuart (2 vols., New York, 1910), I, 337. Information about church membership is in Hofstadter's *America at 1750,* Ch. 6.

The opening quote is from Patrick M'Robert, *A Tour Through Part of the North Provinces of America 1774-1775,* ed. Carl Bridenbaugh, in *Pennsylvania Magazine of History and Biography,* LIX (1935), 171-2.

CHAPTER II

The best account of the revolutionary movement through 1774 is Merrill Jensen, *Founding of a Nation,* supplemented by his *English Historical Documents,* IX. Some interpretations in this chapter I expressed previously in my "Goals and Enforcement of British Colonial Policy, 1763-1775," American Neptune, XXVII (1967), 211-20. The definitive work on the Stamp Act is Edmund S. and Helen M. Morgan, *Stamp Act Crisis* (Chapel Hill, 1953). Samuel Adams has many biographers. The most useful for me were his great-grandson, William V. Wells (3 vols., Boston, 1865-6). Ralph V. Harlow (New York, 1923), and the neo-Tory sketch by Clifford Shipton in *Sibley's Harvard Graduates,* Vol. X (Boston, 1958). The role of the mob in revolutionary America is beautifully explained in Pauline Maier's *From Resistance to Revolution* (New York, 1972). The Boston Committee of Correspondence is the subject of Richard D. Brown's excellent *Revolutionary Politics in Massachusetts* (Cambridge, Mass., 1970). The final section of this chapter owes everything to Benjamin Labaree's *Boston Tea Party,* one of the great books about the American Revolution.

The opening quote is in *The Adams-Jefferson Letters,* ed. Lester J. Cappon (2 vols., Chapel Hill, 1959), II, 455.

CHAPTER III

Ths most exhaustive account of the passage of the Coercive Acts is Bernard Donoughue, *British Politics and the American Revolution: The Path to War, 1773-75* (London, 1964). Also useful is Jack M. Sosin, *Agents and Merchants* (Lincoln, Neb., 1965), chs. 6-8. The acts themselves and most of the debates in Parliament are in Force's *American Archives,* 4 ser., I, 4-224. Franklin's career and ordeal before the Privy Council are well recounted in Carl Van Doren, *Benjamin Franklin* (New York, 1938). The British view of the Coercive Acts comes from Fred J. Hinkhouse, *The Preliminaries of the American Revolution as Seen in the English Press 1763-1775* (New York, 1926), and Dora Mae Clark, *British Opinion and the American Revolution* (New Haven, 1943). The French-Canadian view of the Quebec Act is in Gustave Lanctot, *Canada and the American Revolution 1774-1783* (Cambridge, Mass., 1967), Chs. 1-3.

The opening quotes are from *The Letters of Horace Walpole,* ed. Mrs. Paget Toynbee (16 vols., Oxford, 1914), VIII, 439; *The Correspondence of King George the Third with Lord North from 1768 to 1783,* ed. W. Bodham Donne, Vol. I (London, 1867), 164; and Donoughue, *British Politics,* 47.

CHAPTER IV

This chapter used many collections of letters and diaries. The most important single source is the "Letters of John Andrews, Esq., of Boston, 1772-1776," ed. by Winthrop Sargent, in the Massachusetts Historical Society *Proceedings,* Vol. VIII (1864-1865), 316-412. Next in importance is *The Correspondence of General Thomas Gage,* ed. by Clarence E. Carter (two vols., New Haven, 1931-33), especially the letters between Gage and Dartmouth. Other important sources, in addition to the ever-useful Force's *American Archives,* include the following: *Diary and Autobiography of John Adams,* ed. L.H. Butterfield (Cambridge, Mass., 1961), especially Vols. 2 and 3. "Diary of Mr. Thomas Newell," Massachusetts Historical Society *Proceedings,* XV(1876-77), 347-63, has, among other things, the weather and temperature in Boston for most days. *Letters and Diary of John Rowe,* ed. Anne Rowe Cunningham (Boston, 1903). Ms. letters of Vice-Admiral Samuel Graves, Admiralty Papers, Class l, Vol. 485, in the British Public Records Office, London. Thomas Hutchinson's *History of the Colony and Province of Massachusetts Bay,* ed. Lawrence Shaw Mayo, Vol. III (Cambridge, Mass., 1936). *Peter Oliver's Origin and Progress of the American Rebellion,* ed. Douglass Adair and John A. Schutz (San Marino, 1961). For the Whig view, the histories of the Revolution written by the Reverend William Gordon (4 vols., London, 1788), and Mercy Otis Warren (3 vols., Boston, 1805). Hancock's Massacre Oration is in *Chronicles of the American Revolution,* ed. Alden T. Vaughn (N.Y., 1965), 76-80.

Indispensable secondary accounts include Jensen's *Founding of a Nation* and Brown's *Revolutionary Politics,* both supplemented by the photostats of the records of the Boston Committee of Correspondence in the Massachusetts Historical Society, Labaree's *Boston Tea Party,* and Bridenbaugh's *Cities in Revolt.* The Malcom affair is in Frank W.C. Hersey, "Tar and Feathers: the Adventures of Captain John Malcom," Colonial Society of Massachusetts *Publications,* XXXIV (Boston, 1943), 429-73.

Opening quotes are from Carter, ed., *Correspondence of General Thomas Gage,* I, 355, 356; 364; 371.

CHAPTER V

The most important single source for resolutions of meetings, governors' reports, and private correspondence during the summer of 1774 is Force's *American Archives.* Fortunately in this instance, Force's index under the individual colonies is reliable. The most complete secondary accounts, taking up all the colonies, are Volume XII of Gipson's *British Empire Before the American Revolution,* Chs. 6-9, and Arthur M. Schlesinger, *The Colonial Merchants and the American Revolution* (N.Y., 1917), Chs. 8-9. Gipson is obviously sympathetic to the conservatives, Schlesinger to the radicals. Shorter, but still extensive, is Ch. 18 of Jensen's *Founding of a Nation.* Shorter still, but excellent, is Chapter 12 of Labaree's *Boston Tea Party.*

Diaries quoted in this chapter include those of Landon Carter (Charlottesville, 1965), Nicholas Cresswell (London, 1925) Philip Vickers Fithian (Williamsburg, 1943), and Christopher Marshall (Philadelphia, 1839).

In addition, the following accounts of individual colonies were particularly useful in writing this chapter:

New Hampshire: Jere R. Daniell, *Experiment in Republicanism* (Cambridge, Mass., 1970); Richard F. Upton, *Revolutionary New Hampshire* (Hanover, 1936).

Rhode Island: David S. Lovejoy, *Rhode Island Politics and the American Revolution* (Providence, 1958).

Connecticut: Oscar Zeichner, *Connecticut's Years of Controversy* (Chapel Hill, 1949).

New York: Carl L. Becker, *History of Political Parties in the Province of New York* (Madison, 1909); Roger Champagne, "New York and the Intolerable Acts, 1774," *New-York Historical Society Quarterly,* XLV (1961), 195-207.

Pennsylvania: David L. Jacobson, *John Dickinson and the Revolution in Pennsylvania* (Berkeley, 1965); Charles H. Lincoln, *The Revolutionary Movement in Pennsylvania* (Philadelphia, 1901).

Maryland: John A. Silver, *The Provisional Government of Maryland* (Baltimore, 1895); William Eddis, *Letters from America,* ed. Aubrey C. Lamb (Cambridge, Mass., 1969)

Virginia: Thad W. Tate, "The Coming of the Revolution in Virginia, " *William and Mary Quarterly,* 3d series, XIX (1962), 323-43; Gordon S. Wood, "Rhetoric and Reality in the American Revolution, Ibid., XXIII (1966), 3-32; Douglas S. Freeman, *George Washington* (New York, 1951), III.

The opening quotes are in Labaree, *Boston Tea Party,* 220-21; Force, *American Archives,* I, 384, 618.

CHAPTER VI

The *Journals of the Continental Congress,* edited by Worthington C. Ford, Volume I (Washington, 1904), contains the official journals and resolutions of the First Continental Congress, but only the sketchiest account of the debates. It must be supplemented with the *Letters of Members of the Continental Congress,* edited by Edmund C. Burnett, Volume I (Washington, 1921), one of the finest collections of documents in existence. For secondary accounts, Burnett's own *Continental Congress* (New York, 1941) is the standard work, though Burnett spends relatively little time on the First Congress. The best interpretation is Jensen's *Founding of a Nation,* ch. XIX.

Opening quotes from Force, *American Archives,* I, 1194; Carter, ed., *Correspondence of General Thomas Gage,* I, 384.

CHAPTER VII

Most of the sources cited for Chapter V were also used for this chapter. In addition, for the War of Words, I used the colonial newspapers and the Early American Imprints. The most important secondary works on this topic are Philip Davidson, *Progaganda and the American Revolution* (Chapel Hill, 1941), and Bernard Bailyn, *Ideological Origins of the American Revolution* (Cambridge, Mass., 1967). Most of the material on treatment of the Tories came from Force's *American Archives,* with figures on emigrations in 1774 from Mary Beth Norton, *The British-Americans* (Boston, 1972). Useful interpretations included Pauline Maier, *From Resistance to Revolution* (New York, 1972), and Herbert Aptheker, *The American Revolution* (New York, 1960).

Opening quotes from Force, *American Archives,* I, 976-77; Early American Imprints microcard #13 682.

CHAPTER VIII

For the view from England, Donoughue's *British Politics and the American Revolution, The Letters of Horace Walpole,* Van Doren's *Franklin,* and Jensen's *Founding of a Nation.* Of the many military histories of the American Revolution, the works I found most useful include John Shy, *Toward Lexington* (Princeton, 1965). and his "A New Look at Colonial Militia," *William and Mary Quarterly,* 3d series, XX(1963), 181-84; Don C. Higginbotham, *The War of American Independence* (New York, 1971); Allen French,

The Day of Concord and Lexington (Boston, 1925), and *The First Year of the American Revolution* (Boston, 1943); Neil R. Stout, "The Spies Who Went Out in the Cold," *American Heritage,* XXIII, no. 2 (Feb. 1972); and especially John R. Galvin, *The Minutemen* (New York, 1967). Sources include Force's *American Archives;* Carter's *Gage Papers; Naval Documents of the American Revolution,* edited by William Bell Clark, Volume I (Washington, 1964), and *Journals of Each Provincial Congress of Massachusetts,* edited by William Lincoln (Boston, 1838). I also used many of the sources cited in Chapter V, and, as always, Jensen's *Founding of a Nation* was invaluable.

Opening quotes are from Carter, ed., *Correspondence of General Thomas Gage,* I, 387; II, 180; and Toynbee, ed., *Letters of Horace Walpole,* IX, 107.

Index